KAYAKING

Puget Sound, the San Juans, and Gulf Islands

50 Trips
on the
Northwest's
Inland Waters

SECOND EDITION

RANDEL WASHBURNE

Edited by R. CAREY GERSTEN

THE
MOUNTAINEERS

Published by
The Mountaineers
1001 SW Klickitat Way, Suite 201
Seattle, WA 98134

© 1991, 1999 by Randel Washburne

First edition, 1991. Second edition, 1999.

Published simultaneously in Great Britain by Cordee, 3a DeMontfort Street, Leicester, England, LE1 7HD

Manufactured in the United States of America

Copyediting by Crystal Thomas
Map design by Jerry Painter
Cover and book design by Kristy L. Welch
Layout by Alice C. Merrill

Cover photograph: Joel W. Rogers
Frontispiece: *Kayak sails at the Sea Kayak Symposium, Port Townsend*
Carey and Jeanne Gersten

Library of Congress Cataloging-in-Publication Data
Washburne, Randel.
    Kayaking Puget Sound, the San Juans, and Gulf Islands : 50 trips on
the Northwest's inland waters / Randel Washburne ; edited by R. Carey
Gersten. — 2nd ed.
        p.   cm.
    Includes bibliographical references (p.237) and index.
    ISBN 0-89886-607-3
    1. Sea kayaking—Northwest, Pacific—Guidebooks. 2. Northwest,
Pacific—Guidebooks. I. Gersten, R. Carey. II. Title. III. Title: Kayaking.
GV788.5.W396   1999
797.1'224'0979—dc21   98-54811
                                                              CIP

TABLE OF CONTENTS

Acknowledgments ———— 9
Introduction ———— 10

THE PACIFIC NORTHWEST PADDLING ENVIRONMENT ———— 15
Weather, Water, and Marine Shipping ———— 15
Tides and Currents ———— 22
Going Ashore ———— 30
Going Paddling ———— 40
Emergencies ———— 51

SOUTH PUGET SOUND ———— 54
1 Hammersley Inlet ———— 54
2 Hope Island (South) ———— 58
3 Eld Inlet ———— 62
4 McMicken Island ———— 65
5 Carr Inlet ———— 67
6 Henderson Inlet ———— 69
7 Nisqually Delta ———— 75
8 Commencement Bay ———— 77
9 Maury Island ———— 81
10 Blake Island ———— 86
11 Eagle Harbor to Bremerton ———— 90
12 Eagle Harbor ———— 93
13 West Point, Shilshole Bay, and Golden Gardens ———— 96
14 Port Madison and Agate Passage ———— 100
15 Lake Union ———— 104
16 Duwamish Waterway ———— 108
17 Elliott Bay ———— 112

NORTH PUGET SOUND ———— 115
18 Everett Harbor ———— 115
19 Port Susan ———— 119
20 Whidbey Island ———— 122
21 Skagit River Delta ———— 126
22 Hope and Skagit Islands ———— 130
23 Deception Pass ———— 133

SAN JUAN ISLANDS AREA ———— 139
24 Burrows Island ———— 139
25 Padilla Bay ———— 141

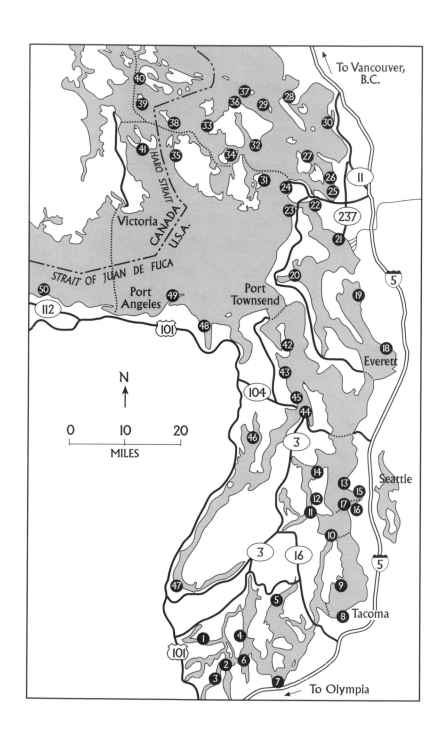

26 Saddlebag Island —— 144
27 Cypress Island —— 146
28 Lummi Island —— 151
29 Clark Island —— 156
30 Chuckanut Bay —— 159
31 James Island —— 162
32 Obstruction Pass —— 166
33 Jones Island —— 168
34 Shaw Island —— 175
35 South and West San Juan Island —— 178
36 Point Doughty on Orcas Island —— 184
37 Patos, Sucia, and Matia Islands —— 187
38 Stuart Island —— 191

GULF ISLANDS (BRITISH COLUMBIA) —— 197
39 Portland Island —— 197
40 Pender, Saturna, and Mayne Islands —— 200
41 D'Arcy Island Loop —— 204

OLYMPIC PENINSULA —— 208
42 Indian Island —— 208
43 Mats Mats Bay —— 214
44 Port Gamble —— 216
45 Hood Head —— 218
46 Central Hood Canal —— 220
47 Southern Hood Canal —— 223
48 Sequim Bay —— 225
49 Dungeness Spit —— 229
50 Crescent Bay to Freshwater Bay —— 232

APPENDIX I: Useful Publications —— 237
APPENDIX II: Quick Trip References —— 242

INDEX —— 251

Western campsite, Blake Island (Randel Washburne)

ACKNOWLEDGMENTS

To those who contributed their expertise: Dr. David Burch (Starpath School of Navigation), Dr. Harold Mofjeld (National Oceanic and Atmospheric Administration), Dave Castor, Will Lorentz, Doug Peznecker, Tom Snyder (all Washington State Parks), John Garrett (Washington Department of Wildlife), Judy Friesem (Washington Department of Ecology), Dave Duggins (Nature Conservancy), Rick Kiesser (Washington State Ferries), and Ellie Henke (U.S. Fish and Wildlife Service).

To those willing to share their local knowledge: Tom Carter, Tim Davis, Oscar Lind, Chris Mork, Judy and Lee Moyer (Lee's efforts to improve paddling opportunities along the Duwamish Waterway are a service to us all), Tom Myers, Stan Reeve, Neville Richter, Bill Ross, Marion Slater, Tom Steinburn, Kelly Tjaden, and Bill Turner.

To those who assisted me in my explorations: Kevin Cron, Linda Daniel, Mike and Susan Huffman, Dwight Jacobson, Keith Maclean, Mitch Press, Hank Snelgrove, Bill Turner, and Mom.

To those who helped me make this book: Margaret Foster, Steve Whitney, Miriam Bulmer, Marge Mueller, and (for her advice on my becoming a book writer in the first place) Linda Daniel.

And to my wife, Gunvor, for her patience and support.   —R.W.

Without assistance from others, updating this guidebook would not have been possible or nearly as much fun. Trying to nail down all the facts for such a large, ever-developing region is a challenge. Often it seemed like trying to catch a salmon with bare hands from a kayak in midocean.

The staff and volunteers of the Washington Water Trail Association are due thanks first. Laura Woodcock, access intern, provided the "up-to-the-minute" information on launch sites. Mary Monfort and Zoe Rothchild responded to my numerous queries or pointed me to the right people.

Bruce Grey of Saltspring Kayaking and Cycle and his friends reviewed the accuracy of the Gulf Island trips. The many staffers and employees at the Washington State Parks, Department of Natural Resources, our national wildlife refuges, Washington and Canadian ferries, local county and city parks, as well as the occasional private resort or business, were all patient in dealing with my questions and getting me straightforward answers. And so were my helpful paddling partners and friends.

Then there is Jeanne and "The Ginzel," who let me roam and paddle about Puget Sound and the San Juans to gather firsthand information.

Thanks to all for your valued assistance.   —C.G.

INTRODUCTION

The Pacific Northwest has a national reputation as prime boating country. Its extensive inland waterways are considered among the best in the world for sea kayaking. The attributes that make good boating of any kind also make good paddling—beautiful scenery, intricate and protected waterways, clear and clean water, abundant marine life, and a lot more. On shore there are ample public parklands, many on islands where the original wild charm still is strong, along with a campsite network for human-powered boaters.

The kayaker's perspective on his or her surroundings is a bit different from that of other boaters. From the close-to-the-water and close-to-the-land perspective, the Pacific Northwest reveals an extra, appealing dimension.

For self-propelled boaters the shoreline is everything. It is along the shoreline that most of us prefer to direct our travels rather than heading out across open water. We experience it at touching distance within the intertidal zone: latching onto a rock while drifting by on a calm afternoon . . . leaning back to look straight up at the brick red trunk of a madrona against the blue sky . . . lingering beneath the city's piers on a quiet Sunday morning to watch the sun illuminate the anemone-coated pilings below.

Shorelines in the Pacific Northwest have "texture," a word that expresses all the things that make it interesting: the spongelike eroded sandstones of Sucia Island; the crumbling canneries along Guemes Channel; the tiny channels that, at high tide, meander inland for miles through the Nisqually Flats' marshlands. Few other boaters know this texture as kayakers do. In these places we meet the creatures that other boaters scarcely see at all, such as myriad sea- and shorebirds, river otters, and orcas. Kayakers share a special relationship with their most common traveling companion, the shy but curious harbor seal, and experience humorous aspects of the seal's character, such as his embarrassment when they make eye contact with him.

Just as kayakers look to the land for enjoyment, we also look to the sea—and we like how it treats us in the Pacific Northwest. Sea kayakers from the stormy, unsheltered British Isles coast comment that paddling is so easy here. With our winding inland channels and frequently docile winds, that is a valid observation. At least during the warmer months, sunny highs drift in to stay for weeks, breezes are languid, and kayakers overtake sailors too stubborn to motor.

Particularly in the San Juan and Gulf Islands' powerful tide races, kayaks can pass sailboats with hardly a stroke by threading behind the kelp beds in back eddies along the shores. Our currents are at once a threat and a blessing, contributing significantly to the Northwest's paddling identity with their free rides and perilous tide rips. Probably more than for any other kind of boater, kayakers are engaged by both the positive and negative aspects of moving saltwater. In the Northwest we quickly learn the currents' workings, for an opposing current can make rough seas murderous. In these waters the whitewater paddler can find something reminiscent of the river drops back home, while the more contemplative sightseer can regard currents through streaming, swaying kelp beds on long downstream runs.

In short, saltwater kayaking hardly needs selling to Pacific Northwesterners. Thousands have already discovered its charms and sea kayaks are becoming a significant craft among the pleasure vessels that ply the waterways. New kayakers come to it from diverse backgrounds. Many aficionados of self-propelled terrestrial travel—backpackers, cross-country skiers, cyclists—have found in kayaks an agreeable and reasonably priced way to explore a whole new realm. Marine channels open up to them like an unexplored network of trails. For whitewater river paddlers, many skills transfer easily.

Even experienced saltwater boaters have discovered the comparative simplicity of kayak travel and its special relationship to the surroundings. An ex-sailor recalls his dissatisfaction with experiences under sail—boredom liberally laced with exasperation at our typically fluky winds. His experiences with paddle in hand are uniformly more interesting, less sedentary, and less stressful. Other converts speak of the new level of intimacy with the seashore that kayaking brings:

"In the San Juans there were so many places I'd passed countless times but had never seen, being too busy worrying about staying off enough to avoid scraping my keel. And it was just too much trouble to anchor and go ashore. It's like I have a whole new place to explore!"

Others revel in trading the cramped accommodations on board for spacious campsites on shore, gladly swapping 16 hours of motoring from Seattle to the San Juan Islands (after waiting in line at the Hiram M. Chittenden Locks) for 2 hours on the highway, perhaps followed by a ferry ride. And not least, monthly loan and moorage payments for a large boat cannot compare to a one-time, $2,500 investment in a kayak and associated gear which stores free of charge behind or in the garage.

More than a few sailors and powerboaters in Washington and British Columbia's inland waters have found kayaks to be excellent shore boats—either stowed on decks of larger yachts or towed behind smaller ones.

These boaters enjoy the best of both worlds—a quiet evening of solitary paddling along shore plays pleasing counterpoint to the challenges or sedentariness of a day under sail or power. Kayaks do have limitations as shore boats. They are poorly suited for carrying bulky gear such as ice chests; can take only as many adults as there are cockpits; and are tricky to get in and out of from boats without a boarding step on the transom.

Kayaks can be towed successfully by sailboats, not faster powerboats, in varying weather conditions—though some admit not wanting that additional concern if things get nasty. Most kayaks track well under tow, and are best kept empty and as light as possible. A kayak should have a tightly fitting cockpit cover that will stay on if the kayak should flip. One sailor brings his kayak's bow right up onto his transom in difficult following seas; he says it rides well there. Two kayaks can be towed side by side, with short poles connecting bows and sterns to keep the boats apart and in line with each other.

However, this book is not about sea kayaking in general. The focus is confined to saltwater paddling as it relates to this particular region. Despite the focus, this book is not intended to compete with the several fine guidebooks for water goers in this area, which are listed under Useful Publications. All of the history and much of the shore-based descriptions are too well documented to merit repeating. General boating guides, however, often lack specific information for sea kayakers, information that other boaters find unnecessary and perhaps even peculiar. A few of the guides include a good dose of each local sea's personality. I too have tried to add those aspects that are especially attractive or repulsive to kayakers. I also include a great many things of interest to kayak visitors on shore that I have not found referenced anywhere else. Examples include: beaches prone to freighters' surge; campgrounds that are usually full, sometimes with other kayakers; the way you should turn to launch your kayak as you stroll off the ferry at Friday Harbor or Winslow; and which shore has the eddy that can get you from here to there.

The trips described in this guide are by no means all of the suitable places to have superior sea-kayaking experiences along Pacific Northwest inland waterways, but they are among the best. I used the same criteria in selecting them as in deciding where to dip my own paddle. I focused on loop-trip possibilities so that you might experience new shorelines all the way, though some out-and-back trips are included for their own merits. Wild scenery is always desirable, but I also chose places where development is dominant, yet attractive for its antiquity, interesting for its marine/industrial culture or for the intricacy that over-the-water construction can sometimes present, or perhaps just as a contrast to some

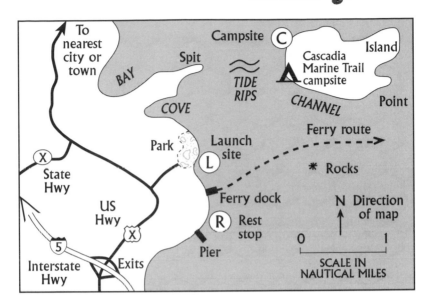

tiny pristine enclave. And, because most kayakers are also campers, opportunities for 2- or 3-day cruises with overnight stopovers, usually at the recently established Cascadia Marine Trail sites for human-powered boaters, are heavily represented along with day trips.

A NOTE ON SAFETY

Sea kayaking entails unavoidable risks that every paddler assumes and must be aware of and respect. The fact that an area or route is described in this book is not a representation that it will be safe for you. Trips vary greatly in difficulty and in the amount and kind of preparation needed to enjoy them safely. On the open ocean and even within the confines of Puget Sound and adjacent waters, conditions can change from day to day or even from hour to hour owing to weather, currents, tides, shipping activity, and other factors. A trip that is safe in good weather or for a highly conditioned, properly equipped kayaker may be completely unsafe for someone else or unsafe under adverse weather conditions.

You can minimize your risks by being knowledgeable, prepared, and alert. There is not space in this book for a general treatise on sea-kayaking technique and safety, but there are good books and public courses on these topics and you should take advantage of them to increase your knowledge. Do not attempt even the easier routes described in this guidebook unless you have developed basic boat-handling and seamanship skills. The maps in this book are intended for general guidance only, not for navigation. Proper nautical charts and tide tables should always be used in conjunction with this book (see Tides and Currents and Going Paddling, The Pacific Northwest Paddling Environment).

Finally, always be aware of your own limitations and of existing conditions when and where you are traveling. If conditions are dangerous or if you are not prepared to deal with them safely, change your plans! It is better to waste a few hours or perhaps even abandon a long-planned-for trip entirely than to proceed in the face of dangerous conditions and pay a high price for your insistence.

These warnings are not intended to keep you off the water. Many people enjoy safe sea-kayaking trips in Northwest waters every year. Just remember that one element of the beauty, freedom, and excitement of sea kayaking is the presence of risks that do not confront you at home. When you go sea kayaking you assume those risks. They can be met safely, but only if you exercise your own independent judgment and common sense.

In my travels around these sounds and islands, the vast majority of times have been good ones. The dangers stay well in the background of my recollections without coloring the pleasures. I hope this book can help turn your kayak explorations of these waters into equally fond memories.

THE PACIFIC NORTHWEST PADDLING ENVIRONMENT

WEATHER, WATER, AND MARINE SHIPPING

The sea-kayaking environment is always characterized by unpredictable elements, the weather being a primary offender. Northwest marine weather patterns do have some consistencies. Paying attention to both visible signs and marine forecasts can reduce uncertainties and risk about what the weather has in store for you. Seawater temperature also deserves cautionary attention. In these waters immersion and the possibility of hypothermia are a problem serious enough to warrant special discussion. Another hazard meriting space in this chapter is the chance of being run down by a ship, especially while crossing main traffic channels. As with weather, knowledge about marine traffic can reduce the chances of having a problem.

MARINE WEATHER

For kayakers the most important variable is wind and the resulting sea state. Unfortunately, winds are difficult for meteorologists to forecast, especially in the Pacific Northwest. Visual cues that you can use to predict what is coming are even less reliable, though there are a few I will take note of in this very brief treatment of our local marine weather. For a more thorough understanding of patterns, I recommend Kenneth Lilly's book, *Marine Weather of Western Washington*, and local TV weatherman and sea kayaker Jeff Renner's book, *Northwest Marine Weather: From the Columbia River to Cape Scott* (both listed under Useful Publications).

The maritime Northwest's year is almost equally divided into two seasonal weather regimes, each with characteristic patterns. The two regimes are governed by two large atmospheric pressure cells. The Pacific High is always present off the California coast, but expands north in the spring to dominate the entire northeast Pacific until early fall. Then the high retreats south and is replaced by the growing Aleutian Low. This low moves south in the fall from the Bering Sea to the Gulf of Alaska to stay through the winter. In spring the low weakens and retreats to the northwest Pacific and the Bering Sea, again replaced with the high. The summer pattern usually eases in during April and gives way in September. Gales (winds stronger than 33 knots) decrease in frequency toward midsummer. This is due to the region becoming dominated by stable Pacific High pressure blocking most disturbances from entering the area. Nonetheless, lows and fronts can bring rain and strong winds, which almost always blow from a southerly direction during bad weather.

Winds can still be quite fresh during fair weather. As the interior land-mass warms, air from high-pressure areas in the Pacific Ocean is drawn in through the Strait of Juan de Fuca. It can blow 25 knots or more in the afternoon. These winds spread to the north and south at the eastern end of the straits, sending southwesterlies up into the San Juan Islands and northwesterlies down across Port Townsend and into northern Puget Sound. Other than as influenced by the Strait of Juan de Fuca, winds tend to be northwesterly during fair weather in the summer regime.

Of course, topography plays an important part in wind direction and force throughout the area. Heating of land creates local onshore winds, called sea breezes, on most sunny afternoons. Hence morning is generally the least windy time for paddling. When the sea breeze direction coincides with the prevailing northwesterly, local winds are intensified.

Mountainous seasides, such as those of Orcas Island, channel winds and deflect them as much as 90 degrees. They may also cause intensified winds where they are forced through a narrow passage or over a saddle between higher hills. For instance, Orcas Island's East Sound often has stronger-than-average winds during prevailing northerlies.

Fog is most common in late July through September, particularly during clear weather when rapid land cooling occurs during the nights. This fog usually clears by early afternoon.

As the Pacific High yields to the Aleutian Low in early fall, prevail-ing winds shift to southeasterly, and disturbances with gale-force winds become increasingly frequent and intense. The first gales of the season usually occur in late September. By late fall no weather pattern can be counted on for very long, as a procession of unstable fronts and depres-sions become the rule through the winter. Strong winds are typically southerly throughout the area, but can blow from almost any direction. One particular wintertime hazard is strong northerly winds on clear days, a result of outbreaks from arctic high-pressure fronts located in the interiors of Washington or British Columbia. On the other hand, periods of very calm weather also occur during the winter regime, particularly

Fog as a ferry approaches the Fauntleroy ferry terminal
(Carey and Jeanne Gersten)

since the low-angle sun has less power to generate local sea breezes. Fog is also possible, especially in January and February, and may persist for several days.

In keeping an eye out for impending weather, there are a few indicators that suggest changes for the worse. Remember that strong winds can develop from very localized circumstances. Weather problems are not necessarily the result of a bad weather system.

In general, be most leery of southerly winds, as these suggest the presence of unsettled weather with potential for strong winds. Oncoming winds often can be spotted on the sea in the distance. Rapid shifts in wind direction, particularly counterclockwise changes ("backing" winds in nautical parlance) to the southeast, suggest the arrival of a front. Whatever the wind direction, weather usually arrives from the west, so note the sky in that direction. The development of high clouds or rings around either the sun or moon is a harbinger of a front.

By far the most effective predictor is the meteorologist's marine forecast via VHF radio. Continuous-broadcast forecasts and local weather reports are always available from at least one of three stations in the United States and two in Canada for the Northwest inland waters of the trips described. Most "weather radios" or hand-held VHF transceivers get at least three of these channels (WX1, WX2, and WX4). Forecasts are reissued every 6 hours, with local-condition updates every 3 hours.

Location	Station	Frequency	Channel
Olympia	WXM-62	162.475 MHz	WX3
Seattle	KHB-60	162.55 MHz	WX1
Port Townsend	WWG-24	162.425	WX4
Victoria, B.C.	—	162.40	WX2
Vancouver, B.C.	—	161.65	21B (also WX4)

In addition, telephone recordings of marine weather are available by calling the United States Coast Guard (USCG), National Weather Service (NWS), or Environment Canada (EC).

Olympia (NWS), (360) 357-6453

Port Angeles (USCG), (360) 457-6533

Vancouver, B.C. (EC), (604) 276-6109

Victoria, B.C. (EC), (604) 656-3978

COLD WATER

Sea temperatures near Seattle vary between 56 degrees (Fahrenheit) in August and 46 degrees in February. Being capsized results in hypothermia—body heat loss that can cause death—unless prompt action is taken to get out of the water. Survival time in 50-degree water can be as little as one-half hour if you are exerting yourself by swimming, especially when immersing your head. Or it might be as much as 4 hours if you have flotation and are able to hold a heat-retaining fetal position to protect the groin and side areas. Clothing provides some in-the-water insulation, particularly tight weaves and cuffs that trap "dead-water" spaces inside, such as a paddle jacket or semidry suit over other garments. Wet or dry suits can extend survival time significantly and are highly recommended. Unfortunately, many paddlers in this region forego them except in cold weather or times of higher risk.

Well-practiced recovery techniques, whether properly dressed or not, are especially important in Pacific Northwest waters. Getting out of the water quickly—either back in the boat or ashore—is critical, though hypothermia may continue due to wind chill.

Early stages of hypothermia include violent shivering, but the individual is lucid and talking clearly and sensibly. Short of a warm shower or bath, dry clothes and a chance to sit quietly and warm up (either in a warm place or wrapped up to prevent heat loss) are probably the best treatment.

If shivering is not present and/or the person's actions become clumsy or speech is slurred, more advanced hypothermia is present and an external heat source is usually needed to help the body rewarm.

Kayak instruction, Alki Beach, Seacrest Boathouse
(Carey and Jeanne Gersten)

Avoid exercise as that may bring "after drop": cold blood from the extremities rushes into the body core with the chance of a heart attack. Likewise, do not rub the arms or legs to encourage circulation. Warm baths are fine, but keep the arms and legs out. Hot drinks also have been known to produce after drop, so they are best avoided unless the condition is clearly a mild one (shivering is present). Warm compresses on the torso, neck, and head; hot water bottles around these areas inside a sleeping bag; or direct body contact with another person may be required. Use artificial respiration and cardiopulmonary resuscitation (CPR) if necessary.

MARINE TRAFFIC HAZARDS

Some kayakers feel that other boats and ships are as much a danger to paddlers as what nature throws at us. Ships could run down a kayak or upset it in a near miss because of their inability to see it or because they spot it too late for avoidance. Pleasure boats could do the same due to inattention at the helm or even in an attempt to come in for a closer look.

Large ships suffer from two disadvantages. Visibility forward from the ship's bridge is partially obstructed by the hull: from some ships a kayaker is not visible at all when less than a half-mile ahead! Also, ships cannot maneuver quickly, and emergency actions, like throwing the engines in reverse which requires some time to accomplish, are slow to have an effect and may put the ship out of control. Many ships require more than a mile to stop, even with full power astern. Tugs pulling barges are especially unable to change course or to stop quickly.

Consider how small a kayak would appear a mile ahead of a ship's bridge. To get some idea of how visible you are from that ship, imagine your kayak on top of the bridge—probably hardly noticeable—then partially obscure it with whatever waves are around you. The chances that the ship will pick you up on radar are slim. Even if you carry a reflector it would be too low to the water to produce a significant signal.

The burden is on you to stay out of a ship's path. As with all other pleasure craft you must stay at least a half-mile from approaching ships and a quarter mile aside from passing ones. Fortunately, where they are going is usually quite predictable. The major shipping routes in Puget Sound, Rosario Strait, and the Strait of Juan de Fuca have defined traffic lanes which are marked in red or purple on nautical charts. Some routes are divided into one-way lanes with a separation zone between the two. Ships are supposed to stay within these lanes. If you can determine where you are in relation to the lane, you can predict where the ship will pass. Though pleasure craft can cross these lanes, they should do so as quickly as possible and otherwise stay out of them. Ships will sometimes deviate from their lane, to pass around a sailboat regatta, for example, so be sure to leave some margin for error for both you and the ship.

Boat traffic, mid-Puget Sound (Carey and Jeanne Gersten)

Suppose you see a distant ship coming down a traffic lane that you wish to cross. Should you try to cross ahead of it or wait for it to pass? Obviously, the latter is safest, but circumstances do arise when you find yourself needing to proceed ahead to get clear or when it seems apparent that you can cross ahead safely. Can you make it?

You need to know something about the ship's speed relative to yours, and your respective distances from your crossing point on the traffic lane. Most ships are much faster than they appear—16 knots is typical in our inland waters, though some freighters may move at their full 20-knot sea speed. Tugs with tows average 8 knots with up to 10 knots possible. Assuming your speed to be 4 knots, ships may be traveling at four to five times that. Make a generous estimate of their speed using the speeds given. Then compare the ship's distance from where you plan to cross with its course to how far you have to go to be clear by a quarter mile on the other side.

Another way to determine what will happen as you approach a ship on a course perpendicular to your own is by watching the ship's position off your bow as you converge. If the interior angle between your bow and the ship's bow gradually increases, that indicates that you will pass the intersection point first—how much sooner is another question. If it stays constant, you are on a collision course. A decreasing angle indicates you will pass astern.

If you find yourself in a situation where you believe you cannot get out of a ship's way, emergency signaling with flares, or orange smoke in sunny weather, may be your only remedy. However, it will probably bring the wrath of the Coast Guard down upon you, as well as the whole maritime community. The most effective solution is a marine VHF transceiver. Call the ship, let them know what and where you are, and then agree on a solution. *Do this before it is too late for them to take evasive action.* Though Channel 16 is the general calling and emergency frequency, ships in Washington's inland waters monitor Channel 14 (Seattle traffic) or Channel 13 (ships' bridge-to-bridge). If you cannot read the ship's name, call it by position (e.g., "the southbound black container ship off Foulweather Bluff").

For pleasure craft you need to rely on visual warnings of your presence. An example includes a flag attached to a fishing pole if you have a rod holder installed on your deck.

Ferries are also a hazard. Generally, the ferries have much better visibility and maneuverability than ships of comparative size, and they will do their best to go around you. When paddling in a group in narrow channels traversed by ferries, or other traffic for that matter, stay close together and avoid getting strung out across their path. If you are taking evasive action, decide on a direction and stay with it so that the ferry can react accordingly. Be especially cautious around docked ferries. Be sure that they are not about to leave as you cross ahead. As a safe practice, give them a wide berth anyhow. Also watch out for their prop wash. Paddling underneath ferry docks is both illegal and dangerous as the prop wash from a docking or departing ferry can easily wrap your boat around a piling.

TIDES AND CURRENTS

In Pacific Northwest waters staying in tune with tides and tidal currents is as important as keeping an eye on the weather and the marine traffic. Adverse currents can slow or stop your progress, but more important are the hazards of rough water created by currents and possibly made far worse by weather.

Tidal currents, the horizontal movement of water, stem from tides, the vertical movement of water. Paying attention to tide cycles is helpful for picking the safest traveling times.

Tides in the inland waters of the Northwest are generally "mixed semidiurnal," which simply means that there are two daily cycles of high and low tides. Typically, one low is considerably lower than the other of that cycle as *Figure 1* indicates. The exact shape of the daily curve changes during the month, and at times the smaller cycle may become little more than an afterthought—just a small deviation in the primary cycle.

The strength of a current is roughly proportionate to the size of the ongoing exchange or the difference between high and low tide. Thus, in *Figure 1*, the flood current between lower low (l.l.) water and higher high (h.h.) will be swifter than that during the exchange from higher low (h.l.) to lower high (l.h.) later in the day. Since the order of this mixed semidiurnal pattern varies from day to day, the tide graphs included in some tide tables such as the *Tidelog* (see Useful Publications), for example, are helpful for getting an overview of the day's current strengths.

Another important factor is the duration of exchanges. Though the average time lapse between high tide and low is about 6 hours, the current-flow interval in some places can be as much as 9 hours on very big exchanges or little more than an hour on very small ones during which there may be hardly any current.

You should also be aware of the bimonthly cycles in tide and current size caused by the alignment of the moon in relation to the earth and the sun. Every 14 days a period of "spring" tides, nothing to do with the season, and bigger-than-usual currents occurs when the moon is either full or new. This happens when the moon is aligned either between or on the far side of the earth in relation to the sun.

In between spring tides are periods of "neap" tides and currents, which are smaller than average, occurring during quarter moons when the moon is out of alignment with the sun and earth.

These cycles exert their biggest influence on outer coast tides and currents. They have less effect on inland tides, though they do affect inland currents to some extent.

More important in Northwest inland waters is the declination of the moon's orbit from the equator, which follows 14-day cycles independent of the spring-neap progressions. The difference between the sizes of the two daily tides and their accompanying currents will be greatest when the moon is at its maximum north or south declination. Since the moon's orbit is elliptical, those periods of the month when it is closest to the earth, "perigee," produce larger tides and stronger currents, particularly on the inside waters.

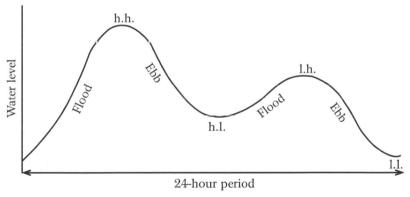

Figure 1

In short, all of these factors can cause dramatic differences in tides and currents, particularly when they coincide. As a consequence, current speeds can be more than twice what they are on another day at the same stage of the tide. So take a close look at your monthly tide tables to keep track of such trends and note that the two daily cycles are somewhat independent of each other. Many tide and current tables include calendars noting the astronomical conditions so that you can see their effects.

Times of no current are called "slack water" or, in some documents, "minimum flood or ebb current," because the water may not completely stop flowing. The length of the slack is related to the strength of the currents before and after it. Slack water times do not necessarily coincide with high or low tide. The characteristics of each waterway greatly affect the differences between tides and currents. Hence, mariners use current tables to predict slacks and times of maximum current. These are far more useful for travel planning than tide tables, though kayakers find the latter useful for timing launches and haul-outs.

PREDICTING NORTHWEST CURRENTS

Predictions for tidal currents are found in two types of documents: current tables, and current charts or atlases.

Current tables are available from two sources. The National Oceanic and Atmospheric Administration (NOAA) publishes *Tidal Current Tables: Pacific Coast of North America and Asia*, a hefty, but inexpensive book that gives current predictions for points between San Diego, California, and the Aleutian Islands, and then west to the Philippines. Because of this range, 90 percent of the volume is worthless if you plan to paddle only the area covered in this book. For those who need only local information, the Island Canoe Company publishes a booklet that includes the

Point No Point Lighthouse (Carey and Jeanne Gersten)

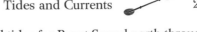

NOAA tables for both currents and tides for Puget Sound north through the Gulf Islands (see Useful Publications). Like the NOAA volume, it is good for one year. The Canadian Hydrographic Service publishes its own tables, which are very similar in format to the NOAA tables.

Current tables are composed of two parts, allowing predictions of slack water and maximum currents at specific places. The first part is a calendar of times for slack water and maximum current with predicted speeds for major reference points. In Washington's inland waters, for example, these are Admiralty Inlet, Tacoma Narrows, Deception Pass, Rosario Strait, and San Juan Channel. Following these are correction factors for many local places based on the major reference points and showing how local currents will differ from those in time and speed. The Island Canoe Company also publishes two current guides that show the local correction factors at their appropriate places on maps, making them easier to find and use during route planning.

Current charts or current atlases show schematic pictures of current flows at different stages of the tide. They are easier to use than current tables and are best for getting an overall picture of the flows during a particular time period when route planning. In some areas such as the San Juan Islands' east/west channels, where flows are far from intuitively obvious, current charts and atlases can be a great help. Another advantage is that these are perennial rather than annual. However, they are less accurate for predicting slack-water times. For critical places, such as Deception Pass, use the current tables.

For Puget Sound, Hood Canal, and Admiralty Inlet, NOAA publishes two sets of current charts that are used in conjunction with the annual current tables. For the San Juan Islands and the Gulf Islands the Canadian Hydrographic Service's *Current Atlas: Juan de Fuca Strait to Strait of Georgia* accurately locates both current streams and the large eddies that occur in this complex area. It also shows how current streams vary both in strength and location depending on the size of the tidal exchange. The major difficulty with this book is finding the right chart to use. To do so, you must have a Canadian tide table and make some calculations about the tide times and exchange size. As an alternative, consult the annual publication, *Washburne's Tables*, which takes you directly to the right chart for any hour of any day without the need for a tide table, calculations, or daylight saving time corrections.

HAZARDS FROM CURRENTS

The majority of Northwest sea-kayaking accidents have resulted, at least in part, from currents usually aggravated by bad weather. The most

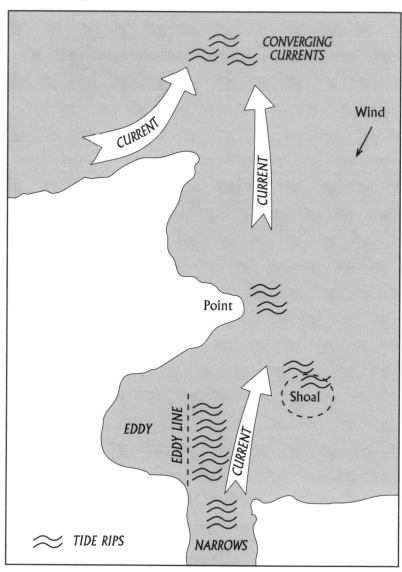

Figure 2

common dangers are those caused by the interaction of wind and currents.

When wind-generated waves encounter an opposing current—one moving against the wind—the waves are slowed down or, if the current is strong enough, prevented from advancing at all. The waves become steeper, larger, and may break heavily. The result is a much rougher and more

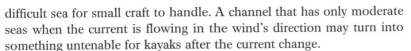

difficult sea for small craft to handle. A channel that has only moderate seas when the current is flowing in the wind's direction may turn into something untenable for kayaks after the current change.

Consequently, kayakers should plan to cross open water when the current and wind are moving in the same direction. Though the wind direction cannot be anticipated with certainty, currents typically can be predicted. It is important to note that in nautical publications, wind and current directions are customarily expressed in opposite fashion to each other: winds in the direction from which they are coming, but currents in the direction toward which they are going.

A kayaker died while crossing from Tumbo Island in British Columbia to Patos Island in the San Juan Islands, a stretch of water known for its strong currents. Though the 50-knot winds that caught the party in mid-channel alone could have caused the fatality, the heavy breaking seas were made worse by a large eddy that resulted in currents contrary to the winds during a time when the general flow was with the wind's direction. This eddy could have been identified only with the Canadian *Current Atlas.*

In certain situations waves are forced to break in quite localized areas called "tide rips." Most tide rips occur where land obstructions or underwater shoals impede or change the current flow, causing the moving water to accelerate because it is being squeezed around a point, through a narrows, or over a shallows (*Figure 2*). Waves may be able to advance against slower currents up to that place, but when they cannot get farther they expend their energy in breaking and become concentrated and trapped in rips such as at eddy lines that result in turbulence.

Where currents intersect, they form an eddy line at their edges. If the difference in current speeds is great enough, waves are unable to cross this barrier and a rip composed of stalled, multidirectional waves forms adjacent to it. The effect is reminiscent of the intersecting waves found near a vertical shoreline where waves are being reflected back through the incoming ones. The waves become irregular and pyramid-shaped. They leap up and disappear unpredictably. A kayak cannot find equilibrium on such a rapidly moving surface, so its movement is jerky. You get splashed a lot with the possibility of losing your balance and capsizing.

Sometimes you encounter rips on calm, windless days. Where do the waves come from? They may stem from very low, widely spaced waves that are barely perceptible until they become trapped and intensified in the tide rip area. Or currents flowing over an irregular bottom may transmit the bottom features to the surface as standing waves—waves that stay in one place—simply another variety of tide rip. Occasionally rips are the result of a large eddy being swept downstream from the place where it was created and persisting with adjacent rips for quite some time and distance.

The rough water in rips may also be created or intensified by the wakes of ships or even pleasure craft. I have seen very minor rips turn into nasty ones after a powerboat passed by. Ship wakes can make such situations far worse.

It is difficult to predict with certainty where rips will be located even if you know the direction and speed of currents; there is just too little information on charts about bottom features. However, the downstream sides of points or islands, shoaling areas, underwater reefs, and places where currents are fastest or currents intersect (such as where they rejoin after flowing around a large island) are all good candidates. In the San Juan Islands, for instance, colliding currents from Spieden Channel and San Juan Channel regularly form dangerous rips. The particularly fast water at San Juan Channel's south entrance usually has rips that are at their worst on ebbs against southerly winds.

From a distance tide rips can be heard as a low roar. Seeing them from the low viewing point of a kayak is harder, particularly on windy days when distant rips are camouflaged by wind waves. If you find yourself heading for a rip, assess your drift in the current and then try to take evasive action while there is still time. Determining your direction of drift can be done with ranges: compare something in the middle ground like a buoy or a rock to a feature in the background such as a hill or tree. Observe their movement in relation to each other. Frequent checking of two ranges at right angles to each other—one ahead and one to the side—will help keep track of what the current is doing to you and how effective your paddling is in countering it.

If you cannot avoid the rip, head straight through it. Remember that you are moving with the current, whereas the rip is stationary. You will soon pass through it. With most rips there is more noise and splashing than real threat to your stability. A suggested defense is to paddle rapidly, each stroke serving as a mini-brace to help maintain equilibrium and direction.

Often, when a current passes along an irregular shoreline or around a point, the flow breaks off from the main current near shore forming an eddy of still water or even a back eddy—water moving in the opposite direction of the current for a short distance. Such eddies usually form on the downstream side of points, islets, or other obstructions. Sometimes the eddy system will extend out alongside the obstruction as well. Sharply defined eddy lines between the current and the still or backward-flowing eddy are often accompanied by swirls, turbulence, or possibly whirlpools. The southeast side of Pass Island in Deception Pass on a strong flood current is a good example of this situation.

Eddy lines can sometimes upset small craft such as kayaks. The primary cause is inertia: crossing from current to eddy or vice versa involves a rapid transition into water going a different direction. Consequently, the rule is to lean and brace downstream. Also, the tremendous turbulence and up- and down-welling in some eddy lines can focus forces of strong torque on a kayak's hull, possibly causing capsize.

Crossing powerful eddy lines is best done quickly and at right angles. Keep paddling at a rapid pace so that strokes can serve as braces.

USING EDDIES TO GO UPSTREAM

Usually, wherever currents are found, there also are eddies along the shore made up of either still water or localized currents moving upstream for some distance. The more irregular the shoreline, the more extensive the eddy system. A good example is San Juan Island's shore along Spieden Channel. During one strong spring-tide ebb, I and a group of young campers in canoes easily traversed this shoreline via its eddy system, while in midchannel two sailboats going the same way stood stationary under both sail and power. We had long since rounded Limestone Point and gone our separate ways by the time the sailors had pulled themselves out of the current's grasp.

The boundaries between the main current stream and an eddy may be marked by turbulence or changes in the texture of the water's surface. These may be difficult to see in slower currents. Within the eddy itself, which may cover an extensive area, water can move in many different directions. Most eddies are actually circling water. A good strategy is to move around when passing through large eddies to find the most favorable currents, using cues such as the direction in which the kelp lies.

More than likely you will be forced to paddle hard to progress upstream from one eddy to the next, usually when you must round a point where, for a short distance, the current sweeps along the shore as fast as in midstream. Such "eddy hopping" requires some positioning, careful boat handling, and perhaps a burst of everything you have for a short, hard pull. Use the still water generally found just downstream from a point to build up some speed and inertia, then break out into the opposing current as far upstream and as close to the point as possible. Head as directly upstream as possible as you enter the main current; otherwise the boat's bow will be pushed out and you will find yourself heading perpendicular to where you intended to go, rapidly losing ground. If this occurs, rather than trying to recover, just continue to turn downstream, reenter the eddy you just left, and try again.

GOING ASHORE

Kayakers are amphibious creatures, at home on both sea and land, with the ability to make the transition easily and frequently. In many other parts of the country, going ashore often puts you in somebody's front yard or private preserve. By contrast, the Pacific Northwest is well endowed with public lands and camping sites hospitable to boaters if you know where they are located. Included is the Cascadia Marine Trail, a "string of pearls," which is a network of dedicated campsites for users of hand-carried, nonmotorized beachable boats throughout Puget Sound and the San Juan Islands.

Many of the trips listed in this book are 2 days long or more, so you will need some camping gear and outdoor skills for these. Though this book offers no primer on camping, a few peculiarities of kayak camping along these inland waters are worth noting, including things that kayakers can do to minimize their effects on these wildlands and their wildlife while ashore or paddling nearby.

Camping at Pelican Beach, Cypress Island
(Carey and Jeanne Gersten)

PUBLIC SHORELANDS

Most public lands are available for use by everyone, but some, particularly national wildlife refuges, are not. The following is a brief description of the different jurisdictions and what kayakers can expect in each.

National Parks. Washington has one national park on its inland shoreline, the San Juan Island National Historic Park commemorating the so-called Pig War of 1859 between Britain and the United States. There are two units, both on San Juan Island: American Camp at the southern end and British Camp on the northwest side. The park has historical reconstructions and interpretive programs, and facilities for picnicking, but not for camping. Camping is also prohibited on the park's undeveloped lands.

National Wildlife Refuges. The Nisqually, San Juan Islands, and Dungeness national wildlife refuges all control shorelines along Washington's inside waters. The Nisqually refuge allows boating close to shore and walking onshore as long as nesting sites are not disturbed. Areas may be closed during sensitive times of year. The Dungeness refuge limits landings to one site, available through advance reservation only. The San Juan Islands refuge includes almost all of the small islets, rocks, and reefs in that area, as well as some larger islands such as Flattop, Skipjack, and Smith Islands. Many of these are also part of the National Wilderness Preservation System. No landings are allowed on any of these eighty-odd places without permission of the U.S. Fish and Wildlife Service. It requests that you stay at least 200 yards from these refuge islands.

Such islands are particularly inviting to kayakers, but this is a case of protecting birds' and seals' rights to peaceful nesting and haul outs. The U.S. Fish and Wildlife Service will not compromise these goals to provide public recreation. You will be cautioned to keep away where units of the San Juan Islands refuge are encountered on routes in this book. They are well marked with signs to that effect. Two islands in the refuge, Matia Island and Turn Island, have portions leased to the Washington State Parks Department. You may camp in these park areas and walk the trails on the rest of the islands, or land on most of the beaches as long as birds' nesting sites are not nearby.

Washington State Parks. State parks provide the most extensive opportunities for both day use and camping throughout Washington's inland waterways. Although most of Washington's park sites are developed, some of the marine (boat access only) state parks are totally undeveloped and overnight camping is not permitted. However, with a few exceptions, camping is allowed at the many small island parks where sanitation such as a pit or solar composting toilet is provided. Most of these also have picnic tables and fire rings, but no drinking water. Examples of such undeveloped camping sites are Blind Island, McMicken Island, and Posey Island State Parks, some of which are also included within the Cascadia Marine Trail system (see below).

Most marine state parks charge a fee collected through self-registration stations. These fees may not be in effect between October and April, though the schedule varies from park to park. A few state parks with more highly developed campgrounds are popular with kayakers. These developed sites, usually with rest rooms and running water, charge more. Most of these parks also have a Cascadia Marine Trail site near the water available for a per-night fee or by purchasing the annual Water Trail Permit (see the Cascadia Marine Trail below).

Establishing your own campsite in the woods, also known as dispersed camping, is not permitted in any of Washington's state parks. This is to prevent spreading the impact that camping has on wildlands. It is also to avoid conflicts with other management goals, such as eagle habitat management in the San Juan Islands.

Be prepared to take your trash home. Many marine state parks now have a pack-it-out garbage program to combat the high cost of removing the mountains of trash left by boaters at the island parks.

British Columbia Marine Provincial Parks. Policies and facilities are like those of Washington's state parks, with "full-service" campgrounds used by kayakers in the Gulf Islands at Montague Harbor and Sidney Spit. Other island parks have a much lower development level (a few have hand pumps for drinking water) and some have none. Camping is generally allowed, though fires are prohibited unless an official fireplace is provided and no fire bans are in effect. In addition, British Columbia is developing its own water trail for users of sea kayaks and other human-powered boats. It is also called the Cascadia Marine Trail.

Washington Department of Natural Resources (DNR) Recreation Areas. The DNR manages some of the best-kept secrets along Washington shorelines, primarily because they are not labeled on most nautical charts. Many DNR camping locations are also designated Cascadia Marine Trail sites. The DNR's recreation areas are picnic and campsites that provide most of the same basic amenities as those of state parks. Facilities are simple (a pit or solar composting toilet and typically no water) and maintenance is infrequent, as the DNR covers a large area with a tiny staff.

Not all undeveloped DNR lands are open to camping. As an example, four-fifths of Cypress Island is undeveloped DNR land, but only two sites at Cypress Head and Pelican Beach are open to camping. You

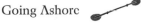

can expect to be evicted by island staff if you camp elsewhere.

The DNR also manages the state's public tidelands which are scattered throughout Puget Sound and the San Juan Islands. More than half of the tidelands in the latter are public, but few in Hood Canal are. Public tidelands are rarely identified by signs, but booklets and maps showing their locations are available from the DNR (see Useful Publications). Almost all of the public tidelands extend only as high as the mean high-tide line unless the uplands are publicly owned too. In general, these are *not* very useful for kayakers except for a quick leg stretch or some clam digging. Remember, you will be trespassing if you wander above the high-tide line.

THE CASCADIA MARINE TRAIL

The Cascadia Marine Trail system augments public waterfront campgrounds by providing a dedicated network of simple campsites located an easy day's travel from the next for sea kayakers and captains of other human- and wind-powered, hand-carried boats. It ranges from south Puget Sound to the British Columbia border.

Since the system's inception in January of 1993, the volunteer organization, Washington Water Trails Association (WWTA), has facilitated the creation of over forty overnight sites as of 1998, with additional innkeeper, restaurant, and other waterside "attraction" partners. About half of the campsites are located within Washington State Parks, with the remainder in DNR, county, and city parks.

The Cascadia Marine Trail is the only Marine National Recreation Trail in the country, conferring status identical to that of the Appalachian Trail. It was also honored in 1996 with an international *Ecotourism for Tomorrow* award, which is supported by major travel associations worldwide and hosted by British Airways.

The Permit System. As of 1995, a permit is required to stay at any site designated as a part of the official Cascadia Marine Trail system. The 1998 annual permit fee of $20 per person is good for the calendar year and grants the purchaser unlimited camping privileges at Cascadia Marine Trail sites. But please note it is not a reservation system and often times, especially during the summer season, you will share sites with others.

The permit is nontransferable and does not preclude the charge of additional site-specific fees. Sites with additional fees are usually noted on signage at the site, by contacting the supervising land manager, or within the Cascadia Marine Trail guidebook available by joining the Washington Water Trails Association.

If you opt not to buy an annual permit, the nightly fee as of 1998 is $7 per person per night of camping. Presently, the permit system makes no differentiation among outfitters, clubs, or individuals. This means that each person, whether camping alone or with any group, needs to have an annual permit or pay the nightly fee. There are no fees for day use only.

You need no permit for children under thirteen years of age, but you will need proof of age. Limited-income senior citizens, people with disabilities, and veterans who hold a Washington State Parks discount pass for camping, receive discounts for Cascadia Marine Trail permits.

Purchasing a Permit. The permit can be purchased from state parks, Washington Water Trails Association, or outdoor retailers. You may call Washington State Parks at 360-755-9231, or Washington Water Trails Association at 206-545-9161, for the name of a retailer close to you or more information about the Cascadia Marine Trail system.

Proceeds from permit sales are deposited to a dedicated Washington State Parks fund used to develop and maintain the system. A Water Trails Advisory Committee composed of seven public agencies and four government agency representatives evaluates projects to be funded by monies from the Water Trails Program Account. It is this committee that sets the fees for the system. If you are interested in attending a meeting or serving on the advisory committee, please call 360-902-8580.

Trail Standards and Guidelines. Maintaining and continuing development of the Cascadia Marine Trail system depends on the good will and cooperative spirit of state, county, and city agencies, port districts, Native American tribes, land trusts, and private citizens. To ensure their support, Washington Water Trails Association asks that its members, users of the trail system, or any other user of a human- or wind-powered, hand-carried boat to practice low-impact, "leave no trace" camping techniques and appropriate camping etiquette.

- Build open wood fires only where fires are permitted. Maximize the use of camp stoves.
- Boat it in, boat it out. Take all the trash whether left by your party or others, and leave a trashless campsite and beach.
- Deposit feces only in proper sanitary facilities. Use only established tent sites.
- Help your group use camping areas in a compact way, and extend a friendly welcome to other users of the trail who arrive after your party.

A WWTA paddle through the Hiram M. Chittenden Locks, Seattle
(Cary Tolman)

■   Strive to preserve the serenity of the camping area and be considerate to others, particularly from dusk to morning.

■   Encourage others, through example and/or gentle correction, particularly members of your own party, to maintain appropriate, courteous behavior.

■   Leave and respect what you find. Avoid trampling vegetation and respect any wildlife you may encounter, including intertidal life.

■   Plan ahead! Know what to expect and use appropriate gear. Also repackage your food before you set out to lessen the burden on remote trash removal systems.

Membership. Membership in Washington Water Trails Association includes the only complete guidebook of the system with descriptions of each site. The WWTA also sponsors a stewardship program for volunteer development and management of these sites. To augment camping opportunities and provide alternatives when weather is inclement, WWTA's Innkeeper Partners program includes member inns and bed-and-breakfasts that cater to kayakers, and are either accessible to the water or will provide transportation for boats and paddler by arrangement.

In addition to the Cascadia Marine Trail, the WWTA has helped with the establishment and continued support of three other water trails. They are the Willapa Bay Water Trail in southwest Washington, the Lewis and Clark Water Trail following the lower Columbia River, and the Lakes to Locks Urban Water Trail ranging from Lake Sammamish to the Hiram M. Chittenden Locks in Seattle.

For information on how to join, contact:

Washington Water Trails Association
The Good Shepherd Center
4649 Sunnyside Avenue North
Seattle, WA 98103-6900

Voice/FAX: 206-545-9161
Web: www.eskimo.com/~wwta
Email: wwta@eskimo.com

CAMPING AND MINIMUM IMPACT

Camping has its own set of requirements and responsibilities. And though we are known by our mode of travel, we need to come ashore each evening to make our temporary home. Though the effect of each sea kayaker is minimal, there are now enough of us that some problem patterns are emerging and will increase with kayaking's popularity unless each of us is aware of the impact on the environment.

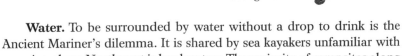

Water. To be surrounded by water without a drop to drink is the Ancient Mariner's dilemma. It is shared by sea kayakers unfamiliar with camping along Northwest inland waters. The majority of campsites along these shores have no drinking water, and those that do, such as Jones Island State Park, often run out midway through the summer or shut it off between fall and spring.

Unless you are going somewhere where you know there will be water, carry your own. Take along enough to tide you over should you have to stay longer because of bad weather, and so you won't be forced to beg water from yachts or head for home in dangerous conditions.

Three quarts per person per day usually is enough if you are careful with it. Wash dishes in saltwater followed by a sparing rinse with fresh water to prevent corrosion. You can also add saltwater to fresh water for cooking. A half-and-half combination is about right for water that will be poured off such as for boiling noodles. One part saltwater to two or more parts fresh water is a good ratio when the water stays in the food such as in cooking rice.

A collapsible two- to three-gallon jug fits well in most kayaks. However, a larger number of smaller water bottles are easier to fit in a small boat to provide better trim and give better protection against water leaking away.

Fires and Stoves. Though most public campsites have fire rings or grates, firewood is not always available. It is also a better practice, environmentally, to use a backpacking stove. The downed wood provides a home for small creatures in the ecological web of things and, ultimately, once broken down returns needed materials to the soil. In most places driftwood is the only option, and during the busy months all pieces have usually been collected.

Beach fires are generally not allowed, both because of the unsightly scars they leave and because they can get out of control and spread to the uplands. Wildfires are a particular fear in drier places such as the San Juan and Gulf Islands during the summer. If you must build an occasional small fire, do so in a designated ring, and never leave it unattended.

Dispersed Camping. Another problem is independent camping in nondesignated sites. One state park ranger told me, "Sea kayakers used to be my favorite user group, but now they're becoming a problem. Too many of them like to find their own campsite in the woods. Even though they are careful about fires and what they leave behind, they tell their friends about it and soon I've got another well-established illegal campsite."

The problem is that Washington's coastline is simply too popular to provide the isolated camping that many kayakers seek. For that, you simply

Solitude on Strawberry Island, at a WWTA site
(Carey and Jeanne Gersten)

must head north into British Columbia or find it in the mountains without your kayak. There are opportunities for legal independent camping on undeveloped DNR lands and in some British Columbia parks, but they are rare and often not very attractive. The rule is to stick to designated campsites and, when in doubt, ask.

Garbage. Kayakers can also cultivate their own best interests by being the most inexpensive and inoffensive user group. Support the pack-it-out garbage programs and avoid using the garbage cans that are provided if you can take it home.

Human Waste. As the number of marine recreations has grown, so has the stress on the land from improper disposal of human waste and the need for the acting land managers to provide adequate facilities to deal with this natural phenomenon. Do not deposit feces anywhere but in a toilet facility or, as is now commonly practiced on some water trails in other parts of the nation, pack it out in a suitable container. Serious health problems from the contamination of ground water and edible marine food sources are best prevented in the first place.

Solitude. An important ingredient to satisfactory camping, solitude may be the most difficult to find during the summer months and particularly on major holidays. I spent one Memorial Day weekend sleeping on the beach at Sucia Island, because all the campsites were occupied. During such peak times, try to aim for places less attractive to overnight boaters: sites without docks, moorings, or protected anchorages. Look to some of the lesser-known DNR sites, especially those with no overland access and poor landings for boats. Or head to the glorious south Puget Sound while everyone else crowds the San Juan Islands.

Wildlife. Marine mammals (particularly seals) and birds are most vulnerable when they are bearing and rearing their young. Mother seals may abandon their pups if they become separated from them or if the pups are handled by humans. Seal pups do not know enough to fear humans, and there have been reports of pups trying to climb aboard kayaks! Stay clear of mothers with young and paddle away from pups if

An orca in Dyes Inlet (Conrad Fiederer)

they approach you. Maintain an adequate distance of 100 yards from seals or other wildlife as prescribed by the Federal Marine Mammal Protection Act.

Birds are particularly sensitive when they are incubating their eggs. Bald eagles are of special concern to wildlife managers, as they may abandon their eggs if there is too much human activity in the vicinity of the nest. This is a major reason that camping is either prohibited or confined to one area in popular eagle-nesting areas such as Patos Island. Eagles are incubating between late March and late May, so be especially unobtrusive on shore or while paddling along shore in eagle country at that time.

Visitors to Cypress Island's Pelican Beach should note that the trail to Eagle Cliffs is closed from January through mid-July to protect peregrine falcon nesting sites in the cliffs area. This closure also affects going ashore on the beaches below Eagle Cliffs.

Cuteness is the sole virtue of the ubiquitous raccoon (*Larcenus pestiferens*). You can expect a visit from these bold and persistent critters at any time, day or night. Their ability to cart off large food packages is notorious.

James Island State Park is home for the commando elite of raccoons, well known for their bravado and larcenous skills continuously honed on park visitors. The tenacity and deviousness of this cadre is unequaled in all the San Juan Islands. They never desist from their mission and apparently never sleep. Neither will you. I recall one winter's night when their persistent efforts to liberate my food from my tent, where I lay clutching it, reduced me to chasing them through the bushes in my underwear with a flashlight, dementedly determined to drive them all into the sea. I failed.

Hanging food is protection only if done cleverly enough to foil these excellent climbers. Another solution, if you have enough stowage space, is to store food in the animal-proof plastic containers commercially available or, as an inexpensive alternative, containers in which foods like Greek olives are shipped. These containers will hold several days' worth of food.

A final note to aid a half-decent night's sleep: bring everything that clanks or rattles such as cookware into the tent with you, or suffer through listening to the raccoons examining it all night.

GOING PADDLING

This section contains information to consider when you prepare for a kayak outing. It discusses general information such as launch sites, carrying kayaks onto the ferries as a foot passenger, and some thoughts about paddling during the off-season on these inland waters. In addition, you also

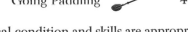

need to evaluate whether your physical condition and skills are appropriate for the trip you have in mind and whether the distances are appropriate for the time you have and the amount of energy you are willing to put out.

CHOOSING A TRIP

New sea kayakers have difficulty identifying trips where the conditions are within their paddling limits. Saltwater trips are more difficult to classify than those on rivers where conditions can be fairly accurately predicted. The water can be mirror smooth on the best of days and a raging sea in the worst of conditions. There is no sure way to avoid the latter. Overconfidence comes easily on those glassy days and many sea kayakers have gotten more than they bargained for by taking on challenging routes after better-than-average weather on early trips. It is wise to start out slowly and experience a range of weather conditions in protected situations before testing your skills in more exposed places.

Carefully review the ratings and descriptions for each route in this guidebook when choosing a trip. Also learn trip planning skills by paddling with experienced kayakers, or through one of the many local clubs or commercial classes frequently offered.

Finally, make note of the mileage provided for each paddling route. Paddling distances are in nautical miles, not the standard land miles you normally think in. A nautical mile equals 1.15 land miles. But please note that all driving directions are in land miles.

TRIP RATINGS

With some trepidation, I have rated saltwater kayak routes in this book by the degree of hazard potential. Though much needed, this was as slippery a task as getting a footing on a kelp-covered rock.

All routes are rated with a *Protected*, *Moderate*, or *Exposed* rating, which reflects the numerous discrete and sometimes ethereal elements that are the sea environment. Unlike easily rated rivers with predictable conditions that are related to a particular rate of flow, sea conditions change by the minute as winds and currents change in intensity independent of one another. My ratings are based on potentials for trouble that may express themselves only rarely, but with perhaps dire consequences: tide rips that spring up from nowhere when the tide changes or a sudden wind that delivers difficult sea conditions during a crossing.

There is a real danger that new sea kayakers, lulled by a placid first trip, might be drawn into traps laid by changing weather or tides with few escape routes. I am particularly concerned about weekend trips where the demands to be home by Sunday night and the lack of a long but easy alternative route lead to "going for it" on a nasty crossing. Sucia Island and its neighboring islands are frequented by weekend neophyte kayakers; my very first overnight paddle was there, yet my criteria led me to rate this trip *Exposed*. (A kayaking fatality has occurred in this vicinity.) My ratings suggest the potential for trouble based on circumstances and paddlers' experiences. How you use them depends on your abilities and judgement.

You might evaluate your own ability to counter the potential sea forces according to your awareness, strength, and survival skills on the water. Awareness is your ability to anticipate and avoid hazards—for example, to spot a dangerous tide rip far downstream and assess which way to paddle to avoid it. Strength is your ability to paddle hard against wind or current to escape a bad situation. Survival skills on the water are your boat-handling reflexes: balance, braces, and rolls. These abilities enable you to keep going in spite of the sea's energies around you with the hope that conditions eventually moderate or you reach calmer water.

I have rated the trips primarily on the potential for trouble from either weather or currents with consideration of the availability of "escape" routes. These ratings take into account the amount of protection provided by land in windy conditions and the distance from shore that paddling each route requires. The ratings also consider currents and the hazards they can introduce, and hazards from marine shipping traffic. Daily paddling distances determined by either a minimum loop distance or the least distance between campsites may be longer for trips with a more challenging rating.

Even the lowest rating presumes some kayak experience—solid instruction, ability to perform assisted and solo rescues, and a saltwater trip with one of the many clubs or commercial outfitters is recommended for your first time or two in a kayak. A first-time kayaker should start by learning basic boat-handling skills, possibly in a pool, lake, or sheltered harbor which is likely to be warmer and smoother than the open Puget Sound.

These ratings are effective from late spring through early fall. Each trip moves up one rating during the off-season, October through April (see Paddling During the Off-season below).

Rating	Description
Protected	A trip designated as *Protected* is suitable for novice kayakers possessing basic boat-handling skills and rescues, as well as rudimentary familiarity with nautical charts. Daily distances are 7 miles or less. Routes mostly follow the shore with no crossings

Moderate

over 1 mile. Waters are largely protected by nearby landforms, and sea currents never exceed 1 knot. Tide rips are unlikely.

A trip designated as *Moderate* is suitable for kayakers who have well-established boat-handling skills, have some previous saltwater paddling experience, are aware of current and weather patterns, and can use current- and weather-prediction resources for planning. Since this rating may commit you to paddling in wind and choppy seas, you should be able to stay on course and keep upright through balance and bracing in these conditions. Daily distances may be up to 10 miles on waters where crossings of 1 mile or more are required. Wind and current could cause dangerous seas. You may need to cross marine shipping lanes. Currents may attain 2 knots or so for short distances with tide rips possible, especially in opposing wind conditions. *Moderate +* indicates the presence of a localized hazard that can be avoided by timing your travel or by choosing an alternate route.

Exposed

A trip designated as *Exposed* is suitable for experienced sea kayakers who have a thorough understanding of weather and currents and can interact with those elements. They also can handle their boats in rough water. The potential for very rough seas is greater on these routes and long open-water crossings may require paddling for some time in these conditions. You may need to cross major marine shipping lanes. Daily distances may be 10 miles or more with travel in exposed seas 1 mile or more from the nearest shore. Currents may exceed 2 knots and tide rips are likely. Trips of this class become very risky during the off-season and should be undertaken only with ample buffer time to await safe weather.

TRIP PLANNING

Trip planning requires the consideration of many factors, including personal kayaking skills, navigation, group dynamics, and much more. It takes time to acquire these skills, but many are translatable from other activities such as bicycling and hiking. What follows is a brief overview of three trip planning topics specifically important to kayak touring.

Nautical Charts. NOAA charts are issued for Washington waters, and the Canadian Hydrographic Service issues charts for British Columbia waters, although there is overlap. These charts are sold in many nautical-supply retailers around the region. Which chart covers any particular area in Washington is shown in *Nautical Chart Catalog 2: United States, Pacific Coast,* a free brochure available wherever the charts are sold. Canada has a similar index for the Pacific Coast.

Two and sometimes three chart alternatives with different scales of coverage are available for any locality in this area. The least expensive coverage is 1:80,000 charts, available in large, single sheets or in folios containing three sheets printed on lighter paper. The folios are called small craft (SC) charts and three of them, 18423 SC and 18445 SC, and the Canadian Hydrographic Service's 3310, cover all the waters discussed in this book. The detail at this scale is adequate, with the Canadian one a bit better at 1:40,000, for cruising. In addition, the light paper and small pages make them easy to fold into a chart case. These small craft charts are usually more thorough in identifying parks than the single-sheet equivalents.

Larger-scale charts such as 1:25,000 give you a more intimate and detailed view of the shorelines, but are more expensive and bulkier, resulting in more frequent turning and refolding. Though the scales of 1:40,000 or larger are preferred for the wilder shores of British Columbia and Alaska in order to spot good landing sites, the 1:80,000 chart is serviceable in Washington. In Washington and southern British Columbia, land ownership is more relevant to getting ashore than shoreline composition and foreshore extent (the area between high and low tide), which shows how far you might have to carry your boat if the tide is out.

Daily Distance. The distance you cover on a daily basis depends on how much time you are willing to spend in the boat. This factor is far more important than your paddling strength or the boat's speed. In general, most people cruise between 2.5 to 4 knots (nautical miles per hour). With stops to look around, rest, and stretch my legs, I average about 2 knots for the day as a whole (time between getting under way in the morning and hauling out for the evening divided by miles traveled). About 12 nautical miles per day seems a comfortable distance for most people in average paddling conditions, barring strong head winds or currents. Using the current can make a dramatic difference. A group of us once clocked ourselves at 5 knots over a 10-mile distance of fairly leisurely paddling with a favorable current.

Weather Allowances and Alternative Routes. One of the most dangerous situations into which kayakers get themselves is the need to be someplace at a certain time. This self-induced pressure prompts them to paddle during unsettled weather in exposed places. For some trips I have included route options offering safer but longer ways back to your launch point or to somewhere from which you could hitch a ride back to your car. The existence of such options is incorporated in the trip ratings for this book.

The more exposed the route and the fewer route options there are, the more time should be allowed for bad weather contingencies. How much time depends on the season and the current regional weather pattern. A large, stable high-pressure area over the Northwest in July probably holds the least likelihood of being weather-bound. In January, however, weather patterns are too changeable to count on forecasted conditions for even a day in advance. During the summer months you may want to consider the forecast for the period you will be paddling and choose a trip rating accordingly. During the off-season, periods of bad weather should be assumed. Either build extra time into the itinerary or choose less exposed trips. Because of the increased hazard potential between September and May, all trip ratings in this book should be considered one rating more hazardous during that time.

LAUNCHING AND PARKING

Finding a place to launch your kayak and leave your car while you are gone can be something of a problem. Some shorelines are well endowed with public facilities providing both access to the water and convenient parking. Others, particularly in certain parts of the San Juan Islands, are limited in public shore access, parking areas, or both. Shaw and Orcas Islands have the least public access and parking, and private property is the probable option—at a cost.

As one solution, the Washington Water Trails Association has published an access brochure. It provides approximately three launch sites convenient to each of the over forty Cascadia Marine Trail campsites. Information included for each access location is the number of parking spaces available, description of the specific type of launch (whether beach, road-end, ramp, or float), amenities at or near the site (such as water availability, rest rooms, groceries, or other), any fees involved, and other useful facts. Whether planning a trip to a Cascadia Marine Trail site, other destinations, or just a day trip, this is a handy resource that can alleviate a lot of headaches.

Etiquette at access locations is very important. While researching

Old ramp, Walker County Park near Shelton
(Carey and Jeanne Gersten)

this book, I encountered negative feelings about kayakers among some Orcas Island residents. Their sentiments have nothing to do with kayakers on the water, only with kayakers getting to the water. One waterfront resident reported finding two kayakers sorting out gear on her lawn in preparation for launching. A marina owner found five kayakers loading their boats on his float, preempting spaces for boats stopping to shop in his store. Another islander summed up her feelings this way: "I identify with kayakers and why they come here and know they appreciate the same things about the islands that I do. But some of them act like the whole place is a park where they have a right to everything at no cost to themselves. They take, but give nothing back; they rarely buy anything in the stores like other boaters do. When they expect to use our property too, that's the last straw!"

Such bad feelings are certainly not in kayakers' best interests, particularly since it is the nature of our means of travel to interact more with people along the way than most other boaters do. The situation is easily redressed when attention is paid to both our actions and attitudes.

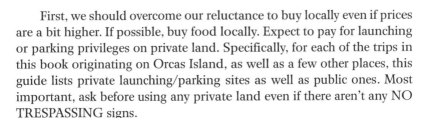

First, we should overcome our reluctance to buy locally even if prices are a bit higher. If possible, buy food locally. Expect to pay for launching or parking privileges on private land. Specifically, for each of the trips in this book originating on Orcas Island, as well as a few other places, this guide lists private launching/parking sites as well as public ones. Most important, ask before using any private land even if there aren't any NO TRESPASSING signs.

Finally, before leaving this topic, it is strongly suggested that you avoid Waldron Island entirely in your San Juan Islands travels. Enough unfortunate incidents involving kayakers have occurred there to prompt the residents' council to formally protest to the state about attracting boating use to the island through the DNR's tideland publications. Be advised that, other than public tidelands, there are no public beaches, toilets, or parklands, and that you are not welcome to visit there. Please paddle elsewhere.

KAYAKS AND FERRIES

Both the Washington and British Columbia ferry systems allow foot passengers to carry kayaks aboard, preferably on a cart or dolly. Washington charges the stowage rate, equivalent to the motorcycle rate, for the boat. Their statewide information number is 888-808-7977.

British Columbia also charges a stowage rate, but it differs from their motorcycle rate, so you need to check for the specific ferries you will travel. Their number is 250-386-3431.

In Washington, a couple with two kayaks car-topped on one vehicle under 20 feet in total length and less than 7.5 feet in total height can save money by driving on. In the San Juan Islands or Vashon and Bainbridge Islands, the round-trip fee structure, collected on the mainland, means a free ride if you paddle out to any of these islands and ferry back.

The savings are not as significant as the flexibility that carrying a kayak on board allows in choosing paddling routes. For example, you can have a fine day excursion paddling from Winslow to Bremerton if you use the Seattle-Winslow and Bremerton-Seattle ferries to start and finish (see the Eagle Harbor to Bremerton chapter). In the Gulf Islands and to a fairly limited degree in the San Juan Islands, you can leave your car on the mainland, ferry to one island, paddle to another, and ferry or paddle back to the car.

As of 1998, opportunities to launch a kayak carried aboard the ferry in the San Juans are limited to Friday Harbor and possibly Orcas Island. Orcas Landing has intermittently allowed launching from a private dock near the ferry landing for a fee, but has suspended it due to congestion caused by kayakers loading inefficiently. Check with the Island Petroleum office. Access to the beach next to the ferry dock at Shaw Island is not allowed.

Carrying a kayak on board also provides a significant bad weather fallback, particularly in the San Juan and Gulf Islands, where paddling to a closer or less exposed terminal and ferrying may be safer than paddling back to your car.

During the summer months large numbers of foot passengers with kayaks make the San Juan Islands ferry run particularly hectic. The ferry staff recommends a few things to make it easier for everyone.

First, arrive at least one hour early. This will give you time to find parking and get your boat and gear ready to board. The biggest problem that carry-on kayaks pose for the ferry staff is the multiple trips that kayakers make to get their gear aboard, which delays loading cars. The staff asks that you consolidate as much as possible and/or use a boat cart to minimize the trips.

Because of the tremendous growth in use of the San Juan Islands ferries in recent years—and because walk-on kayak traffic has increased most dramatically—kayaks now compete with cars for spaces on the ferries. Westbound from Anacortes the crews are able to fit kayaks into "void spaces," those not used by other vehicles, well enough that kayaks readied for boarding ahead of time will stand a good chance of getting aboard. But eastbound from the islands these void spaces cannot be filled readily. Since each island has an allotment of vehicle spaces on each ferry, kayaks must be counted into these and wait their turn to fill them. You will not be required to line up with the cars; kayaks can be staged near the ramp.

Kayakers who carry on their boats need a put-in within walking distance of the ferry terminal where they disembark. In many cases, but not all (including Shaw Island in the San Juans), there is someplace to do that. However, at some there may be a fee for the privilege. Fees are described in trips that involve those ferry terminals.

PADDLING DURING THE OFF-SEASON

For many, paddling in Northwest inland waters during the off-season is just as appealing as during the summer. In fact, there is much about it to be preferred.

During the winter months, there are fewer boats with which to share the waterways. A quiet wildness comes from the scarcity of boats and from having whole marine park islands to one's self as you would never expect in your wildest dreams of summer. Other boaters met are kindred spirits who appreciate the advantages of winter boating to the extent that they are foolish enough to be out there too. Boaters are more inclined to say a few words as they pass one another, acknowledging some sort of bond.

Then there are the many seabird species that are rarely seen in the warmer summer months. There are the overcast November days when the air and the sea are languid, almost paralyzed, from dawn to dusk. Silence is broken only by the distant conversations of floating seabirds or the gentle breathing of a passing harbor porpoise.

However, the question of imminent weather is seldom far from the winter paddler's mind. Winter in these waters is a stern, no-nonsense time of year. You do things on nature's terms or suffer the consequences.

The changeability and strength of the winds during the winter months are major hazards to contend with. Upgrading the trips to a more severe rating for the off-season is entirely justified for this reason alone.

Weather is simply more unpredictable during the off-season. Fronts and low-pressure systems follow each other in much closer succession. Conditions are more extreme and changeable. And you must paddle in rougher and more uncertain situations than you might prefer. As you move along, there is also the pressure of time: twilight lurks never far away. With the stronger winds and the more fully developed seas, tide rips can occur where they rarely do in less windy times. And those admittedly reassuring passing pleasure craft that eagerly watch for the chance to rescue during the summer are now snug in their moorings while winter wilderness isolation is all yours.

I recall one trip from Lopez Island to James Island through Thatcher Pass on an unsettled November day. It bore little resemblance to the placid summer "pond" across which I had lazed my way countless times before. Winds gusted from one direction, settled to flat calm, shifted, and blew hard out of another direction in the space of an hour. Rips popped up where I had never seen them before. The daylight faded far too soon and, through it all, there was nary another boat to be seen.

Other memorable moments of kayak terror have taken place in the winter. The seas may not have been significantly bigger than those of the summer, but with the awareness of the chilling splashes on hands and face and how distant the shore suddenly seemed, there was frequently fear of a medium sea about to become a nasty one.

There are other differences in the winter. Beaches, particularly gravel ones, become steeper. The characteristically bigger waves tend to move the beach material more, piling it up at the current water level so that there is a definite berm or steep drop-off. The consequences are two.

First, launching or landing may result in a raised bow on the beach and the stern in the water, a precarious position that often terminates in a spill. Second, a "dumping" surf, one that abruptly releases its energy close to shore, may hinder entering or exiting the boat.

One January morning a friend and I launched at Clark Island into a heavy chop coming across Rosario Strait. Because of the surf on the beach, we each buttoned up in our boats before launching and paddle-poling ourselves off the steep, slippery beach. I slithered out with no problem, but the sharp stern of my friend's kayak buried itself in the steep berm, leaving him teetering precariously in the surf until he could lever himself off with his paddle.

Daily wind patterns from the summer no longer hold either, particularly the axiom of least wind in early morning. These summer cycles are largely generated by the heating of land masses and subsequent convection currents. But the low angle of the sun in the winter gives it far less heating power. Thus, the land often remains as cold or colder than the sea and generates negligible convection.

Next to weather the biggest constraint on paddling during the off-season is the short daylight. Kayakers need a relatively long time between getting up in the morning and getting under way. In comparing notes, it appears two hours is about the standard.

Hence, trying to make 10 miles a day requires using every minute of daylight during the shortest days of the year. If you hate rising before dawn and it gets light at 8:00 A.M., it means getting a 10:00 A.M. start on the water. Assuming 2 knots for travel speed and a brief lunch stop, you should plan to reach your next camp at about 3:00 P.M. with an hour of fading light left in which to get ashore and set up camp. I am particularly wary of being caught on the water at dusk in the winter since a quick weather change for the worse in the dark is especially unnerving and dangerous.

Off-season camping likewise requires the acceptance of some austerities in return for your own private reserve of gorgeous winter wildlands—perhaps bartering an evening under cover in a continuous downpour for a frosty morning walk along a marine park pathway that shows no recent footprints. And for me the challenge of setting up a warm and comfortable evening's nest in spite of what is going on outside is a large part of the season's appeal.

Clothing for the off-season should be able to shed water and wind. The heavier precipitation and stronger winds mean you will want to wear a paddle jacket or dry-top most of the time. A good barrier against the substantially greater wind-chill factor, even in light breezes, is important for your safety as well as comfort. Many paddlers now wear full dry suits, though they may find them too warm for summer paddling. Here the new breathable materials such as Goretex™ provide relief. Gloves that guard against both wetness and cold air are also important. I have found pogies the one alternative offering the most effective protection without cramping paddling style. Finally, head protection is extremely important; this is where a majority of the body's heat is lost. A wool or synthetic cap under a hood serves most paddlers very well. Wearing neither, one, or both together allows adjustment to a full range of temperature and wetness conditions.

EMERGENCIES

We all hope that an emergency never happens, but we should all be prepared just in case. It is wise to have at least the basics of first aid and cardiopulmonary resuscitation (CPR) training in our repertoire of skills. Classes in these disciplines are taught on a fairly regular basis by local chapters of the American Red Cross, through community service organizations such as the local fire department, and by outdoor recreation groups and clubs.

In addition, the importance of taking classes and practicing to become proficient in performing fundamental sea-kayak rescues, such as the T and X assisted rescues and paddle-float self-rescue, cannot be stressed enough. We never plan to take a swim on a trip, but being prepared with a clear mind and practiced response for that off-chance swim can literally be a lifesaving skill.

Beyond the unmistakable reality that the best help is the immediate aid of your paddling group, you can obtain assistance from a variety of sources when on or near the water. Who to call will depend on the nature of the emergency, your location, and the communications means available to you.

When asking for help, you should be prepared to provide relevant information including:

- Nature of the emergency: injury (exact description), overboard, missing person, etc.
- When the problem occurred and how long people may have been in the water or suffering an injury
- Exact location or direction and distance from recognizable landmarks
- Description of persons and boats involved
- How many people and what equipment, including survival gear and first-aid supplies, are at the scene

- What equipment is needed
- Method of evacuation needed
- Local weather and sea conditions, including currents and wave action
- Names and addresses of members in party and who to notify

Location. Knowing your precise location can be difficult at times, especially due to the nature and stress of the emergency situation. But it is essential if help is to reach you in time. For an exact location, a global positioning satellite (GPS) receiver is ideal. (Note: In the near future, cellular phone systems are planning to provide the location of the caller to 911.) However, batteries and electronic equipment seem to have a predisposition to fail in saltwater environments. For that reason there is no substitute for waterproof nautical charts and a compass to continually track your progress and position.

Communication. In many cases, a telephone is the primary means of communication. In all emergencies when feasible, call 911 for assistance. The dispatcher can contact the appropriate agency for aid. The county sheriff is the standard emergency responder in most areas of Puget Sound and the San Juan Islands. The Coast Guard is tasked with providing emergency aid on the water. Although cellular telephones seem to have become almost universally available, do not rely on them totally, as you may be out of transmission range. A VHF-FM radio is invaluable for this reason alone. But remember: Don't just carry a radio, know how to use it and keep it accessible at all times. Beyond these communications means, you should carry flares and other emergency signaling devices and know when and how to use them for maximum effectiveness.

EMERGENCY CONTACT NUMBERS

U.S. Coast Guard
206-217-6000
cellular telephone: *CG
16 on VHF-FM radio

U.S. Customs: General
800-562-5943 or 360-332-7650 if you have a PIN

U.S. Customs: Port Townsend
360-457-4311

U.S. Customs: Friday and Roche Harbors
360-378-2080

Seattle Harbor Patrol
206-684-4071
16 on VHF-FM radio

County Sheriff
911 dispatcher will contact; use a regular telephone if possible, as cellular phones may go to the wrong county due to the system's configuration and 911 calls CANNOT be transferred.

Paralytic Shellfish Poison Hotline
800-562-5632

SOUTH PUGET SOUND

1 HAMMERSLEY INLET

The skinniest of major Puget Sound inlets, Hammersley is a saltwater river ride if you time the currents right to transport you from one end to the other. There is the possibility of making a fairly easy round trip by coordinating your return with the tidal exchanges, enjoying a snack and exploring the shoreline at your turnaround while you await the current's reversal. Hammersley Inlet was completely overlooked by Peter Puget's expedition and not discovered for another 50 years, possibly due to the overlapping points of Cape Horn and Cape Cod near the inlet's entrance, which mask its true character. Once this inlet was found, the fertile uplands quickly became and still are a primary source of timber.

Duration: Full day to overnight.
Rating: *Moderate* or *Moderate +*. During large tidal exchanges the current can flow at a swift 5 knots. Areas of tricky current and tide rips can be avoided.
Navigation Aids: NOAA charts 18445 SC or 18448 (both 1:80,000) and 18457 (1:10,000). Use current tables for The Narrows with adjustments for Hammersley Inlet.
Planning Considerations: Use the current tables to carefully plan the timing of your trip in either direction, traveling on the flood west to Shelton, and on the ebb east to the Arcadia launch. In this slender inlet it is much more fun and exhilarating to paddle with the current than against, which is impossible at high exchanges. Cape Horn, jutting out from the north shore about 0.5 mile from the inlet's entrance, helps develop a strong tide rip which is avoided by staying to the south shore. Also note that tricky eddies may form at other smaller protuberances along the inlet. If you paddle out to Hope Island, be aware of the strong current that builds on the west side of Squaxin

Island and the long fetch of Totten Inlet which is able to produce stiff southerly winds.

GETTING THERE AND LAUNCHING

Four public launch sites provide access, three in and near Shelton at the inlet's west end, and another one at the Arcadia boat ramp just to the south of the inlet's entrance on Puget Sound.

Shelton: The launch on Shelton's working waterfront is along Pine Street (Highway 3 to Bremerton) just north of the old downtown. You pass under a railroad bridge and immediately on your right is a set of tall fuel tanks. The launch is just on the south side of the tanks. There is room for approximately six cars, more on weekends when the fuel distributor is closed, at this gravel and dirt launch site.

Jacoby Shorecrest County Park: This launch is on the crook of the inlet's elbow across from Shelton. From Highway 3 at the north end of Oakland Bay, head south on East Agate Road, then turn right onto East Crestview Drive. Soon after turn left on East Parkway Boulevard and

Working the logs, Hammersley Inlet at Shelton
(Carey and Jeanne Gersten)

follow it until you reach East Shorecrest Park Way and the county park. You must leave your car one block east of the park, not along the concrete ramp in the park.

Walker County Park: This small wooded Mason County park is on the south shore of the inlet almost across from the Jacoby Shorecrest ramp. Drive Highway 3 south out of Shelton and, as you reach the top of a long hill, turn left onto Arcadia Road. Travel for 1.5 miles turning left onto Southeast Walker Park Road. In another 0.5 mile you enter the park. The park is open daylight hours from 8:00 A.M. to dusk. It is a short walk from the parking lot down the boat ramp, which is no longer maintained, but very useable for kayakers.

Arcadia Boat Ramp: To reach this paved boat ramp, drive just over 7.5 miles from Shelton along Arcadia Road. At Lynch Road turn left and proceed to the launch. Park two blocks away from the ramp on the road's south side. This launch is popular in summertime and parking is limited, so plan accordingly.

ROUTE

Your direction of travel is highly dependent on the current's flow and your timing. The one-way route is just under 7 miles if you travel from Shelton to Arcadia or vice versa. If you prefer to avoid Shelton, Jacoby Shorecrest County or Walker County Parks are pleasant alternatives with picnic tables and sanitary facilities, and will shorten the route about 1 mile.

Starting in Shelton, you immediately recognize this as a logger's town. The Simpson Mill dominates the waterfront, and numerous logs floating on Oakland Bay are normally corralled within booms. The logs are often tended by one-man, lime-green work boats that are best described as pint-sized tugboats. It is fun to watch them push and prod the logs into obedience, but remember to stay a safe distance.

Looking to the north you see the wider expanse of Oakland Bay. Oysters are farmed in its uppermost beds. East lies narrow Hammersley Inlet.

As you paddle down the inlet for the next 4 miles, the shoreline is dominated on both sides by agreeable homes old and new, of various shapes and sizes, many hugging the beach. There is no public access, so be prepared to stay in your boat. The inlet maintains a fairly even but cozy width of less than 500 yards along most of its length.

As you course the remaining 2.5 miles of the inlet after Libby Point, it gradually reverts to a more natural state, primarily due to the higher, steeper banks that discourage building. Nevertheless, houses appear sporadically at the tops, and a few have made inroads down the sides.

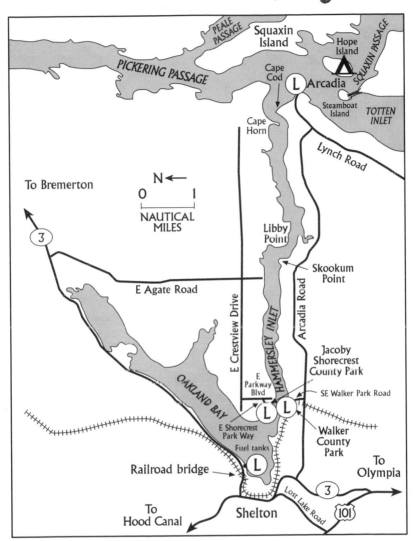

Generally, the land feels a little wilder here and the paddling is pleasant with plenty of shorebirds and waterfowl, often harbor seals and sometimes eagles if you travel during a quieter time of the day or in the winter season.

Just before entering into Pickering Passage from Hammersley Inlet, you pass the jutting prominence of Cape Horn. It helps create a strong rip tide at high tidal exchanges. It is a place to practice paddling technique or to be avoided depending on your skills and intentions for the day.

As you leave the inlet, Squaxin Island appears directly across Pickering Passage, to the southeast is Hope Island, and to the south lies Steamboat Island with its obvious long, low bridge connection to the mainland. Bear south along the western shore of Pickering Passage to reach the Arcadia Boat Ramp in under 0.2 mile.

If your plan is a round trip or overnight, the best spot to relax or camp before the return is the Cascadia Marine Trail site on Hope Island (see the Hope Island trip). However, this requires paddling across Pickering Passage and adds another 2.5 miles to your round-trip journey. Traveling in the other direction, either Jacoby Shorecrest County Park or Walker County Park is the much more comfortable alternative for a picnic compared to the barren launch at Shelton.

2 HOPE ISLAND (SOUTH)

Hope Island is a state park with beaches, meadows, forest trails, and the remnants of a farm homestead. Access from various sides of the South Sound is easy using the Hammersley Inlet, Boston Harbor, or Peale Passage routes described here. Hope Island can be incorporated into a single-day trip around adjacent Squaxin Island or a multiday circumnavigation of nearby Hartstene Island. A Cascadia Marine Trail campsite was established on Hope Island in 1998. Other camping possibilities are the two Cascadia Marine Trail sites at Jarrell Cove State Park and Joemma Beach State Park (formerly known as Robert F. Kennedy) on the Key Peninsula.

> **Duration**: Part day to overnight. The island is currently day use only, with camping facilities for Cascadia Marine Trail permit holders and the general public planned for 1999.
> **Rating**: *Moderate* or *Moderate* +. The Boston Harbor route requires an open-water crossing and exposure to possible tide rips in Dana Passage. Currents on the Peale Passage route may exceed 1.5 knots at times.
> **Navigation Aids**: NOAA charts 18445 SC or 18448 (both 1:80,000). Chart 18456 (1:20,000) covers the Boston Harbor route. Use current tables for The Narrows with adjustments for Dana Passage on the Boston Harbor route, or with adjustments for Peale Passage on that route.
> **Planning Considerations**: Use the current tables to avoid maximum flows in Dana Passage on the Boston Harbor route. On the Peale Passage route, travel to Squaxin Island on the ebb and return

with the flood current. On the Pickering-Peale Passage route, travel south on the ebb and return on the flood.

GETTING THERE AND LAUNCHING

This area sits astride a portion of Puget Sound where island destinations are separated by only a few miles of water and easily accessible by boat, hours apart by highway. Residents of the west side of Puget Sound can start from Latimer's Landing at the Hartstene Island Bridge near Shelton and paddle the Peale Passage route, or launch at the Arcadia boat ramp just to the south of Hammersley Inlet. Those coming from the east will find Boston Harbor near Olympia most convenient.

Latimer's Landing at the Hartstene Island Bridge: To reach the landing, turn onto Pickering Road from Highway 3 about 8 miles north of Shelton (there is a sign for Hartstene Island). Follow this road approximately 5 miles to the bridge. The county landing includes a public ramp, dock, and parking lot located just north of the bridge's western end. There are portable toilets and parking for about twenty vehicles.

Arcadia Boat Ramp: See the Hammersley Inlet chapter.

Boston Harbor: Take Exit 105B (Plum Street) from Interstate 5 in Olympia. Drive north after exiting the freeway; the rest of the route is essentially straight ahead. After passing through several intersections for approximately 1 mile, you will see water on the left. Plum Street becomes East Bay Drive, which eventually becomes Boston Harbor Road. Continue another 7 miles to 73rd Avenue Northeast and turn left. The ramp and parking lot are 0.25 mile beyond, next to Boston Harbor Marina. The paved parking lot across the street is public. The marina store carries basic lunch and snack items. There are also public rest rooms.

ROUTES

Pickering Passage (Latimer's Landing to Hope Island): *Moderate.* One-way distance is 4 miles. Currents can exceed 1.5 knots along this route. Using favorable currents can make a significant difference for travel, although alongshore eddies can be used to travel against the currents in most places. Tide rips are possible, especially when the current opposes the wind direction.

The flood currents coming around both sides of Hartstene Island meet in the vicinity of northern Squaxin Island.

To travel from Latimer's Landing to Hope Island via the west side of Squaxin Island, catch the flood current starting soon after the turn to the flood for Pickering Passage off Graham Point, and return when the current begins to ebb at the same location. If you are circumnavigating

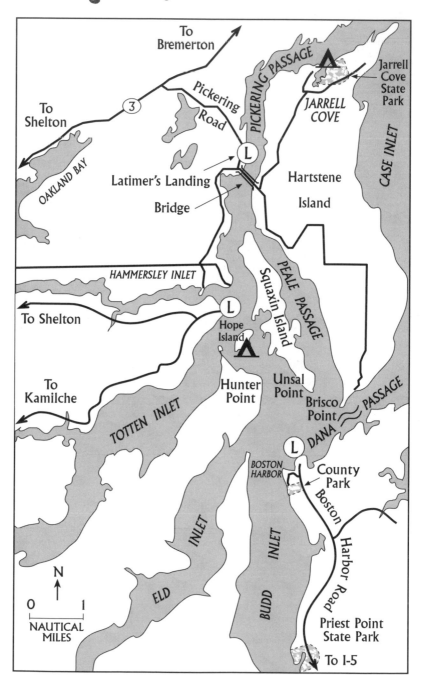

To
Bremerton

To
Shelton

3

Pickering Road

PICKERING PASSAGE

JARRELL COVE

Jarrell Cove State Park

OAKLAND BAY

L

Latimer's Landing

Bridge

Hartstene Island

CASE INLET

HAMMERSLEY INLET

Squaxin Island

PEALE PASSAGE

To Shelton

L

Hope Island

To
Kamilche

Hunter Point

Unsal Point

Brisco Point

DANA PASSAGE

TOTTEN INLET

ELD INLET

BUDD INLET

BOSTON HARBOR

L

County Park

Boston Harbor Road

Priest Point State Park

To I-5

N

0   1
NAUTICAL MILES

Squaxin Island, note that Peale Passage has quite a different schedule, flowing north during most of the flood cycle and south during the ebb. Consequently, plan to head up the east side of Squaxin Island about 2 hours before the turn to the ebb at Graham Point, so as to ride the flood up Peale Passage and then the new ebb the remainder of the distance.

South of the Latimer's Landing, the shores in Pickering Passage alternate between houses and steep tree-lined banks, but the shore of Squaxin Island is a fine oasis of natural beauty. Paddling close to its shore, you can imagine yourself exploring Puget Sound two centuries ago with British explorer Captain George Vancouver.

Squaxin Island is an Indian reservation. Do not go ashore without permission. Squaxin's shoreline has escaped development except for an oyster-rearing operation in the bay midway down the island. Occasional decaying shacks are the only signs of the island's sparse settlement. More evident residents are river otter, blue heron, or even a coyote trotting along the beach.

Hope Island State Park is a 106-acre island that supported a working homestead until the 1940s. This addition to the park system includes meadows, orchards, and an old windmill on the west side, as well as extensive trails leading through the forests on the island. At lower tides, you can hike the approximate 2 miles around the island on the beach. A caretaker's cabin is located above the beach on the flatter west side of the island. This area is also the Cascadia Marine Trail campsite, with several sites for general usage on the south side of the little cove here. There are composting toilets, but there is no water system.

Boston Harbor to Hope Island: *Moderate +.* The one-way distance is about 4 miles. Dana Passage currents can attain almost 3 knots at times, and rips can be lively here, especially with an opposing wind.

The strongest currents can be avoided by crossing directly from Boston Harbor to Squaxin Island. This route, however, involves crossing 2 miles of open water. Also, an ebb current flows southeast from Unsal Point on Squaxin Island most of the time, averaging a little over 1 knot at its peak, making this route most practical for the return.

To avoid open water and the strongest currents, cross Budd Inlet from Boston Harbor, then Eld Inlet entrance where currents there may reach 1 knot at times. Next follow the shoreline north and then west through Squaxin Passage, where the current may exceed 1.5 knots, flowing west during the flood. If you are circumnavigating Squaxin Island, expect either a longer open-water crossing from or to Unsal Point, or take a detour east to Dana Passage for a shorter crossing to Hartstene Island at Brisco Point. Currents in Dana Passage may reach several knots, and tide rips can develop. Try to cross when the current is slack or at least flowing in the same direction as the wind. Note that Peale Passage flows north on the flood.

3 ELD INLET

This is a pleasurable place to lazily paddle with no real destination, or to explore the little mid-inlet coves and southern tidal estuaries. Only one commercial boat ramp, a driveway through a private home's yard, provides direct trailered boat access on Eld Inlet. This factor helps encourage greater tranquillity than found elsewhere. The other access point, at Frye Cove County Park, is only suitable for hand-carried boats.

> **Duration**: Part to full day.
> **Rating**: *Protected* or *Moderate*.
> **Navigation Aids**: NOAA charts 18445 SC (1:80,000), 18448 (1:80,000), and 18456 (1:20,000). Use current tables for The Narrows with adjustments for Eld Inlet entrance.
> **Planning Considerations**: The timing of any trip into the southern tidal estuaries requires care in planning so as to explore only during a high tide. Extending the trip into these shallow channels too long into ebb likely means dragging your craft through deep mud. Current can also be a factor, especially as the channels drain, which creates fast flowing waters.

Budd Inlet near Olympia, Washington (Conrad Fiederer)

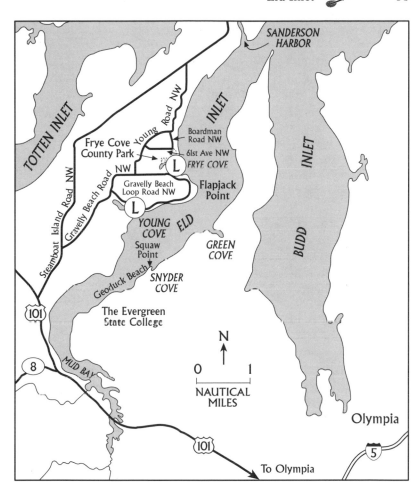

GETTING THERE AND LAUNCHING

There are two launch sites for hand-carried boats, a very small commercial boat ramp open to the public and Frye Cove County Park.

Commercial Boat Ramp: From Highway 101 take the Hunter Point/Steamboat Island Exit and drive north 1.1 miles on Steamboat Island Road Northwest. Turn right onto Gravelly Beach Road Northwest, proceed another 1.6 miles to Gravelly Beach Loop Road Northwest, and turn right. There is a sign at that intersection directing you to the boat ramp. In another 0.6 mile you will come to the boat ramp, a marine repair shop, and boat builder clustered on the same property. The ramp is concrete with a float along the side. There is a portable toilet and very limited parking. Weekend parking is actually a little better, as the boat builders need the spaces during work days. A small fee is charged by the friendly owner of the ramp to maintain the facilities.

Frye Cove County Park: Once on Gravelly Beach Road Northwest, continue past the turn to the commercial boat ramp another 0.8 mile to the junction of Young Road Northwest and the other end of Gravelly Beach Loop Road Northwest. Turn left onto Young Road Northwest and proceed 0.7 mile and turn right onto 61st Avenue Northwest (also known as Giddings Road). In 0.5 mile, at the end of 61st Avenue Northwest where it intersects with Boardman Road Northwest, is the park entrance to the right. Follow the park road to the main parking area. You must carry your boat down a well-maintained path, Cove Trail, about a quarter mile to the small beach at the head of Frye Cove. A cart will work, but you may need help negotiating a couple of short sets of two or three steps. The park itself is delightful. Well maintained with a nice view out over Eld Cove, it has rest rooms, picnic tables, clamming on the beach in season, and a great lawn for lazing on.

ROUTES

Young and Frye Coves: *Protected.* Great for novices, either of these snug little coves makes for a tranquil paddle of an hour or so. It is best to time a trip for higher tides so their inner reaches are accessible. Trees drip with mosses and lichens, while small creatures forage or flit along the sheltered banks.

Mud Bay: *Moderate.* The distance to the head of the Mud Bay inlet and back is 8.5 miles. The route offers pleasant views of homes nestled within a wooded shore backed to the south by gentle mountains. It is an easy paddle with no current to speak of until you approach the southern reaches and tidal channels passing beneath Highway 101. The ebb and flood of the tide creates fairly strong current that is difficult to paddle against, especially in the restricted passages near the highway during a large ebb. But here are the ideal conditions for waterfowl and wading birds. It is likely you will see heron, kingfisher, and numerous other winged hunters in these shallows.

Eld Inlet still produces a reasonable share of oysters, and you may witness markers defining growers' beds in the shallows and shoals here and there. However, the major harvests of old have long since dwindled. You will witness evidence of this once productive past intermittently along the shore as you pass the remnant piers and pilings of oyster shacks identified by the mounds of sun-bleached oyster shells surrounding them.

Geoduck Beach: *Moderate.* Directly across from Young Cove is

Geoduck Beach, the western boundary of The Evergreen State College's campus. This wonderful stretch of shoreline is fully wooded except for a couple of buildings. Together with the beach they comprise the college's Marine Study/Ecological Reserve. Landing is prohibited to protect the marine and shore life for research, but simply paddling this edge of sandy shore and tall forest is pleasure enough. If you must walk the beach, save it for another day—the approach is by land from the bluff above on maintained trails.

A fulfilling round trip is to launch from Young Cove, exploring it first, then paddle south across Eld Inlet to the southern end of Geoduck Beach. Follow the beach north, then recross Eld Inlet rounding Flapjack Point to Frye Cove. Stop for a rest or picnic at Frye Cove County Park, then return south to your start by following the western shore and once again rounding Flapjack Point. The total distance is about 7 miles.

4 Mc MICKEN ISLAND

Located along the eastern shore of Hartstene Island, this little state park is a low-key destination that can be accessed easily from Tacoma or the Bremerton area via the Key Peninsula.

Duration: Full day.
Rating: *Moderate*. Requires a 1.5-mile open-water crossing. Currents along the route are weak.
Navigation Aids: NOAA charts 18448 or 18445 SC (both 1:80,000).
Planning Considerations: As of late 1996, McMicken Island is officially closed to camping. The future addition of a Cascadia Marine Trail site is being considered; check with Washington State Parks.

GETTING THERE AND LAUNCHING
Joemma Beach State Park: This trip originates at this state park (formerly Robert F. Kennedy) and Cascadia Marine Trail site on the Key Peninsula. From Highway 302, turn south in Key Center onto the Gig Harbor–Longbranch Road and follow it to Home. About 1 mile south of Home, turn right on Whiteman Road (there are signs for Joemma Beach here and at the next junction). After another mile, bear left at the fork, and then turn right a little less than 0.5 mile beyond onto Bay Road. This road turns to gravel and then forks. Take the right-hand road and follow it downhill to the recreation area. Generally, there is ample parking in a

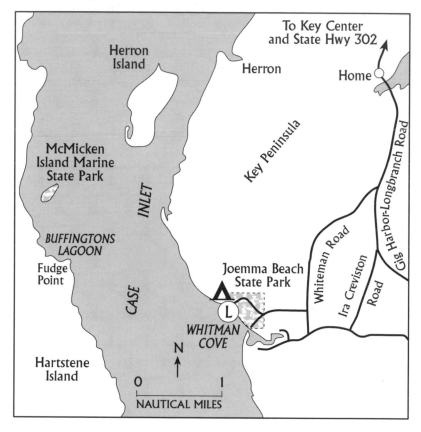

lot just above the beach. Do not leave valuables in your parked car. There is also a campground nearby.

ROUTE

For variety, follow the peninsula's shore north to a point opposite McMicken Island before crossing; on the return leg follow the Hartstene Island shore south and cross opposite Joemma Beach, which involves a slightly longer crossing. The shoreline north of Joemma Beach is pleasantly natural, with a pebble beach below high bluffs, the remains of an old pier, and a shallow lagoon with water that warms to bathtub temperatures during the summer, and, at upper tidal stages, a miniature tide race at its entrance. Hartstene Island's shore offers a similar setting. Buffingtons Lagoon, less than 1 mile south of McMicken Island on Hartstene, is another pleasant detour, though accessible only at high tide. Keep in mind that tidelands on both of these shores are private, so stay in your boat.

McMicken Island is particularly attractive to boaters who like the isolation afforded by low levels of development. There is no dock; a pit toilet is the only facility on shore. No water is available. Landings and access to the island are practical only on the southwest side due to the steep bluffs above the narrow beaches elsewhere. Behind this pebble and shell beach is a meadow with the handiest picnic sites. The fenced-in area and buildings behind the meadow are private land. A trail network circles through the dense forest north of the meadow, with occasional views out over the bluffs. Be alert for poison oak. Fires are not allowed on the island, so bring a camp stove if you plan to cook anything.

5 CARR INLET: RAFT ISLAND, CUTTS ISLAND, AND KOPACHUCK STATE PARK

If you live south of Seattle, this is a short, easy trip, ideal for those with limited saltwater experience or for families. Distances between stopovers are not long, and there are plenty of shore attractions and beaches with

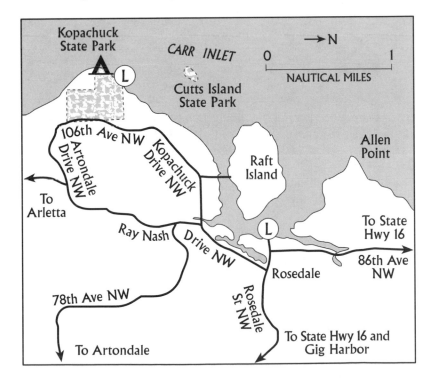

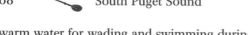

warm water for wading and swimming during the summer months. The route can be altered or shortened if weather is inclement. Camping is available at Kopachuck State Park or the waterside Cascadia Marine Trail site located there.

Duration: Part day.
Rating: *Protected*.
Navigation Aids: NOAA charts 18445 SC or 18448 (both 1:80,000), 18474 (1:40,000); Seattle tide table (add about 30 minutes).
Planning Considerations: Consult the tide table before starting out, as low tides make for long carries to launches in the Rosedale area and may cut off access behind Raft Island.

GETTING THERE AND LAUNCHING

Launching alternatives are a street end in Rosedale, or a longer carry from the parking lot to the beach in Kopachuck State Park.

From Highway 16 in Gig Harbor, take the Gig Harbor City Center Exit. This and subsequent turns have signs for Rosedale and Kopachuck State Park. Turn left to cross over the highway, then right after 0.5 mile onto Hunt Street Northwest, and then right again onto 46th Avenue Northwest. After 1 mile, turn left at the intersection onto Rosedale Street Northwest, following it for 2.5 miles to Rosedale.

Rosedale Street End: To launch from the Rosedale street end, go straight where the road curves left at the store and gas station, passing a dead end sign and a playground on the right. Drive about two blocks past a church on the left and launch at the street's end onto a gravel beach. There is little room for more than one boat at a time to launch here at high tide when the beach is inundated. Parking at the street end is limited to the south side, as the north side is private property. Avoid blocking private residences by parking farther down the street if you have more than one vehicle.

Kopachuck State Park: Follow the above instructions for Rosedale, but turn left onto Ray Nash Drive Northwest and then go straight over the bridge onto Kopachuck Drive Northwest after about 0.75 mile. Another 1.75 miles brings you to the park entrance. You must carry your boat approximately 0.35 mile from the parking lot to the beach. Follow a gravel service road, that is also smooth enough for boat carts, to the beach.

ROUTE

The round-trip loop from Rosedale via Raft Island, Cutts Island State Park, and Kopachuck State Park is 4 miles.

Raft Island is exclusively residential, with gorgeous homes and moored yachts well worth the rubbernecking. What looks like a good launching beach on the Raft Island side of the bridge is not: It is restricted to use by island residents only.

Tiny Cutts Island seems larger than it really is. Steep bluffs, which increase in height toward the south end, partition the use of the island to either strolls in its madrona and fir woods above or beach hikes below. At the north end is a pebble and shell spit that extends almost to Raft Island during the lowest tides; this is steeper and easier on boats than the rockier beaches to the south. A pit toilet is located in the woods near the south end. This attractive little island cannot sustain camping or fires, and both are prohibited.

Kopachuck State Park, barely 0.5 mile from Cutts Island, brings you back to the intensity of road-accessible recreation. On a warm sunny day there are picnickers along the beach and kids splashing in the water. End the day here with a barbecue at one of the shore side picnic sites, or perhaps a car-camping overnight in the campground at the top of the bluff. You may also camp at the Cascadia Marine Trail site if you have launched from another location.

5 HENDERSON INLET: WOODWARD BAY NATURAL RESOURCES CONSERVATION AREA

Henderson Inlet offers a serene place to paddle, especially when compared to other, more trafficked inlets of south Puget Sound. This is partly due to the absence of public beaches or boat ramps excepting a limited launch place for hand-carried boats, and because a fair amount of undeveloped and protected shoreline remains. A reclaimed gem along the western shore, Woodward Bay Natural Resources Conservation Area, transformed from a Weyerhaeuser timber storage and transport facility, is a lush oasis of wildlife. Waterfowl, seals, great blue heron, and numerous other shoreline and marine creatures call this home, consistently providing a prime wildlife viewing destination.

Duration: Part to full day.
Rating: *Protected* or *Moderate* +. Within Woodward and Chapman Bays, and the south end of Henderson Inlet, the paddling is gentle and sheltered. Kayaking around Johnson Point exposes you to the possibility of tide rips and strong winds depending on currents and weather.
Navigation Aids: NOAA charts 18445 SC and 18448 (both

1:80,000). Use current tables for The Narrows with adjustments for Dana Passage.

Planning Considerations: If the Woodward Bay Natural Resources Conservation Area managed by the DNR is your planned launch, be aware that shoreline access is only permitted from April 1 through Labor Day to protect a varied and exceptional mix of wildlife. The alternative launch, from the marina on the east side of Johnson Point in the Nisqually Reach, requires paddling in possibly bumpy and exposed waters when the current is fast, the wind is blowing, or a combination of the two. It is easiest to paddle around Johnson Point into Henderson Inlet and back again by timing your trip with the respective flood and ebb.

GETTING THERE AND LAUNCHING

Two launch sites provide access: one a public site within Henderson Inlet at the conservation area, the other a private marina on the east side of Johnson Point in the Nisqually Reach.

Woodward Bay: This launch provides the most direct access to Henderson Inlet, but, as stated above, it is closed right after Labor Day

Chapman Bay (Carey and Jeanne Gersten)

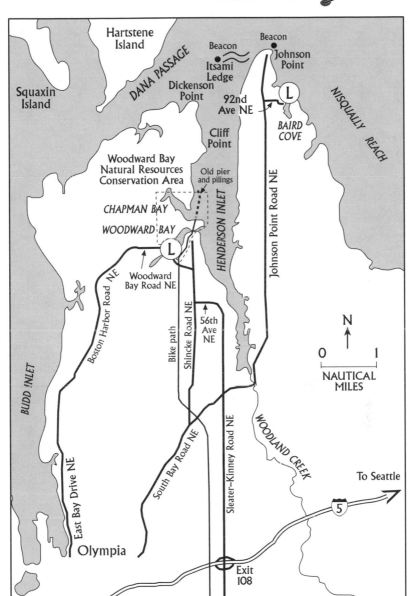

until April 1 to protect wildlife. From Olympia, drive north on East Bay Drive Northeast just over 2 miles. The road then becomes Boston Harbor Road Northeast, and you drive an additional 2 miles. Turn right onto Woodward Bay Road Northeast and follow it for just under 2 miles to a bridge that spans Woodward Bay. Just before the west end of the bridge turn left onto the dead end Whitman Road Northeast, which provides parking next to the grassy launch slope.

Johnson Point: The boat ramp at Zittel's Marina near the end of Johnson Point can be reached from Interstate 5 by turning off at Exit 108. Drive north on Sleater-Kinney Road Northeast for 3.25 miles, turning right onto South Bay Road Northeast. In about 0.5 mile the road turns into Johnson Point Road Northeast where it bends under the head of Henderson Inlet. In approximately another 5 miles turn right on 92nd Avenue Northeast. Follow it to its end at the marina. A fee is charged to use the boat ramp. Parking and toilets are also available.

ROUTES

Woodward Bay Natural Resources Conservation Area: *Protected*. The paddling distance is a round trip as short as 2.5 miles from Woodward Bay to Chapman Bay and back again, or longer as self-determined. Launching at Woodward Bay allows easy exploration of the two bays included within the conservation area and is an ideal trip for novice kayakers. High tide is best for launching, as the bank is a potential slippery mud slide at lower waters. High water also allows you to explore the bays to their fullest extent.

After launching, begin by investigating Woodward Bay with the option of paddling southwest under the car bridge back into its farthest reaches. From Woodward Bay pass under the trestle railroad bridge to the open water of Henderson Inlet, rounding to the north the peninsula separating the bays. There is a beach on the north side of the peninsula with picnic tables that makes for a nice rest spot. Here also is a building used by caretakers of the preserve. Continuing on you may explore the numerous pilings, docks, and a rusting crane left by Weyerhaeuser's former timber operation before heading into Chapman Bay. Return to your launch point by retracing your route.

The conservation area is the perfect place to immerse yourself in the intimate sanctuary these two bays provide for marine wildlife. The bays are well sheltered with a thick blanket of tall trees and natural vegetation guarding their perimeters. In places, the overhanging branches and fallen trees drip with lichens and mosses, dappled with sunlight highlighting their various greens, producing an almost southern feel of bayou. From either bay when the skies permit, the white cone of Mount Rainier can be spied sitting atop the forest canopy on the opposing shore of Henderson Inlet.

You may spot smaller upland, perching, and clinging birds flitting within the branches and shrubs, while heron, eagle, or hawks deck the upper branches. Waterfowl grace the bays' surface, including ducks, waders, and gulls. Seals and jellyfish are two of the marine creatures likely to be encountered lurking within the water.

Woodward Bay to the Head of Henderson Inlet: *Protected* or *Moderate*. An option for wildlife exploration and close-in shoreline viewing is to paddle south to the head of the inlet. This is a round trip from the Woodward Bay launch point of 5.75 miles or more, given how deeply

Zittel's Marina, Baird Cove, Nisqually Reach
(Carey and Jeanne Gersten)

you explore the bay and its shoreline convolutions. It is best to visit at higher tides to gain maximum entry into the tidal lands. If winds are strong from the north, seas can build over the long fetch and make the return trip a difficult one. Remember also that there is no public access along these shores, so you must be comfortable in your boat.

Here you can wander in the little channel formed from Woodland Creek emptying into Henderson Inlet and explore remnants of log booms left from the timbering days. Seals often inhabit these booms and breeding also takes place. Remember to maintain an adequate distance of 100 yards from seals or other wildlife as prescribed by the Federal Marine Mammal Protection Act.

Johnson Point to Henderson Inlet: *Moderate* or *Moderate* + (depending on current and wind). The approach to Woodward Bay Natural Resources Conservation Area from the marina ramp adds 4.75 miles (one way) to the trip. The tidal flood and ebb passing between Johnson Point and the Key Peninsula, along with the long fetches of Case Inlet and Nisqually Reach, means you must plan your travel to and from with the current's direction and an eye to the winds. Ideally you would like a flood in the morning, high tide at midday, and an ebb in the afternoon for a full day round trip. Of course, a one-way trip in either direction is also easily accomplished with a shuttle.

Zittel's Marina is a pleasant place, as it is well kept and has a small store for last-minute provisions. You might even want to investigate among the docks or poke around a bit in Baird Cove.

As you leave the marina, you will see Mount Rainier looming up from the southeast across Nisqually Reach. Look to the right of the big volcano and you may also see a somewhat smaller one, Mount Saint Helens. Proceeding north around Johnson Point, you will be facing the Olympic Mountains strung out across the far horizon.

A marker is just off Johnson Point where cormorants often perch to dry their wings. As you head west around the point into Henderson Inlet, be aware that Itsami Ledge is midwater between Johnson and Dickenson Points, marked by another light. If conditions are right, it can produce sharp waves. It is easily avoided by staying along the gravel shore of Johnson Point.

Once you enter Henderson Inlet, you have two basic options. You may head diagonally across to Woodward Bay Natural Resources Conservation Area, passing by Cliff Point jutting from the opposing shore, or paddle south along the eastern shoreline to the bottom of the inlet, admiring modest and grand structures alike as you go. There are a couple of interesting little coves to explore as well.

7 NISQUALLY DELTA

The Nisqually Delta is one of the finest estuaries in Puget Sound, and a good place for kayakers who like to exploit their craft's shallow water abilities and explore brackish back channels as few other boaters can. Needless to say, this is a prime place for birders.

Duration: Part day.
Rating: *Protected*.
Navigation Aids: NOAA chart 1844S SC (1:80,000); Seattle tide table (add 30 minutes).
Planning Considerations: Most channels are negotiable at midtide or above; high tide opens up many others. A Department of Fish and Wildlife conservation license is required to use the Luhr Beach Public Access site. Nisqually Delta can be unpleasant in wind because of steep seas in the shallows and the chance of getting wet at the unprotected launch site. Waterfowl hunters are present in the Department of Fish and Wildlife portions of the delta from mid-October to mid-January.

GETTING THERE AND LAUNCHING

From Interstate 5, take Exit 114 (Nisqually). Just south of the freeway, turn right on Martin Way and follow it for just under 1 mile to Meridian Road Northeast. Turn right here and follow it for almost 3 miles to 46th Avenue Northeast. Turn right again and go 0.25 mile to D'Milluhr Road on the left with a sign pointing to public fishing. Follow it downhill for about 0.5 mile to the parking area.

The Department of Fish and Wildlife's ramp at Luhr Beach has a moderate-size lot and a beach next to the ramp for launching. At high tide there is limited launching space on the rocky beach, which becomes sandy at lower tides and offers more space. To park here you will need a Department of Fish and Wildlife permit, which can be purchased at most sporting goods stores that sell hunting licenses. Next to the parking area is the Audubon Society's Nature Center, which is open on selected days of the week depending on the season.

ROUTE

Choose your own route and distance. This area is managed by the U.S. Fish and Wildlife Service and the Washington Department of Wildlife. The federal Nisqually National Wildlife Refuge includes the lower

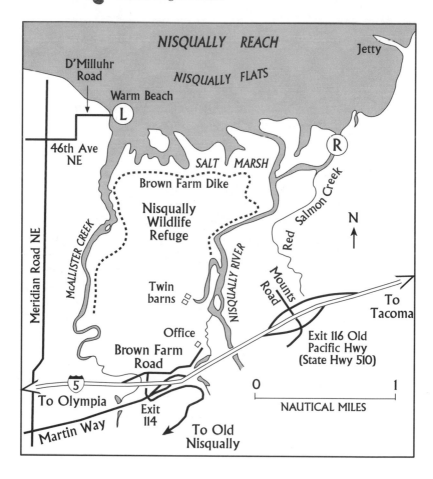

delta's tideflats and the meadows and woods of old farmland in the central portion above the dike that extends between McAllister Creek on the west and the Nisqually River on the east. State Wildlife lands include most of the lower salt marshes and most of the land along McAllister Creek.

If you arrive near high tide, you may wish to explore the myriad channels that wander across the salt marshes in the lower delta. At highest tides you may be able to pick your way through shallow channels near the dike, though a spring tide is required if you are to make it all the way across the delta by this inner route. Otherwise, head north to the lower flats to find your way to the eastern side of the delta, where you can head upstream on the Nisqually River or explore the connecting channel to Red Salmon Creek, farthest to the east. At the very northeast corner of the flats, still within federal refuge boundaries, is a sand jetty of old pilings and a beached barge that makes a nice lunch and sunbathing stop.

If you care to venture inland, McAllister Creek at the western edge of the delta offers the possibility of many miles of small stream paddling, using the last of the flood tide to assist you on the way in and then riding the ebb back out. The creek can be paddled easily to well inland of the freeway overpass.

8 COMMENCEMENT BAY

Here you will find a pleasant contrast to expectations of a polluted industrial wasteland. Commencement Bay has a bit of everything. There are the wooded bluffs of Point Defiance, the "downtown" feel of the Thea Foss Waterway with its yachts and workboats, the melancholy quiet along the slag shores of the abandoned Asarco smelter site, and the intense activity of loading and off-loading ships in one of the busiest ports in the Northwest. Within the bay and adjacent waterways is enough to fill many days of exploration.

Duration: Part to full day.
Rating: *Protected* or *Moderate.* The *Moderate*-rated Commencement Bay Loop requires crossing about 2 miles of open water.
Navigation Aids: NOAA charts 18445 SC (1:80,000), 18474 (1:40,000), or 18453 (1:15,000).
Planning Considerations: As Commencement Bay is a port of commerce, always stay alert to other watercraft and their movements.

GETTING THERE AND LAUNCHING

Launch sites around Commencement Bay are scattered unevenly.

Thea Foss Waterway: In downtown Tacoma, the waterway is accessible via the floats at the city dock. Located behind Johnny's Seafood, between private marinas north of the 15th Street bridge, the waterway is marked with a sign on Dock Street. Parking may be scarce.

Thea's Park: This park (also known as Northwest Point Park) at 405 Dock Street, just at the north end of the Thea Foss Waterway, has a ramp and approximately twenty-five parking spaces.

Tacoma to Point Defiance Shoreline: There are many alternatives

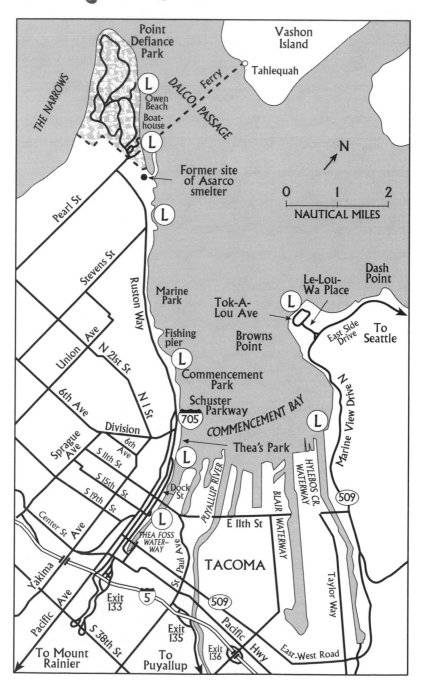

to choose from on the shoreline between Tacoma and Point Defiance. The closest to the city is Commencement Park, located at the point that Schuster Parkway becomes Ruston Way, a little less than 2 miles from downtown. There is a good sand and gravel beach here. Similar parks are located at intervals along Ruston Way between Commencement Park and the old Asarco smelter site.

Point Defiance Park: You can set off from the launching ramp or the adjacent public floats at Point Defiance Waterfront Complex. Follow Ruston Way to Pearl Street, then go right and down the hill. Or use the sand-and-gravel beach at Owen Beach. To reach it, continue into the park, past the zoo and aquarium, and drive along the bluffs to a side road that drops down to the right to the beach.

North Side of Commencement Bay: The launches closest to the docks and industrial points of interest in the waterways are an unimproved wayside and a marina just northwest of the entrance to Hylebos Waterway on Marine View Drive. To reach them from downtown Tacoma, take Route 509 east from its junction with Route 705. As Route 509 skirts around the south end of the waterway industrial area it also becomes known as East-West Way and Marine View Drive. The total distance is about 11 miles.

Browns Point: Farther west along the north shore of Commencement Bay is Browns Point, an appropriate launch for a loop tour of the entire bay and the closest access from north of Tacoma. From Tacoma, follow Marine View Drive North west from the East 11th Street intersection for 3 miles to Le-Lou-Wa Place Northeast. Turn left, then go about 0.75 mile, curving around to the right as the road becomes Tok-A-Lou Avenue Northeast. Boats must be carried about 100 yards to the gravel beach. Note that the park and lot close one hour after dark.

To reach Browns Point from the Seattle area, take Exit 143 (Federal Way) from Interstate 5. Go west on 320th Street for 4.5 miles until it intersects 47th Avenue. Go right for 0.5 mile and then left on Dash Point Road. Follow this road for 3 miles, passing Dash Point State Park, after which it becomes East Side Drive. Proceed to Le-Lou-Wa Place Northeast. Turn right and go 0.75 mile to the park.

ROUTES

South Shore Local Paddling: *Protected.* Choose your own distance. Pick any of the launch sites described along Ruston Way to Point Defiance Park.

One possibility is a short trip from Owen Beach west toward Point Defiance, following the gravel beach beneath steep wooded bluffs that restrict access to the beach except for occasional trails. The current here usually flows west, which is strongest during the flood, and can be quite swift near the point.

Also consider paddling between Point Defiance Waterfront Complex and one of the parks along Ruston Way, perhaps in conjunction with a car shuttle. Many new restaurants have sprung up along the shoreline, offering dock space to lure passing boaters in for a meal. This route also skirts the former site of the Asarco smelter, beginning with its reeflike tailings of slag and cinders. This forms a steep and jumbled shoreline that is surprisingly pleasant and interesting: seaweeds grow profusely and waves have eroded sea caves large enough to paddle into cautiously.

A third and more urban alternative on Commencement Bay's south shore is the paddle from Commencement Park southwest into Thea Foss Waterway, with a round-trip distance of up to 4 miles. As an option, a much shorter exploration of the waterway can be made from the city dock at Thea's Park, perhaps on a Sunday morning when parking is easiest to find. You pass bulk carrier freighters being loaded as you enter the waterway and the buildings of downtown Tacoma come into view. Thea Foss Waterway is the hub of recreational boating in the bay, so there are plenty of yachts to view in the many marinas along both shores. Commercial fishing boats have their own floats on the northeast side of the waterway.

Commencement Bay Loop: *Moderate* (due to 2-mile crossing). Loop distance is about 7 miles, plus any exploration into the waterways, but can be shortened to about 5 miles by cutting across parts of the bay at any point. You can start from Commencement Park on the south shore or from Browns Point Park on the north, depending on the direction from which you approach the area. This description begins at Browns Point.

Begin with the crossing from Browns Point toward downtown Tacoma via Commencement Park if you care to make a stop there first—these are the only public facilities along the route. This course should take you past ships that usually are at anchor there. Perhaps after a look into Thea Foss Waterway, start northeast across the old Puyallup River estuary, now among the most active maritime industrial areas in the region. There may be a fairly strong current outflow as you cross the Puyallup Waterway.

Beyond are the Blair and Hylebos Waterways, where large container ships and car carriers unload. At the mouth of the Hylebos Waterway is a small military station with Army Corps of Engineers vessels. The north shore is mostly private marinas, one of which has interesting old ships positioned to form a breakwater.

9 MAURY ISLAND

A narrow isthmus connects Maury Island to Vashon Island providing an age-old portage. The most challenging route here combines the quiet charm of Quartermaster Harbor with a more arduous paddle along the "island's" south coast to produce a circumnavigation that will leave you feeling you have seen a great deal as well as had a good day's exercise. For a more relaxed alternative, dabble in the harbor. If you wish to start from south Seattle, launching from Saltwater State Park involves a more demanding crossing, traversing shipping lanes and possible tide rips.

> DURATION: Part day or full day.
>
> RATING: *Protected*, *Moderate*, or *Exposed*. The *Moderate* route may require committing to several miles of paddling in wind and choppy water. The *Exposed* area has potential tide rips and shipping traffic.
>
> NAVIGATION AIDS: NOAA charts 18445 SC, 18448 (both 1:80,000), or 18474 (1:40,000); Seattle tide tables (add 15 minutes).
>
> PLANNING CONSIDERATIONS: Windy weather can make the east side of Maury Island unpleasant; the shallow beaches make offshore seas steep and landings wet and rough. If you are going to circumnavigate, plan for high tide to make the portage at Portage and to avoid the extensive tide flats on the Quartermaster Harbor side.

GETTING THERE AND LAUNCHING

Maury Island routes can be reached via Vashon Island by launching at either Portage, Burton Acres, or Dockton County Parks. It can also be reached from the east shore of Puget Sound from Saltwater State Park, which requires a 2-mile crossing.

To reach Vashon Island from Seattle, take Exit 163 from Interstate 5 and follow the West Seattle Bridge. In West Seattle, this becomes Fauntleroy Way and leads to the Fauntleroy ferry terminal. Exit the ferry at Vashon Island and drive south to the town of Vashon.

To reach Vashon Island from Tacoma, follow Ruston Way to Pearl Street, then turn right down the hill to the Point Defiance ferry landing. Take the ferry to Tahlequah, and follow the Vashon Island Highway north to the Quartermaster Harbor area.

Dockton County Park: To reach Maury Island from the town of Vashon, follow 99th Avenue Southwest south about 3 miles to Southwest 225th Street, where you turn left for Maury Island. For Dockton

County Park, continue past Portage on Dockton Road Southwest about 3.5 miles. Parking is ample with a gradual sandy beach.

Portage: This launch is a popular beginning and end for an island circumnavigation. There is usually parking along both of the two roads that cross this isthmus, which are connected by Southwest 222nd Street. The carrying distance between high-tide lines is approximately 200 yards. A high-tide launch or takeout on the Quartermaster Harbor side is particularly desirable, since it becomes a large mud flat at low tide. A store is open year-round and has plenty of snacks and some groceries.

Burton Acres County Park: Continue ahead on 99th Avenue Southwest to Southwest 240th Street, turn left, and then right onto Bayview Road. Turn right into Burton Acres at the sign for the park. There is usually plenty of parking. The park has a ramp, toilets, and a beach that gently slopes into Quartermaster Harbor. Additionally, a Vashon Island Parks District boathouse is being built with completion set for 1999. It will be managed by Puget Sound Kayak Company and house their Vashon Island Kayak outpost which will offer rentals and lessons. It will also become an official Land, Lunch and Launch site along the Cascadia Marine Trail.

Saltwater State Park: From Interstate 5, take Exit 147 and go 0.8 mile on South 272nd Street. Turn right at 16th Avenue South (Route 509) and proceed 0.7 mile. Turn left onto Woodmont Beach Road South (Route 509). In 0.3 mile, bear right onto South 265th Place (Route 509). Continue another 0.3 mile and turn right onto Marine View Drive South (Route 509). At 2.3 miles, turn left onto South 250th Street (which becomes South 251th Street) for one-half block, then turn left onto 8th Place South, which leads to the park's entrance. Saltwater State Park has vault toilets and easy access to a sand and gravel beach. Despite its nearly 300 parking spots, the lot may fill quickly on summer weekends. A fee is charged for overnight parking. There are also primitive campsites along the forested hills at the east end of the park and a group camping area on the bluff above the beach.

ROUTES

Quartermaster Harbor: *Protected.* Choose your own paddling distance. Quartermaster Harbor is a fine place for a leisurely paddle year-round. It features warm waters with the opportunity to swim during the summer and the quiet of still, overcast days in winter. The Burton Peninsula effectively breaks up the fetch, so seas are not likely to develop extensively. Both Burton Acres and Dockton county parks are good for a picnic, though Dockton offers more shoreside seclusion with its longer beach. Tables and rest rooms are available at both.

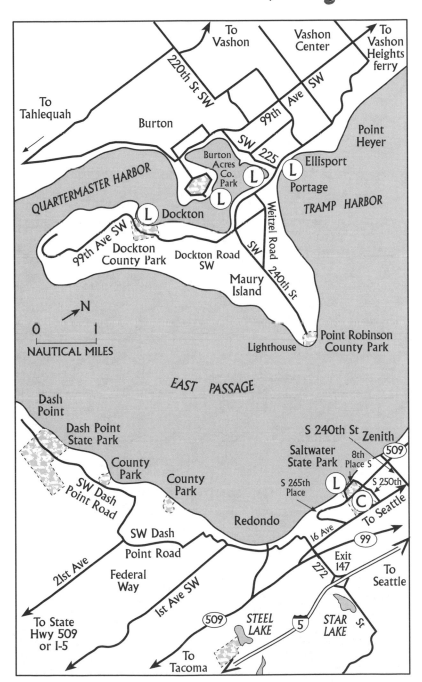

To Vashon

Vashon Center

To Vashon Heights ferry

220th St SW

99th Ave SW

To Tahlequah

Burton

SW 225

99th Ave SW

Point Heyer

Burton Acres Co. Park

L

L Ellisport

L

Portage

TRAMP HARBOR

QUARTERMASTER HARBOR

L Dockton

99th Ave SW

Dockton County Park

Dockton Road SW

Weitzel Road SW

240th St

Maury Island

N

0   1
NAUTICAL MILES

Lighthouse

Point Robinson County Park

EAST PASSAGE

Dash Point

Dash Point State Park

County Park

County Park

SW Dash Point Road

SW Dash Point Road

Redondo

21st Ave

Federal Way

1st Ave SW

S 240th St   Zenith

Saltwater State Park

8th Place S

509

S 265th Place

L

S 250th

C

To Seattle

16 Ave

99

Exit 147

272

To Seattle

To State Hwy 509 or I-5

509

STEEL LAKE

5

STAR LAKE

St

To Tacoma

Maury Island Circumnavigation: *Moderate.* The total paddling distance is 12 miles. The long shallow bight of Maury Island's south side is an unusual mix of wildness amid the development of the central Puget Sound area. Though about half of the shoreline is occupied by residences, the remainder is grassy or wooded bluffs that invite a climb for a magnificent view of East Passage, Commencement Bay, Tacoma, and Mount Rainier in the distance. A large part of this shoreline and the bluffs behind are occupied by gravel and sand pits. However, these do not detract in the least from the overall attractiveness or interest of the area. Grass, alder, and madrona are rapidly reclaiming most of the pits, while rusty, derelict conveyer systems descend through the brush to rotting terminals where barges once loaded. There are no public uplands or tidelands along this shore, so respect private property rights.

The south and north shores of Maury Island can turn into rough paddling in southerly or northerly winds, so you might want to plan a circumnavigation to cover the portion most exposed to prevailing winds early in the day. Though currents for East Passage are described as weak and variable, tide rips are known to form off Point Robinson, and are perhaps at their worst when ship wakes cross them. (See the Saltwater State Park to Point Robinson route below for information and cautions about Point Robinson.)

Saltwater State Park to Point Robinson: *Exposed.* The total paddling distance is 5 miles. The crossing from Saltwater State Park, about 2 miles at the narrowest point, is easy in moderate weather. Currents in the area are listed as weak and variable, though they do accelerate around Point Robinson as water is compressed around it. Rips are possible. The primary hazard on this crossing is marine shipping bound to and from Tacoma. The traffic lanes separate to either side of the midchannel buoy; northbound ships pass to the west. Wakes from ships and the many pleasure boats that ply this channel can create quite choppy seas. Surf at Point Robinson from a passing ship's wake can be nothing less than outer Pacific Coast magnitude. Look well before landing or launching, particularly at Point Robinson where ships pass close by. Pull your boat well up onto the beach when ashore.

The beach at Point Robinson and the grassy area behind the Coast Guard's lighthouse are open to the public during the day only. Up the hill northwest of the lighthouse is a county park, restricted to day use only.

Kayakers gathering at Quartermaster Harbor, Vashon Island
(Carey and Jeanne Gersten)

10 BLAKE ISLAND

Come to Blake Island for either a pleasant day trip or for one of the most unusual kayak-camping experiences on Washington shores. Pitch your tent at Tillicum Village, take a shower in the heated rest room, then stroll over to the longhouse for a salmon dinner followed by Indian dancing. Too civilized for you? Choose the Cascadia Marine Trail site on the northwest corner or the even more primitive campsite on the southern shore.

>**Duration**: Full day to overnight.
>**Rating**: *Exposed*, *Moderate*, or *Protected*. Tide rips may be encountered on the *Moderate* route; the *Exposed* route involves 4 miles of open water across shipping lanes, with the potential for rough seas in southerly or northerly winds.
>**Navigation Aids**: NOAA charts 18445 SC or 18448 (both 1:80,000), and 18449 (1:25,000); Seattle tide table.
>**Planning Considerations**: Call ahead if you want a salmon dinner at Tillicum Village (see the route description for specifics).

GETTING THERE AND LAUNCHING
From Seattle, launches can be made at either Alki Beach or Lincoln Park.
Alki Beach or Alki Point Light Station: Take Exit 163 from

A WWTA campsite on Blake Island (Carey and Jeanne Gersten)

Interstate 5 and follow the West Seattle Bridge to the Harbor Avenue Southwest Exit, then follow the road north and around Duwamish Head to where it becomes Alki Avenue Southwest. Continue west along Alki Avenue to the designated launch site between 54th Place Southwest and 55th Avenue Southwest, or proceed further to access at the far west end of Alki Beach or just south of the Alki Point Light Station. Public rest rooms are available near each launch site at 58th Avenue Southwest and 63rd Avenue Southwest, respectively. On-street parking is extremely difficult to find in the summer, so be prepared to launch early before the crowds arrive to avoid a long walk.

Lincoln Park: It has the unique advantage of being near the Fauntleroy ferry landing, so you can return on the ferry if necessary. Park

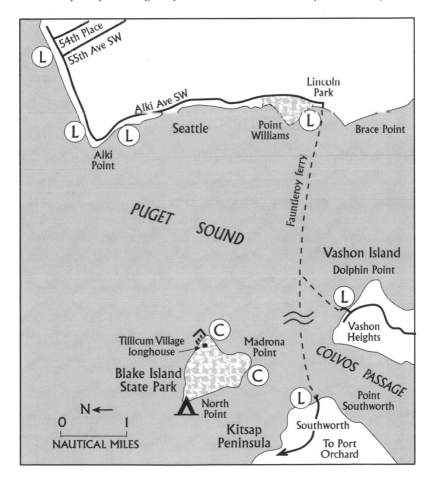

in the south lot and follow the path at the park's southern boundary about 150 yards to a defunct boat ramp and the sand and cobble beach. Rest rooms are close by. Note that the park closes at night.

For ferry access to Vashon Island and Southworth, take the West Seattle Bridge and follow the signs to the Fauntleroy ferry.

Vashon Island: To launch your kayak use the small ramp just east of the north-end ferry dock. Parking next to the ramp is private, so unload and move cars as soon as possible to the ferry parking area up the hill. There is no beach on either side of the ramp at higher tides, and you must be prepared to launch quickly from the ramp itself at those times without delaying other users. Do not try to get to the beach from west of the ferry dock: this is private land.

Southworth: Park in the ferry parking lot just east of the dock and follow a short path on the left side of the parking lot fence to a sandy beach. Please be courteous as private homes closely border this put-in.

ROUTES

West Seattle to Blake Island: *Exposed*. The paddling distance is over 3 miles one way from either West Seattle launch point, across open water with heavy shipping traffic. Currents in this area usually are less than 1 knot; they are strongest on the ebb. Be prepared to use one of the alternative routes or to return to West Seattle by ferry if the weather takes a turn for the worse.

Vashon Island to Blake Island: *Moderate*. The paddling distance is approximately 1.5 miles each way, with about 1.25 miles across open water. Currents in this area rarely exceed 1 knot, but rips can occur between the two islands, particularly near the Allen Bank off Vashon Island. Colvos Passage is unique in that the current flows only on the ebb (moves north), and becomes weak and variable at other stages of the tide. Hence, this area becomes roughest on northerly winds when the ebb current opposes it.

Southworth to Blake Island: *Protected*. The paddling distance is approximately 1 mile each way, with about 0.75 mile across open water. Currents here are weak and variable as long as you stay west of Colvos Passage and head for the more westerly shore of Blake Island.

Blake Island is roughly triangular, with a paddling circumference of about 5 miles. Most of its shoreline consists of low bluffs above rocky beach, but there are sandy beaches and a shallow high-tide lagoon at the west end. Once ashore, you can hike an extensive network of paths and trails.

There are three camping areas, all of which bear a camping fee year-round. On the northwestern corner of the island is the Cascadia Marine Trail site and general public camping with water, normally shut off during winter months, and rest rooms located up the hill. The primitive camping rate is charged for the public sites. On the southern shore are two more campsites, which charge the same rate but have no water. A pit toilet is located about 100 yards east along the trail.

The eastern point, Tillicum Village, is more developed and crowded with boaters and boat-in campers during the summer months. A breakwater encloses a boat basin with floats for the boaters who come here year-round. The campground is between the boat basin and the stony beach to the south. If you are camping here, land on this beach unless there is a strong southerly wind and waves; in that case use the beach in the boat basin. Most of the campsites here have little or no southerly wind protection. Campsites here cost the higher full-service rate because of the heated bathrooms with coin-operated showers and other amenities.

Nearby are semi-enclosed shelters for group picnics; they also can be used for cooking and shelter during the day if not already reserved. A large central fireplace can make them cozy in cooler weather.

The most interesting element in this cluster is the Tillicum Village longhouse, featuring Indian-style baked salmon followed by demonstrations of traditional dance. The clientele is primarily people arriving by tour boat from Seattle, but boaters may reserve a place for themselves by signing up at the longhouse at least one hour prior to mealtime. Service is daily during the summer and on weekends during the off-season. Call 206-443-1244 for more information.

Tillicum Village, Blake Island (Carey and Jeanne Gersten)

11 EAGLE HARBOR TO BREMERTON

This is one of the most interesting and long-range day trips in Puget Sound, and the ability of foot passengers to carry kayaks aboard ferries allows 10 miles of one-way paddling. Leave your car in Seattle, walk your boat aboard the Winslow ferry, paddle through Rich Passage and Port Orchard to Bremerton, then take the ferry back to the city. State parks along the way make nice picnic stops with old military installations to explore. To make this into an overnight, stop at one of three Cascadia Marine Trail sites: Fort Ward on the south end of Bainbridge Island, Manchester State Park on the south side of Rich Passage, or add a 2-mile side trip to Blake Island (see the Blake Island chapter).

Duration: Full day.
Rating: *Moderate*. Involves current with possible tide rips and heavy boat and shipping traffic in Rich Passage.
Navigation Aids: NOAA charts 18445 SC or 18441 (both 1:80,000), 18446 (1:25,000); Admiralty Inlet current tables corrected for Rich Passage.
Planning Considerations: Ferry schedules dictate timing here, but runs are frequent. A favorable current in Rich Passage is desirable as it can reach 3 or 4 knots. The flood flows toward Bremerton in Rich Passage.

GETTING THERE AND LAUNCHING

If coming from Seattle, weekends are the preferred days for this trip because parking close to the Seattle ferry terminal at Colman Dock is easier, especially early on Sunday morning. If nothing is available under the Highway 99 viaduct across from the terminal, you may have to look some distance south along Alaskan Way.

Eagle Harbor: After leaving the ferry in Winslow, turn left on the first street beyond the toll booths and look for a walkway to the left just before the Eagle Harbor Condominiums. This leads to a small beach just south of the ferry terminal. Total carrying distance is about 300 yards.

Bremerton: There is easy access to the ferry at the First Street public dock, just north of the ferry landing. Carrying distance from the floats to the ferry is about 100 yards. A tavern and a seafood restaurant are handy while you wait for the return connection.

ROUTE

Paddling distance from Eagle Harbor to Bremerton is 10 miles. Add 4 to 6 miles for a side trip to Blake Island State Park depending on which part you visit.

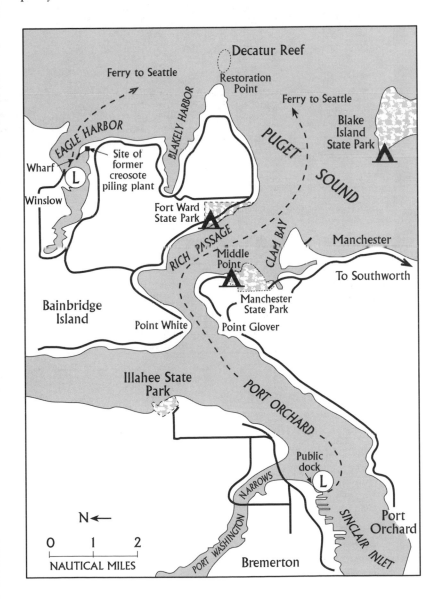

Members of the Washington Kayak Club take a rest stop in Eagle Harbor, Bainbridge Island (Carey and Jeanne Gersten)

Eagle Harbor is a worthy destination in its own right and you may want to return on another day to explore it (see Eagle Harbor chapter). But for this route, cross to the south side and out of the harbor, passing a massive wharf that served what was once the world's largest plant for creating creosote-treated pilings. Head south.

Continue along shore to Restoration Point, being careful to stay out of the way of the ferries that run fairly close to this shore for some way before turning east toward Seattle. Off Restoration Point is Decatur Reef, a long rocky spine that can produce breaking waves or tide rips. Swing wide around the navigation marker if conditions inside of it warrant.

Both Fort Ward and Manchester State Parks provide a Cascadia Marine Trail campsite, picnic tables, water, and rest rooms, as well as interesting things to explore in the vicinity. The two parks are located across Rich Passage from each other. Look for the picnic tables at Fort Ward just beyond the salmon aquaculture pens and pier along the north shore. Old buildings from this fort, one of the first settlements in Puget Sound, are nearby and up the hill.

Manchester State Park, on the south shore west of Middle Point, also has military origins, with gun emplacements and a large brick picnic shelter that originally housed torpedoes. Beach your boat at either side of this shallow bight (the center dries to a muddy foreshore). Be wary of boat and ferry wakes.

Rich Passage makes a dogleg to the south and narrows just beyond the two parks, and currents become much swifter. Keep in mind that you could encounter an incredible array of large or small vessels coming through here—even huge aircraft carriers coming or going to the naval base at Bremerton.

Currents themselves are not likely to be dangerous unless interacting with adverse winds; use them to your advantage while keeping an eye out for large vessels like the Bremerton ferry that must keep up some speed in order to stay in control in this flow. If you should encounter an opposing current, there are eddies north of Point White on the north shore and smaller ones along the south shore. The latter may be preferable since you can continue along shore, avoiding marine traffic into Port Orchard, where the currents weaken. Cross to the East Bremerton shore 1 mile or so beyond the eastern end of Rich Passage.

The ships often moored at the Bremerton Shipyard, such as the *Turner Joy*, make it an impressive place to visit. But remember that it is a military installation, and you must keep a minimum of 600 feet from the perimcter of all naval vessels, piers, and other Navy facilities.

12 EAGLE HARBOR

This excursion is for sea kayakers who love looking at all sorts of boats, exploring pockets of wildlife, and viewing picturesque waterside structures old and new. They are all on Seattle's doorstep, yet far from the urban bustle.

Duration: Part day.
Rating: *Protected*.
Navigation Aids: NOAA charts 18445 SC (1:80,000 with 1:25,000 Eagle Harbor inset) or 18449 (1:25,000); Seattle tide table.
Planning Considerations: Higher tides allow exploration of the back bay and side coves in Eagle Harbor, which dry at lower tides.

GETTING THERE AND LAUNCHING

If you are driving from the Winslow ferry dock, turn left at the first traffic light onto Winslow Way, right if you're coming south on Highway 305, and into downtown Winslow. After 0.3 mile, going through the "downtown" shopping area, take the first left onto Madison Avenue at the four-way stop, then the next immediate left onto Bjune Drive. In less than 0.1 mile turn right onto Shannon Drive and follow it down to the ramp at the water.

Public parking for Winslow Waterfront Park is located along Bjune Drive. Parking is limited to 4 hours along the park, so you may need to move your car to another street within Winslow. Do not park in the trailered boat parking lot, or suffer a stiff fine. (Be aware, Bjune Drive and

Eagle Harbor, Bainbridge Island, at sunset
(Carey and Jeanne Gersten)

the park are scheduled for redevelopment in 1999 and may change significantly.) Launch on the gravel beach or at the boat ramp in the park.

You may also wheel your kayak onto the ferry at Colman Dock in Seattle. When you exit the ferry take the first left onto a road signed for Eagle Harbor Condominiums. Follow it down a slight hill a very short distance. You may take either the left or right footpath. The left footpath leads past the condo complex to public beach access right next to the ferry terminal. The right footpath leads to Winslow Waterfront Park and along to the public ramp and dock in about 0.1 mile. You have to negotiate three small, low steps along this path, but they are manageable.

A final option is to rent a sea kayak from Puget Sound Kayak Company, which runs an outfitting and guide service in Winslow. They are members of the Washington Water Trails Association and with prior arrangement will store your kayak if you paddle to Eagle Harbor planning to stay overnight.

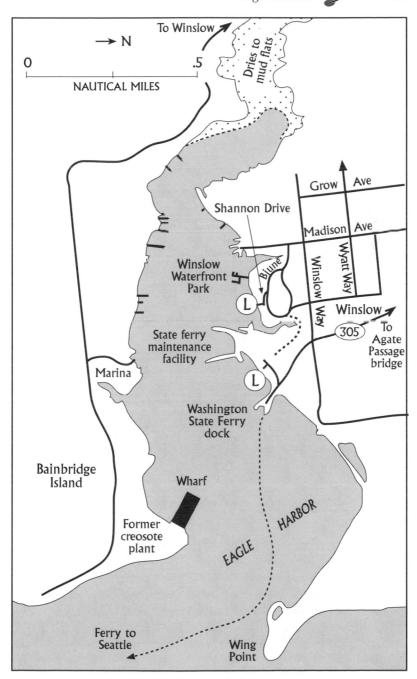

→ N

0   .5
NAUTICAL MILES

To Winslow

Dries to mud flats

Grow   Ave

Shannon Drive

Madison   Ave

Wyatt Way

Winslow

Biune

Winslow
Waterfront
Park

L

Winslow Way

Winslow

305

To
Agate
Passage
bridge

State ferry
maintenance
facility

Marina

L

Washington
State Ferry
dock

Bainbridge
Island

Wharf

Former
creosote
plant

EAGLE   HARBOR

Ferry to
Seattle

Wing
Point

ROUTE

Choose your own route and distance. From Winslow Waterfront Park, there are things to see in any direction. Just east are the state ferries' maintenance facilities, where out-of-service ferries dock. Here is a chance for a close-up look at the old veterans and the superferries. Before approaching them, look carefully for activity suggesting that one of them may be about to move.

Several marinas, one directly across from the ferry docks and the others just west of the park, hold a wide assortment of fantastic yachts as well as unusual boats and barges that have been converted into live-aboards. Eagle Harbor also is popular with boaters, some of them live-aboards who prefer to anchor out. Their craft are concentrated in the middle third of the harbor and include floating houses on barges or rafts, old tugs and fishing boats, and yachts.

Along shore are the remnants of past industry including, at the harbor's entrance, a plant site with major wharf still remaining that once produced creosote-treated pilings to build the Panama Canal. Many other relics remain from the past—sheds and warehouses on pilings, some abandoned and some still in use. A tiny, shallow cove across from the ferry dock is particularly picturesque for its shoreline structures as well as its seclusion.

The very back of the harbor is quieter and less popular with boats because it dries on lowest tides, but it is worth exploring when the tide is in. Midway back in the harbor are warehouse pilings that are all that remain of the vigorous berry-farming industry that once thrived in the vicinity. You can often spot eagle, osprey, heron, and other birds dependent on a productive water environment.

13 WEST POINT, SHILSHOLE BAY, AND GOLDEN GARDENS

This area, west of Seattle's Ballard neighborhood, is a good place for both cautious sea outings for new kayakers during calm weather and more lengthy and challenging routes for the experienced. It includes popular and secluded sunbathing beaches, pleasure boats galore at the extensive marina, and sunset views of the Olympic Mountains. The Lake Washington steelhead run at the locks in Salmon Bay attracts a notable "chorus" of sea lions. The West Point beaches are lightly used and are backed by the woods and bluffs of Seattle's largest natural reserve, Discovery Park. The park includes a gigantic shoreside sewer treatment facility that has been

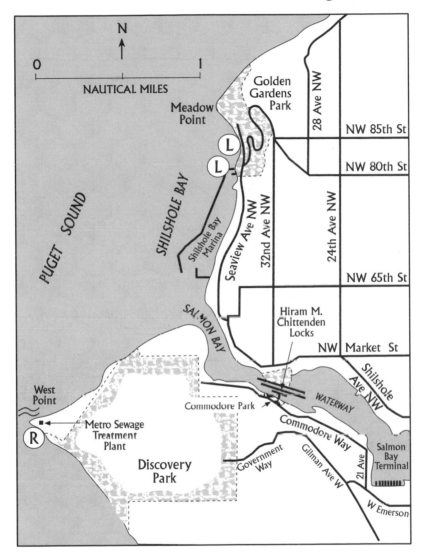

landscaped to blend into the scene. From West Point the route can also be extended into Elliott Bay to connect with the launch points and routes described in the Elliott Bay chapter.

Duration: Part to full day.
Rating: *Protected* or *Moderate*. The *Moderate* route may require committing to a distance of rough paddling to return to the launch site.

Navigation Aids: NOAA charts 18445 SC (1:80,000), 18446 (1:25,000), or 18447 SC (1:10,000); Seattle tide table.

Planning Considerations: Winds can create breaking waves to produce rough paddling conditions, especially around West Point. Lower tides offer more beaches, and many are backed by rock riprap that makes unsuitable landing places at high tide. Allow plenty of leeway for larger boats and ships entering and leaving the Ballard Locks.

GETTING THERE AND LAUNCHING

The launch site is Golden Gardens Park at the north end of Shilshole Marina. Take Exit 172 for 85th Street from Interstate 5 and go west on 85th Street for about 3 miles. Where it ends turn right on Golden Gardens Drive Northwest and wind down the bluffs to the beach area.

At Golden Gardens, use the parking lots just behind the beach or, if they are full, park along Seaview Avenue Northwest. Launch at the beach or at the ramp just inside the marina breakwater to the south. The parking lots are closed at night.

Sea lions hauled out on a buoy in Shilshole Bay
(Randel Washburne)

A moonlight paddle, mid-Puget Sound (Carey and Jeanne Gersten)

ROUTES

Golden Gardens to Salmon Bay and Return via Shilshole Marina: *Protected.* Choose your own paddling distance; the full round trip from Golden Gardens to Commodore Park at the Ballard Locks is about 4 miles. Novice paddlers may prefer to stay in the bay just off Golden Gardens beach, which gets some protection from both northerly and southerly seas. However, sustained northerly to northwesterly winds can produce breaking waves just the same. As an option, explore inside the marina, being especially watchful for traffic entering and exiting at the breakwater entrance. Landings to use the rest rooms or restaurant at Shilshole can be made at the dock closest to the parking lots behind the gas docks.

An outflowing current is always present in Salmon Bay due to the drainage from the Lake Washington Ship Canal. Most of it can be avoided by using eddies close inshore, particularly in the shallows on the south side. Boat traffic may be very heavy in this area, so alongshore routes are the safest for kayakers. Pleasure craft waiting for the locks may be numerous just below the railroad bridge.

Sea lions, especially in the spring months, are very active between Commodore Park and the dam. Stay close to shore when approaching the park and do not paddle closer to the dam.

Golden Gardens to West Point: *Moderate.* The round-trip distance is 4 to 5 miles. Keep in mind launching is prohibited from the West Point beaches, but making a rest stop is allowed by Seattle's Department of Parks and Recreation. Tide rips are possible off West Point, and the bar can produce breakers some distance from the point. Be especially watchful for ships' wakes when landing along this route.

Popular landing spots are at the gravel and cobble beach just north of the rock riprap at the sewage plant and at West Point itself; choose whichever side is sheltered from the wind. Rest rooms are located 0.25 mile up the road from the point. For more seclusion continue about 1 mile past the point and into the bight below the bluffs, beyond where most beach walkers from West Point usually venture. The foreshore here is very flat, so you will likely have to carry your boat some distance if spending time ashore. Watch for the many boulders scattered throughout this intertidal area.

If you follow the route within the marina on the way out, consider a straight course back across the bay toward Golden Gardens from West Point if conditions are conducive. Sea lions sometimes haul out on the buoys or riprap of the marina breakwater. At midtide a sandy beach appears on the outside of the marina breakwater providing the most secluded stop in this area, as it is not accessible by land.

14 PORT MADISON AND AGATE PASSAGE

The northern shores of Bainbridge Island and the adjacent Kitsap Peninsula make an easy "impulse" paddle for local dwellers and are easily accessed from Seattle by car ferry too. Though the area's shores are primarily residential with an emphasis on ritzy homes, there are two state parks and an Indian museum along the winding course of a narrow inlet and the fast waters of Agate Passage. Possibilities for short or longer paddles, perhaps with a car shuttle, are numerous.

> **Duration**: Part day.
> **Rating**: *Moderate* or *Moderate* +. The *Moderate* + route involves crossing Agate Passage in current up to 3 knots with possible heavy pleasure boat traffic.
> **Navigation Aids**: NOAA chart 18446 (1:25,000) or 18445 SC (1:80,000); Admiralty Inlet current tables with corrections for Agate Passage.
> **Planning Considerations**: Strong wind, particularly from the south, can make a wet launch or landing on the beach at Fay Bainbridge State Park. Agate Passage currents are the only significant ones in this area, but they are strong enough to be worth planning around.

GETTING THERE AND LAUNCHING
Launch choices are Fay Bainbridge State Park on the northeast corner of the island or, for the Agate Passage area, the Suquamish Museum, Old

Man House State Park, or Suquamish Center. The car shuttle distance between Fay Bainbridge Park and the Agate Passage launch sites is about 8 miles.

Fay Bainbridge Park: Turn north from Highway 305 about midway between Winslow and the Agate Passage bridge on East Day Road. Watch for signs to Fay Bainbridge State Park. After 1.5 miles, go left onto Sunrise Drive Northeast. Go another 1.7 miles and turn right into the park. Rest rooms, drinking water, and picnic facilities are provided.

Launching at Fay Bainbridge Park is from a gravel beach facing east onto Puget Sound. A slight bulge in the shoreline offers some protection from northerly wind waves, but the launch is exposed to ship wakes and waves from the south. This state park also has a Cascadia Marine Trail campsite at the south end of its beach, so you could also make an overnight excursion if you launch from another location.

Old Man House State Park: Turn north from Highway 305 about 0.25 mile west of the Agate Passage bridge on Suquamish Way. Old Man House Park is 1.35 miles down this road at Division Avenue. Turn right there and go another 0.35 mile.

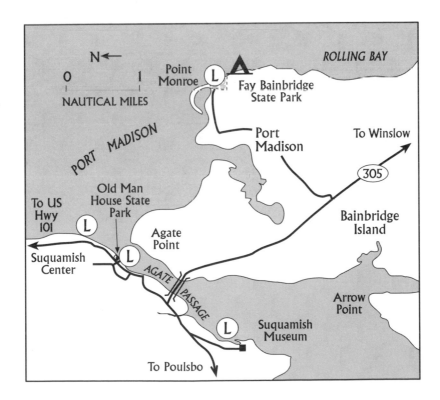

A WWTA campsite at Fay Bainbridge State Park
(Carey and Jeanne Gersten)

This small state park has very limited parking, for just four cars, but fortunately it is little used. There is also a vault toilet, drinking water, and picnic facilities. Interpretive displays describe Indian dwellings that were located here, including Chief Sealth's. A sand beach for launching is located about 100 yards from the parking area.

Suquamish Center: Continue by Old Man State Park for another

0.35 mile along Suquamish Way and turn right where the road makes a dogleg to the left as it enters this small town. Park in the small lot and launch next to the boat ramp on a gravel and cobble beach. Cars can be driven to the water's edge briefly to unload. Cafés and grocery stores are located nearby.

Suquamish Museum and Tribal Center: Turn south off Highway 305 about 0.5 mile west of the Agate Passage bridge onto Sandy Hook Road, and go 0.35 mile to the entrance on the left. From the parking lot, carry boats around the left side of the museum building, and take a path with wooden steps down a 5-foot bank, leading to a gravel beach. It's about 50 yards' carrying distance. Facilities here are available during the museum's open hours.

ROUTES

You can choose between local paddling west of Bainbridge Park or at Agate Passage, or connecting the two areas for a 5- to 7-mile round trip (or half that distance using a car shuttle for the return).

Fay Bainbridge Park: *Moderate* or *Moderate* + (dependent on wind waves). You might explore the high-tide lagoon at Point Monroe. The entrance is on the west side, close to the Bainbridge Island shore, and then paddle into Port Madison to see the exclusive shoreside homes there. The round-trip distance is about 4 miles. There are no public shorelands or facilities on this route after the park.

Agate Passage: *Moderate* or *Moderate* + (dependent on current). You might launch at any of the three sites described and paddle locally, or arrange a shuttle (the road distance between the museum and Suquamish Center is about 2.5 miles) and paddle along the 3 miles of shoreline through Agate Passage. The sandy beach and picnic site at Old Man House State Park make a nice stop along the way. From the water, look for the park on the west shore between the inshore navigation marker and the "2" buoy at the north end of Agate Passage.

Currents in Agate Passage can attain almost 4 knots under the highway bridge, but are rarely as much as 2 knots in the northern portion. You may cross between Agate Point and Old Man House State Park if the currents are strong and unfavorable. A current flowing against either a north or south wind could make dangerous seas here, and the combination of strong currents, eddies around the highway bridge abutments, and heavy pleasure boat traffic could give less experienced kayakers problems. Most difficulties and hazards can be minimized by paddling as close to the beach as possible. However, the currents under the highway bridge can sometimes be strong enough to make slow progress against them.

15 LAKE UNION

If you are an experienced Seattle paddler, chances are you have already explored Lake Union, as the majority of resident paddlers probably took their first strokes here. Lake Union has perhaps the highest year-round density of sea kayaks, perhaps nation- or even worldwide! It is usually smoother than local saltwater destinations. The water is warmer than the Sound in the summer months, making it a good place to develop skills. The fascinating shoreline of shipyards, houseboats, yachts, and shore-accessible eateries and shops makes it a repeat destination for any Seattleite with a few hours to spare. A tour of Lake Union could be combined with excursions either east or west along the ship canal, perhaps with a shuttle to launch points in Ballard or the Arboretum.

> **Duration**: Part day.
> **Rating**: *Protected.*
> **Navigation Aids**: NOAA chart 18447 SC (1:10,000). A Seattle street map is probably as useful.
> **Planning Considerations**: Go anytime.

GETTING THERE AND LAUNCHING

There are several public shoreline areas suited for launching and three sea kayak renters waterside of Lake Union proper and Portage Bay just to the east. Some parking is available near all of them, though often on the street curb. In general, it is difficult to find space on nice summer weekends.

For the north shore of Lake Union, take Exit 169 (45th Street) from Interstate 5. Go west on 45th Street 1 mile to Stone Way North. Turn left and follow Stone Way almost another mile to the lakeshore. Go left on Northlake Way past Gasworks Park to the launch site along the north shore.

For the south, west, or east shores of Lake Union, take Exit 167 (Mercer Street) from Interstate 5. Take the first right onto Fairview Avenue North and go one block to the lakeshore. The Chandler's Cove complex is at this location. Continue straight for the east shore, or bear left onto Valley Street for the west shore, turning right after about three blocks onto Westlake Avenue North.

NORTH END OF LAKE UNION

Gasworks Park: Park in the park's lot or along Northeast Northlake Way at the park's eastern boundary. The designated launch point is a small,

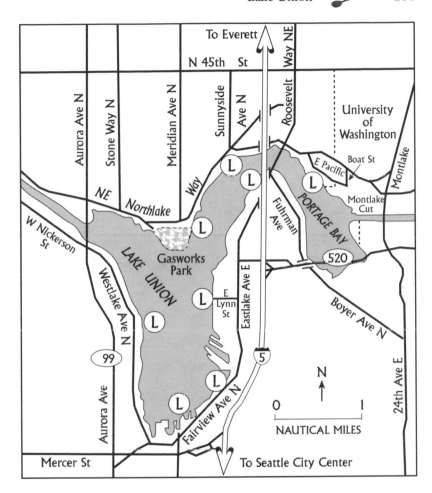

protected beach at the extreme eastern edge of the park, requiring a 100-yard carry from the lot, less from a signed boat drop-off parking zone.

Sunnyside Ramp: Use the boat ramp off Northlake Way at the foot of Sunnyside Avenue North. Please park along the bike trail.

WEST SIDE OF LAKE UNION

Northwest Outdoor Center: There is no public access along Westlake Avenue North. The Northwest Outdoor Center rents kayaks at the water's edge and allows access to owners of hand-carried non-motorized boats at the wooden stairs leading to their facility.

Picking raspberries at the Arboretum (Carey and Jeanne Gersten)

EAST SIDE OF LAKE UNION

South Passage Point Park: This little park, maintained by the Pocock Rowing Center in cooperation with Seattle City Parks, is at the foot of Fuhrman Avenue below the freeway bridge. Parking may be scarce. Beaches are rocky except for a small gravel beach centered under the freeway bridge. You may also use the westernmost float if it is not in use.

East Lynn Street Minipark: The launch is a small, narrow beach 3 or 4 feet down from the sidewalk at the foot of East Lynn Street. Expect to get wet feet as you step down. Parking on side streets may be difficult.

Lake Union Steam Plant: Along Fairview Avenue North, just 0.3 mile east of Chandler's Cove, is a public float specifically designed for kayakers and other human-powered boaters. At the west end there are six parking spaces.

Chandler's Cove Development: This launch is located at the junction of Fairview Avenue North and Valley Street, just east of a Burger King. Some public parking is nearby, but be sure not to use that reserved for local businesses. Use the gravel beach just below the lawn. Moss Bay Rowing and Kayak Center, located on the docks, rents shells as well as kayaks.

Portage Bay: Another option is renting a sea kayak at Aqua Verde Paddle Club located just south of the University of Washington on Boat Street.

ROUTES

The lake is slightly less than 2 miles in length and about 4.5 miles around if you follow the shores between the freeway bridge and the Fremont Bridge. All shores have restaurants with dock access, ranging from burgers to seafood to gourmet dining. The north shore has Gasworks Park, shipyards, and plenty of yachts to view. The west side is primarily yacht moorage. The Lake Union houseboat community comprises much of the east shore, along with NOAA's research-ship facility and a shipyard. The south end has a seaplane base, the Naval Reserve Center, the historic lumber schooner Wawona, and the Center for Wooden Boats, where all manner of small wooden craft can be rented. Just west is the Chandler's Cove area, a good place to go ashore at the small beach to purchase a snack or window shop.

Lake Union's mood changes with the pulse of the city. Try it on a fair summer's evening, when the myriad sails of the Duck Dodge race frame the sunset, or on a calm Sunday morning in winter, when both city and water are quiet and you will meet few others besides hardy kayakers like yourself. On a stormy day, Lake Union is a good practice place for experienced paddlers who want to work on their wind-paddling technique in a reasonably safe setting.

A working boat on Lake Union (Carey and Jeanne Gersten)

16 DUWAMISH WATERWAY

Among shipyards, barge landings, ship hulks, the roar of factories, and
foundations of long-gone activities is Kellogg Island—a remnant of the
original meandering Duwamish River and the last natural shoreline in
the Elliott Bay area. Though a portion of the island was covered with
dredging spoils, vegetation now grows thickly. Herons, cormorants, and
other waterfowl abound. The Port of Seattle is keeping the island in its
natural state and has an ongoing program to develop a number of nearby
shore access points and mini-parks in the lower Duwamish Waterway.
Pick your own route depending on your interests, or combine one with
the nearby trips described in the Elliott Bay chapter, especially Harbor
Island.

Duration: Part day.

Rating: *Protected*. Although the paddling is easy, ship and barge
traffic is heavy in this confined waterway. Novice kayakers should
ensure that they have sufficient boat control to stay out of the way
before venturing into the waterway, especially during the times of
ebb current.

Navigation Aids: NOAA chart 18450 (1:10,000) or 18445 SC
(1:80,000, see 1:40,000 inset); Seattle tide table.

Planning Considerations: A strong ebb current (the flood current
is negligible) can make upstream travel harder and may pose problems
for novice kayakers around pilings or when avoiding ship or barge
traffic. Consequently, you may wish to avoid these currents during
periods of a falling tide. At low tide the shoreline is quite muddy.

GETTING THERE AND LAUNCHING

There are six launch points on both sides of the lower Duwamish
Waterway. Different sites can be used with a shuttle, making possible a
one-way paddle through the entire lower Duwamish. A trip could begin,
for example, at the First Avenue Bridge and end at the Alaskan Way Public Access. Launch sites are listed in order of preference.

End of Diagonal Street: This is the closest access for visiting
Kellogg Island, which is directly across the waterway. Follow Highway
99 for about 0.25 mile south of the Spokane Street overpass and turn
west on Diagonal Street. If northbound, turn at the next light after the
hedges on the left of Federal Center South; if southbound, turn at the
second light after the overpass. Follow this street about three blocks to its
end at the waterway. Public access and parking are to the left and center

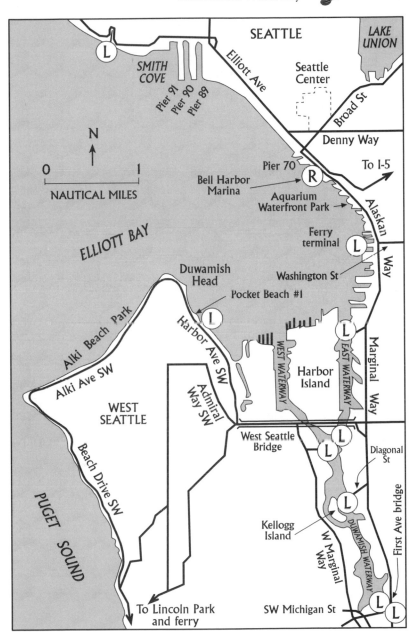

of a tiny bay. An easy launch with drop-off area for portable boats is right at the head of the parking lot where it meets the waterway. Portable toilets and picnic tables are provided.

East Waterway Junction: A little difficult to find due to its placement, it is located beneath the West Seattle Bridge across from Harbor Island at the junction of the East and Duwamish Waterways. Coming from West Seattle take the old Spokane Street drawbridge across the Duwamish. Travel across Harbor Island and turn right immediately after crossing the East Waterway bridge. Westbound traffic must follow Spokane Street onto Harbor Island, make a U-turn, and recross the East Waterway bridge to reach the launch. There is parking and a gravel ramp that makes launching easy at any tide.

Jack Perry Memorial Viewpoint/Alaskan Way Public Access: This access allows launching near the middle of the East Waterway and is also a launch point for exploration of Harbor Island and Elliott Bay. Located about 0.65 mile south of the Coast Guard facility, just south of South Massachusetts Street, it is at the point where Alaskan Way South becomes East Marginal Way South. Look for the Jack Perry Memorial Viewpoint sign only visible when traveling south. Access to the water is across rock riprap, which can be difficult at higher tides as you must launch from it.

Terminal 105 Viewpoint: Located off West Marginal Way Southwest less than 0.25 mile south of the West Seattle Bridge interchange, and just north of Southwest Dakota Street. This park includes parking, a picnic shelter, and portable rest rooms. Those launching boats are asked to use the access point at the south end of this facility by following the path to a side channel. At low tides this launch becomes nothing but mud: plan accordingly. Be especially careful of shipping traffic that cuts very close to the north end of the park, and a barge operation just to the north.

Terminal 115 Viewpoint: This is another minipark located off West Marginal Way Southwest, just north of the First Avenue bridge. Turn east on Southwest Michigan Street and follow it to the parking area at the end. As of 1998 major construction closed access, but when completed the launch is to be reopened with improvements.

First Avenue Bridge Boat Launch: This launch is located just east of the First Avenue bridge, off South River Street. This concrete ramp is owned by the Muckleshoot Indian Tribe and may be crowded during the warmer months or the salmon season when it is the base for Indian gillnetters. Limited parking is nearby and no facilities are provided.

ROUTES

Choose your own route in the waterway; there are shipyards, barge loading docks, cement plants, derelict ships, and much more.

Be sure to include Kellogg Island and the channel west of it. The island is close to the west side of the waterway, across from and slightly south of the Diagonal Street launch point. Just to the north are derelict ships. Kellogg Island was originally much larger Anderson Island and the approximate northern edge of the Duwamish estuary before the filling of Harbor Island and the development of the south Seattle industrial area. The waterway was dredged to the east of the original channel bend, creating the island. Kellogg Island's original height, formerly just above high tide, was raised by dredging spoils dumped on the south end. This miniature wilderness of brambles, brush, and hidden grassy glens is worth a gingerly stroll on a sunny spring day. Late in the summer a cornucopia of largely unpicked blackberries makes a fully sufficient reason to visit.

The shore on the west side of the old channel bend behind Kellogg Island is also a park, with the Duwamish bike path quite close to the shore. Steep banks make it an impractical launching spot, though you could certainly scramble up for a picnic at the top. There are no facilities at Kellogg Island.

The old channel course behind Kellogg Island may dry on low tides. Though the ebb current in the Duwamish can run up to 1 knot, the flow in the old channel is slight and makes a good way to get upstream, riding back down in the main channel.

A ferry in the Harbor Island dry dock (Randel Washburne)

17 ELLIOTT BAY

Shipyards with naval frigates or an Alaska ferry in drydock create an engaging scene, one that is in constant motion and change. There are also routes deep under the waterfront's piers and the opportunity to make a stop along Alaskan Way for fish and chips. You are sure to find plenty if you like seaport cities. A longer outing could be made by exploring south around Harbor Island and the Duwamish Waterway (see the Duwamish Waterway chapter), or around Magnolia and West Point to Shilshole Bay (see the West Point, Shilshole Bay, and Golden Gardens chapter).

Duration: Part day.

Rating: *Moderate*. Ship and ferry traffic is heavy, landings are not allowed along much of the waterfront, and the circle route involves crossing 2 miles of open water and busy traffic.

Navigation Aids: NOAA chart 18450 (1:10,000) or 18445 SC (1:80,000, see 1:40,000 inset); Seattle tide table.

Planning Considerations: High tide is more pleasant, but some riprap shores provide small low-tide beaches where landings are not possible at higher tides.

The skyline from the Seacrest Boathouse pier
(Carey and Jeanne Gersten)

GETTING THERE AND LAUNCHING

There are four launch sites spaced around Elliott Bay, and one downtown marina.

32nd Avenue West in Magnolia: This launch provides access near Smith Cove at the north end of Elliott Bay. From downtown Seattle drive north on Elliott Avenue and bear right onto the overpass for the Magnolia area (15th Avenue West). From the overpass follow West Garfield then West Galer Streets a total of 0.9 mile to Magnolia Boulevard West. Bear right on Magnolia Boulevard West and follow it 0.4 mile before turning left on West Howe Street. Take the next immediate left onto 32nd Avenue West, following it downhill to the water. There is usually parking available in the small lot. A portable toilet is provided.

Downtown Seattle: Launch at the public docks at the foot of Washington Street. Parking nearby may not be easy; look for a spot to the south along Alaskan Way.

Jack Perry Memorial Viewpoint/Alaskan Way Public Access: Farther south, along Harbor Island, use the Jack Perry Memorial Viewpoint located at the point where Alaskan Way South becomes Marginal Way South. See the Duwamish Waterway chapter for details.

Pocket Beach #1: On the west side of Elliott Bay, launch at this little pebble and sand beach on Harbor Avenue Southwest. From the West Seattle Bridge, take the Harbor Avenue Exit and drive north about 0.75 mile to the beach. Rest rooms are provided just to the north at Seacrest Boathouse. As an option, Puget Sound Kayak Company is located at the Seacrest Boathouse, and rents kayaks and other human-powered watercraft.

Although not a launch site, this is an attractive option for a rest stop. The Port of Seattle has made provision for kayakers at the new Bell Harbor Marina to moor for a few hours or overnight. The fee is insignificant, generally less than parking a car, and a special bargain when you consider there is security for your boat at all times.

ROUTE

Paddle locally from any of the launch points, or make a circle tour of as much of the bay as desired. A good option is to launch at Pocket Beach #1, then paddle straight across Elliott Bay toward Pier 70 or a point farther south. Follow the waterfront south and take a break at either Bell Harbor Marina or the Washington Street floats, perhaps sending one member of the party north along Alaskan Way for fish and chips. Beyond is the container terminal, Pier 46, which has a cavernous space beneath with plenty of room to paddle between the cement footings.

Along Alki Beach (Carey and Jeanne Gersten)

This seemingly endless straight tunnel is one of the more unusual sea kayaking experiences possible.

But a note of caution about paddling under any piers: technically you are trespassing on leased tidelands and doing so at your own risk. Because of safety and liability concerns, the Port of Seattle cannot condone this use and could prohibit it at any time. Use common sense. Be sure that there is plenty of headroom, look for wires that could be live, and avoid nearby ships, container-loading operations, and *definitely avoid the ferry dock entirely*. Never paddle between any ship and a dock.

At the Harbor Island shipyards, you must stay at least 100 feet to seaward. That is still close enough to ogle the dry-docked ships with propellers, bow thrusters, and sonar domes exposed for all to see.

NORTH PUGET SOUND

18 EVERETT HARBOR: JETTY ISLAND AND VICINITY

Just beyond the mills and marinas of Everett's waterfront, Jetty Island has both wildness and antiquity: seabirds and sea lions can be seen near the rotting barges that were beached long ago to stabilize the shifting sandbars of the Snohomish River estuary. This island also offers an excellent opportunity for a solitary beach hike in the Seattle area—winter months guaranteed. The Navy's homeport facility on the east side of the Snohomish River channel south of the marina provides other big sea-going attractions, but doesn't detract from the nature of Jetty Island or interfere with access to the river's channels.

Duration: Part day.
Rating: *Protected.*
Navigation Aids: NOAA charts 18423 SC, 18441 (both 1:80,000), 18443 (1:40,000), or 18444 (1:10,000); Seattle tide table.
Planning Considerations: Extensive tide flats make avoiding the lower tides essential. The highest tides give you access to small lagoons and backwaters on Jetty Island and make circumnavigation of the island shorter. Currents in the Snohomish River channels can be strong on both the ebb and flood tides.

GETTING THERE AND LAUNCHING

From northbound Interstate 5, take Exit 194 for Pacific Avenue. Turn left under the freeway and go about five blocks on Hewitt Avenue to Broadway Avenue. Turn right and drive two blocks. Turn left and follow Route 529 through downtown Everett and downhill toward the waterfront. About three blocks short of the mill buildings on the shore ahead, turn right onto West Marine View Drive (Route 529). Follow this street for

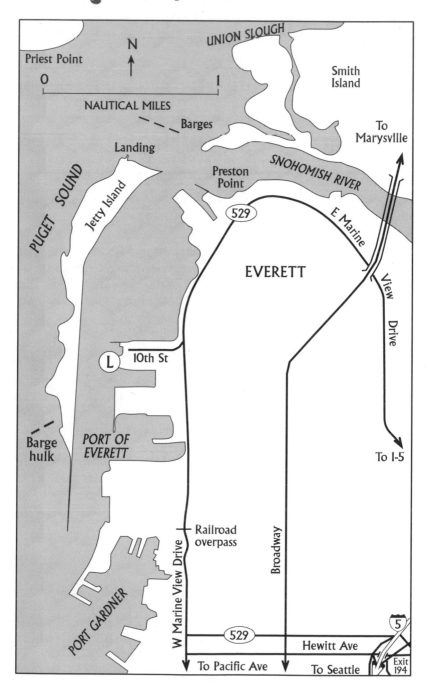

almost 2 miles, bearing left at the Y and railroad overpass, and passing the marina on the left. Turn left onto 10th Street for the public launch ramp and marine park. Use the launch ramps and docks or, if they are very busy, the shoreline on either side. No fee is charged for hand-carried, human-powered boats. Note the closing hours for the park and be sure to return before then.

ROUTE

The Jetty Island circumnavigation is approximately 4 miles. Shorter excursions to northern Jetty Island and the vicinity are attractive in themselves. For the circumnavigation, plan the direction in accordance with the Snohomish River channel flow direction, which is stronger than that on the west side of Jetty Island.

From the launching ramp, traveling counterclockwise around the island, follow the main Snohomish River channel upstream, passing extensive log storage facilities on the right. Across the channel is Jetty Island. Its shore here is used for log storage too, but less actively. At high

A contented paddler at Port Gardner, Everett
(Carey and Jeanne Gersten)

tide you may be able to find routes behind the logs along the island's shore, winding through shallow passageways among the rotting pilings and derelict, forgotten logs. Eventually, the water opens up to the left as you round the north end of Jetty Island.

The elevations of seabed and land barely differ in this river outwash area. Jetty Island itself is hardly more than a long sandbar covered with salt grass, Scotch broom, and an occasional tree. Over the years, wooden barges have been beached to control the movement of sand and silt. Walk inland toward the navigation marker tower at the north end of the island and you will find the old timbers and iron drift pins and bolts of barges that were beached and burned here long ago and are now completely surrounded by land.

Better-preserved barges are located about 0.5 mile north of Jetty Island. They are beached in a line that extends, along with countless pilings, most of the way across to Tulalip's shore to the north. If you appreciate wooden ships, the barges are worth the visit for a close look. These oceangoing vessels have all the workmanship that shipwrights of that era put into the more memorable sailing ships—diagonal triple planking, huge scarph joints, wooden treenail fastenings, and massive one-piece timbers no longer obtainable at any price.

The western edge of Jetty Island is an unbroken beach, with shallow waters warmed enough by the summer sun for a swim at high tide. At low tide, it becomes a sandy tide flat a mile or more wide. More hulks of old barges are found here and there along the beach.

A large colony of sea lions resides in this area during the late winter and spring, usually from February to May. At lower tides they move offshore, often floating in large somnambulant clusters. When the tide is in they like the beached barges or even the logs behind Jetty Island in the Snohomish River channel. Beware—they have little fear of humans and are apt to make threatening gestures to kayakers. In fact, many paddlers feel sea lions are potentially the most dangerous of all the marine mammals.

The southern end of the island narrows to become a stone jetty for the last 0.5 mile. If currents are strong against you for the paddle back upstream, you may want to shorten the loop by portaging across the island north of the stone jetty. This is a distance of 100 yards or less, depending on tides and logs stored on the east side.

Once in the river channel, you have the choice of following the wilder island shoreline or crossing to inspect the marina's fishing boats and yachts. There are a variety of shops here with groceries, food, and assorted beverages.

19 PORT SUSAN: THE STILLAGUAMISH RIVER AND KAYAK POINT

The productive estuary of the Stillaguamish River offers the winding channel of Hat Slough through a lush delta of grasses, trees, and farmland attractive to wildlife that floats, flies, and strides. With views across Port Susan to Camano Island and the distant Olympic Mountains beyond, and a relatively direct route between the estuary to a Cascadia Marine Trail site at Kayak Point, this area offers a relaxing half-day paddle.

> **Duration**: Part day.
>
> **Rating**: *Protected* or *Moderate*. Generally this is protected paddling with the exception that a good steady south wind on Port Susan can make for choppy seas in these shallow waters.
>
> **Navigation Aids**: NOAA charts 18423 SC (1:80,000 with 1:30,000 insets) and 18441 (1:80,000). The current for Saratoga Passage is typically weak and variable. Use the tide tables for Kayak Point to estimate the chance of current at the mouth of the Stillaguamish River.
>
> **Planning Considerations**: The ebb and flow of the tide can produce about 1 knot of current in Hat Slough. The river itself typically produces a very mild outflowing current at what would otherwise be slack. The northern portion of Port Susan from Warm Beach north drains to mud flats at low tide and requires a high tide to be paddled.

GETTING THERE AND LAUNCHING

Hat Slough, Lower Stillaguamish River: From Interstate 5 take the exit for State Route 531 (172nd Street Northwest) west. At 2.3 miles it turns right at a stop sign onto Lakewood Road. Continue another 6.3 miles to Marine Drive (92nd Drive Northwest). Turn right, north, onto Marine Drive and follow it 3.6 miles, passing over Hat Slough. Just beyond the bridge on the left is Boe Road, a dirt road. Turn onto it and in 0.2 mile turn left to the signed Washington State Fish and Wildlife launch. A launch permit is required for this day use only ramp.

Kayak Point: At the junction of Lakewood Road and Marine Drive turn south. Follow Marine Drive 2.2 miles to the entrance to Kayak Point Park on your right. The park road descends 0.6 mile through forested lands down to the ramp and beach. A minimal combined day use and launch fee is required. A Cascadia Marine Trail site is located at the far

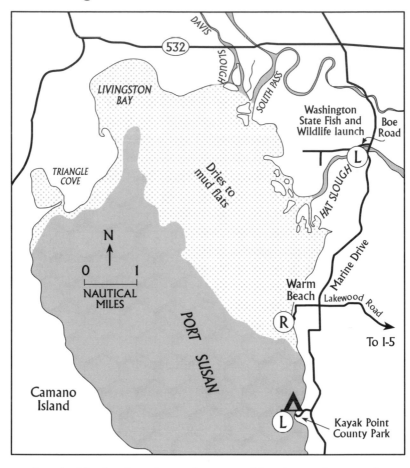

north end of the beach and must be reserved in advance for a maximum of one night's stay.

The shuttle distance between the two points is an easy 6.6 miles, mostly along Marine Drive.

ROUTE

From the north bank of Hat Slough paddle the slowly winding channel in a generally southeast direction for 1.75 miles toward the open water of Port Susan. Both sides of the slough have been bermed up to protect the farmlands, creating a cozy feeling with the bordering trees overhanging the slough. Though the banks limit close views, through the trees you can spy the Olympic Mountains in the far distance ahead and Mount Baker, the Three Fingers, and other mountains of the Cascade range peaking over the foothills behind you. Birds such as the kingfisher

Pier at Kayak Point County Park, a WWTA site
(Carey and Jeanne Gersten)

enjoy this environment, and so do otter, muskrat, and other water-happy mammals.

As Hat Slough enters Port Susan your view opens to a panorama with Camano Island to the west and north, and rich farmland to the east backed by thickly wooded hills. The distant Olympic Mountains come clearly into view. If you paddle about 1 mile west out into Port Susan, you can also spot Gedney Island to the south, about 10 miles away. Due to the shallowness of this end of Port Susan, waterfowl and land birds feed here in abundance. Heron, eagle, tern, seagull, and many others are easy to spot, especially as the tide lowers to offer them what seems effortless dining.

It is another 1.4 miles to the community of Warm Beach. In 0.3 mile more, at the south end of Warm Beach, is public access at a road end. It is hard to spot through the shrubs; a small, yellow cottage of concrete brick marks its northern edge. The access is only 50 feet in width and the tidelands are privately held on either side. If a snack break or food for an evening meal is needed, you can walk 0.5 mile to the small grocery store up the hill.

From Warm Beach the direct paddling distance to the boat ramp and pier at Kayak Point County Park is 1.75 miles. The entire shoreline along the way has sandy beach with homes dotting the land above. The park itself has a gradual sloping beach, is well manicured, and provides a pleasant place to picnic or camp overnight. All the sites border the beach and most have sheltered picnic tables. You will often find fisherman at the pier casting their lines or dangling crab pots.

The naming of Kayak Point is attributed to two differing explanations. A resort lodge that once stood here many years ago either rented sea kayaks for guests to use, or displayed Aleut kayaks in the main hall that the sons of the owners brought back with them from an Arctic trip. No matter which explanation, the locals simply started referring to the point as Kayak Point, and over time it stuck.

20 WHIDBEY ISLAND: OAK HARBOR, CRESCENT BEACH, AND PENN COVE

Big magnificent views down Saratoga Passage, a snug harbor, a gorgeous 3-mile-long sandy crescent beach backed by a luxuriant meadow alive with raptors, and a charming wharf with delightful treats at the heart of Coupeville make this area a joy to paddle. In addition, a Cascadia Marine Trail campsite at Oak Harbor City Park offers a convenient base from which to explore.

> **Duration**: Part to full day.
> **Rating**: *Protected* or *Moderate*.
> **Navigation Aids**: NOAA charts 18423 SC (1:80,000 with 1:30,000 insets), 18428 (1:10,000 for Oak and Crescent Harbors), 18441 (1:80,000), and 18471 (1:40,000 for Penn Cove). The current for Saratoga Passage is typically weak and variable.
> **Planning Considerations**: A strong south wind can build rough swells as it sweeps up Saratoga Passage into Oak and Crescent Harbors.

GETTING THERE AND LAUNCHING

Oak Harbor City Park: Traveling either north or south on Highway 20 within the Oak Harbor city limits, at the major junction of Highway 20, Pioneer Way, and Baywatch Street, turn south onto Baywatch Street, then immediately left into Oak Harbor City Park. The boat ramp is clearly marked; no fee is required. Besides the Cascadia Marine Trail site at the southwest corner of the park, there are tent camping and RV sites, rest rooms with showers, and the town with all its amenities. Unique to the city park is a windmill at one end and a decommissioned naval jet at the other.

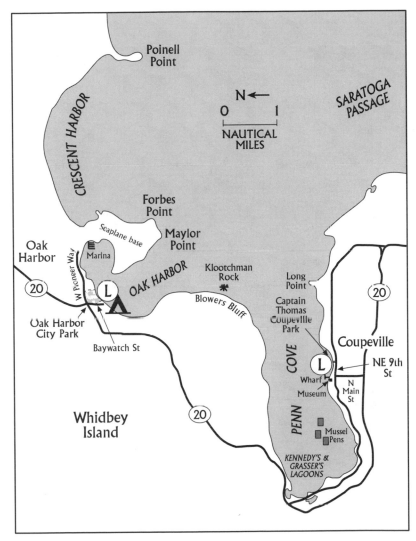

Captain Thomas Coupeville Park: From Highway 20, turn north onto North Main Street and go 0.5 mile taking a right onto Northeast Ninth Street. Go 0.1 mile to Captain Thomas Coupeville Park on the left. There are rest rooms, picnic tables, and drinking water. A ramp and float serve for launching boats in this day use only park.

ROUTES

Several basic trips are possible. Staying within either Penn Cove or Oak Harbor offers a protected setting for novice paddlers, whereas traveling between the coves and harbors allows for moderate one-way or round trips.

Oak Harbor: *Protected.* Paddling the shoreline of Oak Harbor offers a surprising variety. Along the park and city waterfront is a sandy beach with commerce just behind. At the harbor's east end is the fair-sized Oak Harbor Marina beside the Whidbey Naval Air Station's Seaplane Base. Continuing your circumnavigation to the south brings you to another strip of sandy beach with a more natural flavor where naval personnel often jog and kids play. Crossing the entrance of the harbor west, you come to steep bluffs with homes perched on top. The total circle is 2 miles or more depending on how close you stick to the shore.

Oak Harbor to Crescent Harbor: *Moderate.* By rounding Maylor Point and then Forbes Point at the end of the peninsula on which the

seaplane base resides, you can explore Crescent Harbor and Crescent Beach where reality lives up to its name. The clean, sandy beach stretches over 3.5 miles from end to end in a smooth curve. Due to its southern exposure, storms coming up Saratoga Passage stack all types of timber and driftwood above the light coffee-colored strip of sandy beach. Behind the beach is meadow and marsh protected to enhance wildlife; birds abound, including raptors such as hawks and eagles. Common loons are also spotted as they float and chortle in the harbor. The one-way paddle from the launch at Oak Harbor City Park to the western end of Crescent Beach is 3.4 miles.

Oak Harbor to Penn Cove: *Moderate.* The relatively direct paddling distance from the city park to Captain Thomas Coupeville Park is 4.2 miles. Keeping to the western shoreline, at 2 miles you pass by Klootchman Rock, a fair-sized erratic boulder left behind as the last glaciers melted, sitting beneath Blowers Bluff. On days when a south wind blows, the seas can build along this stretch, possibly breaking as they reach the shallow beaches.

The barn-red Coupeville Wharf is easy to spot, making it a good target at about 0.35 miles beyond the ramp at Captain Thomas Coupeville Park. This trip can be done as a one-way from either end, with an easy car shuttle of only 11 miles between the two city launches, or as a round trip. There are plenty of choices for food and drink at either end. Particularly fun is the very complete deli at the end of Coupeville Wharf where they also rent sea kayaks.

Penn Cove: *Protected.* Penn Cove, only open to the larger water of Saratoga Passage at its east end, is well sheltered from most major blows. Starting from Captain Thomas Coupeville Park, you can explore the docks, wharfs, and overhanging buildings comprising Coupeville's waterfront. Coupeville is the oldest town on Whidbey Island and it, along with the surrounding shoreline of Penn Cove, is within the Ebey's Landing National Historical Reserve that stretches to the west side of Whidbey Island. You might want to secure your boat and visit the Whidbey Island Historical Society's Museum at the foot of the wharf.

From Coupeville you can paddle west and visit the many floating pens growing the famous and delicious Penn Cove Mussel. Remember not to disturb or climb on the pens. Beyond this at the head of the cove, you can poke around Kennedy's and Grasser's Lagoons in search of waterfowl, raptors, deer, and other creatures that habituate the shoreline. The one-way distance from the ramp to the lagoons is 2.6 miles.

Wharf at Coupeville on Penn Cove (Carey and Jeanne Gersten)

21 SKAGIT RIVER DELTA

The Skagit River Delta is a birder's paradise and more. A maze of marshland channels, river dwellers' shanties and floating houses, and even overgrown pre-World War II coast artillery emplacements are included in the rich estuary country within the Skagit Wildlife Area.

Duration: Part to full day.
Rating: *Protected.*
Navigation Aids: NOAA chart 18423 SC (1:80,000) or USGS 7.5 Minute Series (1:24,000) topographic map for the Utsalady Quadrangle; Seattle tide table (add about 20 minutes).
Planning Considerations: Midtide or higher, at least 4 feet above mean low water, is required for paddling outside the main Skagit River channel and outside Swinomish Channel. Both Skagit River and Swinomish Channel reverse their currents with the tide. This occurs for the channel at least one hour after the tide change for the river, but in practice the channel current is not easily predicted. Currents affect paddling efforts to and from all launch locations.

You may wish to avoid the heavy bird-hunting period from mid-September through December; contact the state Department of Wildlife for specifics. Each member of your group must have a Department of Wildlife conservation license in his or her possession to go ashore in Skagit Wildlife Area. These can be purchased at stores that sell fishing and hunting licenses.

GETTING THERE AND LAUNCHING

Choose from launch sites along the Skagit River or in downtown La Conner. An approximately 10-mile car shuttle could be made between them.

Skagit River: From Interstate 5 take the La Conner–Conway Exit and within a short distance branch right to Conway. Continue about 5 miles on Fir Island Road. For the lower river launch at Blake's Skagit Resort and Marina, turn left on Rawlins Road. Located approximately 1 river mile above the delta area, Blake's is the lowest launch point on the North Fork of the Skagit River. The resort charges a launch fee, which also covers parking for the first day. Their number is 360-445-6533.

A state Department of Wildlife launch site is located farther upriver. Turn right off Fir Island Road onto Moore Road about 0.35 mile beyond Rawlins Road, just before the North Fork bridge, then take the

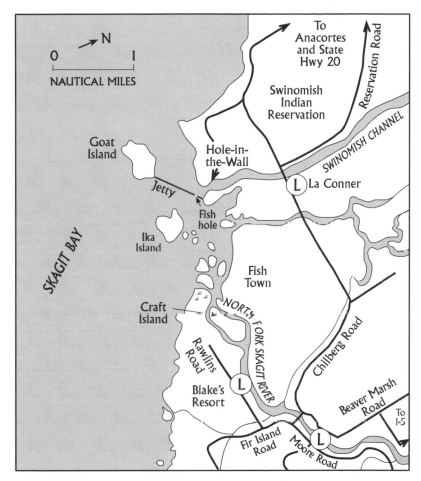

first unsigned dirt road to the left 0.25 mile beyond at the S-curve. Department of Wildlife conservation licenses are required to use this launch site.

La Conner: To launch from La Conner follow the above directions on Fir Island Road, which changes to Chilberg Road, and continue 5 miles beyond the North Fork bridge to La Conner. The La Conner public boat ramp is located below and just north of the Rainbow Bridge. After entering La Conner, turn left on Maple, then right on Caledonia Street, left on Third, and finally right on Sherman Street. The ramp is straight ahead at the waterfront. There is a fee for the use of the ramp. Parking in summer is difficult. Use the lot across the street or along the street beyond if space is available.

ROUTES

Skagit River to Craft Island: *Protected.* The paddling distance is 3 to 5 miles each way. Time your start to ensure that you will have mid to high tide in the delta once you get downriver. The distance to the shallow delta area from Blake's is about 1.5 miles, and about 3 miles from the upper river launch. There is a downstream current from both river launch sites during the ebb and an upstream flow as far as the upper launch on larger flood tides (except during heavy river runoff), though this begins as much as an hour after low tide.

Heading downriver approximately 1 mile below Blake's, you reach a sharp bend to the right; just beyond are pastoral farm buildings and river dwellers' houses and shacks on the right bank. This is the community of Fish Town. Just downstream on the left is the first side channel into the delta. Take this channel for Craft Island and keep bearing left. The distance is a little more than 1 mile after leaving the river.

Craft Island is really a hill jutting up from an otherwise flat marsh and tidelands west of the river as it nears the mouth. From the top you can see a sweeping panorama of the marshlands to the north and south and, at low tide, the vast gray tide flats to the west. This and other upland islands are a particularly sensitive habitat for raptors, including bald eagles and red-tailed hawks. If you go ashore, avoid approaching or disturbing these birds, particularly when the nesting sites are in use.

The La Conner waterfront (Carey and Jeanne Gersten)

Timing for the Craft Island excursion is important, as the side channel to it is dry below midtide. If you have the time, you may wish to head downriver at early ebb, paddle to the island, and spend the last of the ebb and early flood lunching, exploring, or just enjoying the view. If your tide timing is off for paddling to Craft Island, you can walk there after returning to the launch point. Drive to the end of Rawlins Road beyond Blake's. A rough trail about 0.75 mile is accessible on lower tides leading across the marsh meadows to the island.

La Conner to Goat Island to Skagit Delta: *Protected.* The paddling distance for the loop is 7 miles; additional side trips are possible.

Most of this loop can be paddled at tide heights of 3 feet or more. Avoiding a lower tide is not as critical here as for the Craft Island route. However, you will be scooping sand much of the way in a foot or less of water; getting out to wade and tow your boat may prove easier in spots. Spending the low-tide interval exploring Goat Island is worthwhile if you can afford the time.

From the public launch at La Conner, follow the channel south through the twisting narrows of Hole-in-the-Wall. Beyond, the channel opens to flats with intertidal islets and shallow waterways that invite exploration if the tide is in. To the south is a log storage area bounded by a stone jetty extending to Goat Island. The route later returns through a tiny gap in this jetty.

Goat Island has both the dense forest and the grassy meadows with madrona trees that are typical of the more arid San Juan Islands. On the northwest end is Fort Whitman, a component of the extensive coast artillery defenses for Puget Sound built at the turn of the century. There are mounts for three guns in the emplacements, with associated rooms and tunnels similar to those found at Fort Worden and Fort Casey State Parks. Such defenses were obsolete by World War II, when aircraft became more effective than coast artillery against invading fleets.

To reach the emplacements, look for the old dock along the island's north shore. Behind it is a rocky, muddy beach and the start of a rough trail that climbs to the right. Follow this about 250 yards to the battery.

As with other islands in the Skagit Wildlife Area, this is a particularly sensitive habitat for resident raptors. The Department of Wildlife asks that you respect the privacy of these birds, particularly during spring nesting. As elsewhere within the Skagit Wildlife Area, no camping is allowed.

Paddling around the south side of Goat Island brings you into the shallowest part of this route, though enough water can be found in the shifting channels of the Skagit River on all but the lowest tides. On ebb tides and the first portion of floods, downstream currents will make moving up into the delta hard and slow work, with few eddies to assist your progress.

At this point, you could take time to explore the many sloughs off the Skagit River's channel and perhaps cut through the delta to Craft Island, about 2 miles to the east, if the tide is high enough.

The return to Swinomish Channel from the Skagit River is via the "fish hole" in the jetty, a small opening allowing migrating salmon that made a wrong turn into Swinomish Channel to get back to the river. Located about 200 yards from the eastern end of the jetty, this gap is not visible as you approach from upriver, but follow the jetty and you will find it. The hole is dry below midtide.

22 HOPE AND SKAGIT ISLANDS

Though currents are swift in this area, the protection of nearby Fidalgo and Whidbey Islands makes Hope and Skagit reasonable destinations when other places are a bit on the rough side. Ashore on these state park islands are grassy hillsides with flowers in season, forest trails, and plenty of sand and gravel beaches for sunbathing. To preserve these fragile islands, camping is no longer permitted by Washington State Parks. However, nearby Ala Spit is a Cascadia Marine Trail campsite offering easy access and a wonderful place to stay.

Skagit Island, looking toward Deception Pass
(Randel Washburne)

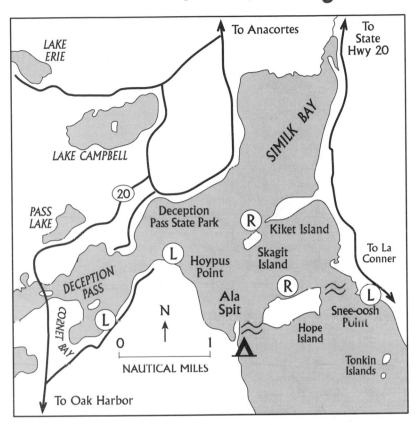

Duration: Part day to overnight.

Rating: *Moderate* +. Currents can produce turbulence in certain areas and rough seas when opposing southerly winds. Avoid strongest currents at the west end of Hope Island unless you have the skills to handle strong eddy lines and tide rips.

Navigation Aids: NOAA charts 18423 SC, 18421 (both 1:80,000), or 18427 (1:25,000); current tables for Deception Pass.

Planning Considerations: Currents here are dependent on those in Deception Pass. The flood flows south. If possible, plan to catch the flood current going to the islands and the ebb for the return.

GETTING THERE AND LAUNCHING

Deception Pass: Launch from the Cornet Bay area of Deception Pass State Park. Follow signs to Cornet Bay from Highway 20 about 1 mile south of the bridge and go about 1.25 miles to the launching ramp area. Use the gravel beach just below a timbered bulkhead in front of the parking area or, if the tide is high and covers the beach, use the launching ramp or floats. For overnight parking, use the lot across the road from the boat launch.

For day trips, you could continue 1 mile past Cornet Bay boat launch to the end of the road at Hoypus Point. This was the old ferry landing before the bridge over the pass replaced its purpose. Launching here cuts at least 1 mile from the one-way distance. Overnight parking is not allowed here; use the overnight lot at Cornet Bay.

Snee-oosh Beach: A pleasant alternative that avoids most of the current on the west side of the islands is this gentle beach near La Conner. Drive west from La Conner over the Swinomish Channel bridge on Pioneer Parkway for 0.6 mile to Snee-oosh Road; turn left and proceed another 1.9 miles. Bear left onto Hope Island Road for 0.3 mile, then bear left onto View Lane. After 0.2 mile turn left onto Chillberg Avenue and then make an immediate U-turn onto the dirt access road to the beach. There are no amenities, but a beautiful view across to Hope and Skagit Islands.

Snee-oosh Beach near Deception Pass (Carey and Jeanne Gersten)

ROUTE

From Cornet Bay to Hoypus Point, the state of the current dictates how far offshore to paddle—head out 100 feet or so to catch a ride on the flood current. If it is ebbing, there are eddies that make easy paddling along the tree-lined gravel beach to Hoypus Point, but you will have to fight the brunt of the current as you round the point. Likewise, there are some eddies south of the point toward Ala Spit that will help against an ebb.

You may wish to cross directly from Hoypus Point to Skagit Island, adjusting to offset the effects of the current as you go across. Its strength diminishes during the second half of this 1-mile crossing.

Skagit Island is rocky and steep along its north and western shores. There are gravel and shell beaches at the east and southeast ends. A trail circles the island, winding through fir and salal forest on the north side. The south side of the island is a series of rocky meadows interspersed with madronas, with lots of nice spots for lunch in the sun.

Hope Island is far larger. Trails circle this island, but most visitors prefer hiking the beaches or paddling along shore to walking in the thick forest. Gravel beaches on the south side of Hope Island are the biggest attraction for day use paddling, with chances for walking and secluded rest stops.

During large tidal exchanges, currents at both the east and west ends of Hope Island can be swift and dangerous for anyone not skilled in dealing with moving water. If you are unsure, avoid going around to the south side, or go back around via the east end where currents are a little weaker. Both ends can have sharp eddy lines and possible tide rips. Stay close inshore on the east end where you will probably need to cross only one eddy line, and then paddle in eddies the rest of the way around.

The west shore has a very strong eddy line that has capsized kayaks in the past. The current between Hope Island and Ala Spit, about 0.35 mile distant, may be as swift as you can paddle, requiring hard work to get across against an opposing flow without losing too much ground. The flow along the spit is slower, but still takes hard paddling upstream against a flood current to reach the eddies north of the spit.

23 DECEPTION PASS

Deception Pass offers outstanding beauty that can be explored safely on the fringes of the high-current area in the pass itself. You can also paddle through the pass when currents are weakest if a novice. Beginners should avoid the pass unless certain of correctly identifying the slack current time; there is plenty of easy paddling in areas of little current within view of Deception Pass's full magnificence.

Experienced paddlers eager to expand their skills can expend some adrenaline practicing in Washington's strongest currents—crossing eddy lines, developing bracing reflexes in swirls and turbulence, and maybe descending into a whirlpool! Currents mostly average 5 or 6 knots at their maximum, while the occasional strongest ones exceed 8 knots. Speeds rapidly decrease within 0.5 mile of both sides of the pass.

Routes in Deception Pass can be combined with those in the Hope and Skagit Island area to the east (see the Hope and Skagit Islands chapter). The Cascadia Marine Trail campsite at Bowman Bay also affords the opportunity to make extended trips.

Duration: Part day.

Rating: *Protected, Moderate +*, or *Exposed*. Heavy boat traffic in the pass may create rough conditions.

Navigation Aids: NOAA charts 18427 (1:25,000) or 18423 SC (see 1:25,000 inset for Deception Pass); Deception Pass current tables.

Planning Considerations: Seek or avoid strong current periods depending on your skills and preferences, using the Deception Pass current tables. Launch and takeout locations depend on current flows, described below. The flood current flows east through the pass. Avoid times of strong wind from the west, particularly during ebb currents, which can produce particularly nasty seas and tide rips.

GETTING THERE AND LAUNCHING

There are three launch sites within Deception Pass State Park. Which you use depends on where you wish to paddle and the state of the current in the pass. Tactics for planning with currents are described under routes.

Bowman Bay: The launch is accessed from Highway 20 about 0.5 mile north of the Deception Pass Bridge. This is a good place for protected paddling north of the pass or for one end of a shuttle trip of about 3 miles driving distance from Cornet Bay. Launch on the gravel beach in front of the parking lot. A launch fee is required.

West Beach: This is the easiest access to the pass from the west. Turn off Highway 20 about 0.5 mile south of the bridge and follow signs to the West Beach parking lot. In windy weather or when a large swell is penetrating the Strait of Juan de Fuca, the sand and gravel West Beach can have substantial surf. If it is not to your liking, a 200-yard-long path leads from the parking lot to a protected launch on North Beach just behind West Point.

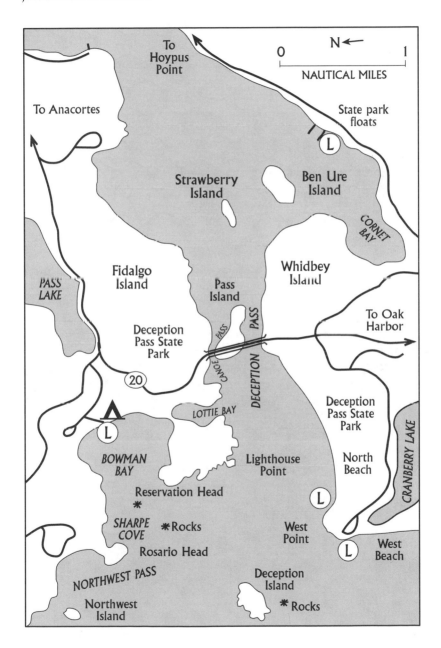

Cornet Bay: This launch serves paddling to the east of the pass. Follow signs to Cornet Bay from Highway 20 about 1 mile south of the bridge and go about 1.25 miles to the boat ramp area. Use the gravel beach just below a timbered bulkhead in front of the parking area or, if the tide is high and covers the beach, use the launching ramp or floats.

ROUTES

Bowman Bay: *Protected.* Paddling anywhere within this bay, located between Rosario Head and Reservation Head, will avoid dangers from currents, and waters should be relatively smooth. There is plenty of rocky shoreline to explore, plus opportunities for lolling on the beaches, exploring ashore at Sharpe Cove to the west or at the spit adjacent to Lottie Bay to the east. Portaging across to Lottie Bay is easy, and Lottie Bay is rated *Protected* to its mouth, where currents can be strong.

West Area Exploration: *Moderate +.* Currents west of Lottie Bay are generally less than half the strength of those predicted for the pass, and probably are suitable for intermediate paddlers with some experience with currents. If there is any doubt about the abilities of members of your party to handle currents, avoid times when the currents in the pass are predicted to exceed 5 knots. Crossing the mouth of the pass from

Deception Pass (Carey and Jeanne Gersten)

Talking with a fisherman off the east side of the Kitsap Peninsula
(Carey and Jeanne Gersten)

Bowman Bay to North Beach should be done cautiously during flood currents that could set you toward the stronger currents in the pass. This area can be extremely rough when swells from the Strait of Juan de Fuca oppose an ebb current flowing out of the pass. At such times or in windy weather, the eastern portion of the pass area (Cornet Bay) is a more prudent choice.

Plan to spend some time exploring the rocky shores between Reservation Head and Lottie Bay where you will find a number of pocket beaches for secluded lunch stops. Ashore, this area is accessed by a trail from Bowman Bay. In one of these coves, a steel ladder leads from sea level to the heights of Lighthouse Point which provides an excellent vantage into Deception Pass.

The park extends north to include part of Rosario Bay, as well as Northwest Island and Deception Island. Neither of the islands is developed and access is not easy. Gravel beaches on the north side of Deception Island offer fairly easy landings on lower tides, but it's a hard scramble to gain access to the island above.

Cornet Bay: *Protected.* Explore this bay as far north as Ben Ure Island (private) or west toward Hoypus Point, about 1 mile from the boat launch. Currents in Cornet Bay are weak and often flow the opposite direction as in the pass to form a long, tapering back eddy on ebbs along the shore toward Hoypus Point. At the latter, currents may be strong while accompanying rips make it unsuited for *Protected*-rated paddling. Likewise, the strong currents and eddies around Strawberry Island are appropriate only for experienced paddlers.

Bowman Bay to Cornet Bay (or reverse) through Deception Pass: *Moderate* ı. You can see it all in this 3-mile traverse through Deception Pass. Timing for at least near-slack in the pass is critical; you may want to arrange your travel to catch the last of the current going your way at the beginning or the new current at the end. Allow plenty of time to explore the coves west of the pass. Stops ashore near the pass are easy on the beaches at Gun Point and another small beach directly north across the channel. Pass Island has fair access ashore on rocks on the east end. Access at Strawberry Island is similar.

Boat traffic in the pass is a significant hazard, especially if the current forces boats to speed up or reduces their control. Canoe Pass, the smaller passage to the north of Pass Island, is the safer and more interesting way through when currents are weak, as little traffic goes this way. However, a bend in this channel reduces visibility for oncoming powerboats.

Deception Pass Current Play: *Exposed.* Depending on the current strength and your skills, capsizing here is probable; a wet- or dry suit is essential. A helmet is a good idea too, due to the rocky shoreline. You should be prepared to rescue members of your party if they should capsize.

A number of Seattle-area sea kayak retailers and outfitters hold classes for intermediate-level paddlers in Deception Pass to give them practice in negotiating currents and bracing. They usually seek current strengths of about 5 knots and may have an outboard-powered inflatable at the ready.

Five knots offers eddy lines strong enough to capsize the kayaker who does not prepare for them, especially in narrower boats. Seven knots requires strong leaning and bracing in all boats when crossing eddy lines, and can create swirl zones and boils that may be intimidating to all but the most blasé whitewater boater. On ebbs, whirlpools form downstream from Pass Island, but do not last. On strong floods, more persistent whirlpools form on the edge of the main channel east of Pass Island. These are a thrill for those who care to chase them down and put one end of their boat into the vortex.

Canoe Pass is preferred to the main channel for eddy play, primarily because of the boat traffic going through the pass at all but the strongest current times. Wakes can make big breakers as they meet eddy lines on either side of the channel. On ebbs Canoe Pass has eddies on both sides just west of the bridge, and ferrying back and forth from one to the other is easy. On floods a series of small eddies forms close to the island's steep rock face, and a long back eddy forms along the opposite shore. Hopping from one to the other is possible, but requires more maneuverability than during ebbs. Watch out for sharp barnacles along both shores that can make capsizing there perilous.

SAN JUAN ISLANDS AREA

24 BURROWS ISLAND

The paddling at Burrows Island is interesting and exhilarating—sheer rock and lively currents. Ashore you will find an abandoned Coast Guard light station that is now a state park. Hike beyond the station to steep grassy shorelines or climb the hill above for a spectacular view of southern Rosario Strait.

Duration: Part day.
Rating: *Moderate*. Currents can exceed 2 knots and tide rips are likely. Wind can make this area quite dangerous during times of strong current.
Navigation Aids: NOAA charts 18423 SC or 18421 (both 1:80,000), or 18427 (1:25,000); Rosario Strait current tables with corrections for the Burrows Island–Fidalgo Head area.
Planning Considerations: Use the flood current to travel west in the channels on either the north or south side of Burrows Island and for rounding Fidalgo Head from the south. Flood currents here are generally stronger than the ebbs.

GETTING THERE AND LAUNCHING

Choices for launching are either Skyline Marina, the closest to Burrows Island, or Washington Park, which adds another mile or so of paddling around Fidalgo Head. These two launch points are about a 0.5-mile walk apart, so consider starting at Washington Park and taking out at Skyline Marina.

Skyline Marina: From Anacortes, follow signs for the San Juan Island ferry, about 4 miles west of town. Continue straight where the ferry traffic curves right down the hill to the ferry landing. After 0.5 mile, turn left for Skyline Marina and go another 0.5 mile. Take Hughes

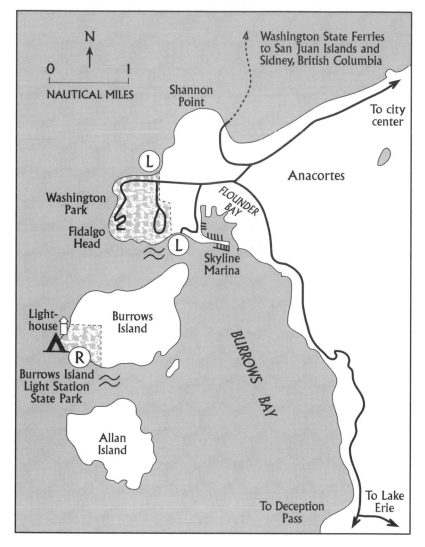

Lane to the right and park along the south side of the street near the end. This is private property, and there is a daily fee to park. Launch at the sand beach just a few yards' carry from the circle at the end of the road.

Washington Park: Continue straight past Skyline Way and go right at the Y intersection. Park in the "A" lot to carry your boat across the lawn to the gravel beach. Then move your car to the "B" lot to park. There is a daily parking fee.

ROUTE

Most of the shoreline of Fidalgo Head, Burrows Island, and neighboring Allan Island is steep rock with grass and madronas growing above and sharp drop-offs that allow close-in paddling. Beaches are infrequent. All of Fidalgo Head west of Skyline Marina is in Washington Park; expect to see lots of people along its shores. Public land on Burrows Island is restricted to the 40 acres and 1,000 feet of shoreline in Burrows Island Light Station State Park on the island's west and southwest corner. Visitors ashore here are rare. There are no public lands or tidelands on Allan Island.

Expect to find strong eddy lines and nearby tide rips in the channels separating Burrows Island from Fidalgo Head and Allan Island. It is possible to ferry across these currents to reach the island, though you may have to work hard to maintain your position as you cross.

The only landing at the park on Burrows Island is on a gravel beach just north of the light station. The challenge here is scaling the steep rocks on the north side to the old supply-landing facility which can be precarious in wet weather. Above are the equipment shed and residence building which have been boarded up since the station was automated. The lighthouse and a horn that operates in all weather are located at the point.

A Cascadia Marine Trail campsite is planned for Burrows Island beginning in the 1999 season. Please check with WWTA or Washington State Parks before planning to camp.

To the south are wild and rugged grassy slopes above cliffs that drop to the water, a chance for exploring where few others go. If you would like an excellent vantage point, follow this shore a few hundred yards around to the east and climb up the rocks and grassy slopes to the hilltop. To get there from the light station, walk on the path behind the lighthouse into the trees, as the shoreline here is not negotiable. Beyond, the trees and brush thin out as you continue. Be wary of steep drop-offs to the cliffs below. This is no place for small children.

25 PADILLA BAY

One of a handful of national estuarine sanctuaries, Padilla Bay is a vital rest and feeding stop for migratory waterfowl, particularly black brants. It is also a nursery for countless intertidal creatures. Due to the mixture of fresh water from its sloughs and saltwater from the bay, its tidal marsh habitat hosts a rich diversity of plants and animals. At low tide, Padilla Bay's mud flats extend for miles, so timing for high tide is essential to explore its tidal marshes and sloughs. For a better understanding of what to see here, stop at the sanctuary's Breazeale Interpretive Center just north of Bayview State Park.

Duration: Part day.

Rating: *Protected*. The hazard is low here because the waters are almost never too deep to stand in. However, winds in this area can be strong and seas in the shallows steep.

Navigation Aids: NOAA charts 18423 SC, 18421 (both 1:80,000), or 18427 (1:25,000); Port Townsend tide table (add 30 minutes for high tide time and one hour and 15 minutes for low tide time).

Planning Considerations: A high tide of at least 5 feet is essential to explore these huge tide flats and adjacent sloughs. A falling tide could leave you stranded with a mile or more of soft mud between you and the water. This area is often windier than the surrounding area. Most of the bay is open to bird hunting from mid-October through January.

GETTING THERE AND LAUNCHING

Launch at either Bayview State Park on the bay's east side, Indian Slough on the southeast side, the Swinomish Channel boat ramp on the southwest side, or March Point on the west side.

Bayview State Park and Indian Slough: From Interstate 5, take the Anacortes Exit (Highway 20) and go west 16 miles to Bayview-Edison Road, opposite the Farmhouse Restaurant. Go north on this road for Indian Slough or Bayview State Park. The road crosses the slough after about 1 mile; park at the trailhead for the Padilla Bay Shore Trail just beyond it. At Bayview State Park, turn right into the park and then take the underpass down to the picnic area. Launch at the sand beach. The sanctuary's Breazeale Interpretive Center is located about 0.5 mile farther north along the highway. It is open 10:00 A.M. to 5:00 P.M. Wednesday through Sunday, all year. Their phone number is 360-428-1558.

Swinomish Channel Boat Ramp: Continue west on Highway 20 another 1.5 miles and turn right just before the bridge. There is a small daily donation to Skagit County Parks and Recreation who maintain the ramp.

March Point: The turnoff to March Point is about 0.25 mile west of the Swinomish Channel bridge. For more details on March Point, see the Saddlebag Island chapter.

ROUTE

Though the entire bay makes for interesting and scenic paddling, there are some portions that you should avoid. The Department of

Wildlife has identified two areas where wintering brants are vulnerable to disturbance. One area extends north from Bayview State Park almost to Joe Leary Slough. Confine paddling to south of the park. The second area is just north of the railroad bridge in Swinomish Channel and east along the dike for about 0.5 mile. Give the tidelands in this area a wide berth if you launch from the boat ramp in the channel, and paddle east to explore the areas in and around Telegraph and Indian Sloughs. Or go west from the channel to find more salt marshes and sandy spits resulting from dredging the channel.

There are no public shorelands other than the launching points in the estuary sanctuary, and most of the tidelands are still in private ownership pending litigation. Two good routes would be from Swinomish Channel to either Bayview State Park or March Point, using the facilities there (minimal at March Point). Both involve about 6-mile round trips, more mileage if you explore the sloughs on the way to the state park.

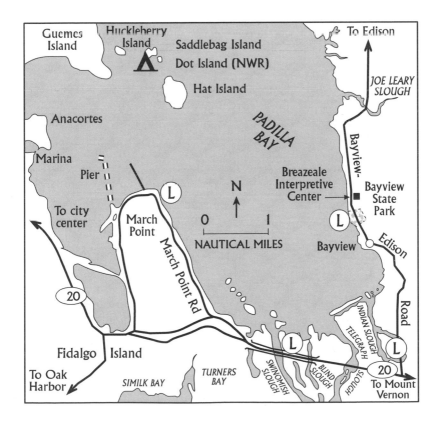

26 SADDLEBAG ISLAND

So named because it is almost two islands with a connecting isthmus, Saddlebag Island has both meadow and forest for walking in, and a Cascadia Marine Trail campsite along with other primitive campsites in the low area between. The short paddling distance makes it suitable for a last-minute camping decision. It can be combined with further exploration of nearby Padilla Bay.

Duration: Part day to overnight.

Rating: *Moderate*. Requires crossing open water where tide rips are possible.

Navigation Aids: NOAA charts 18421 or 18423 SC (both 1:80,000), or 18427 (1:25,000); Port Townsend tide table (add one hour).

Planning Considerations: Though all tides are fine for the Saddlebag Island route, lower tides add some carrying distance at the March Point launch and restrict access to other parts of Padilla Bay.

GETTING THERE AND LAUNCHING

The easiest and closest launch is from the end of March Point, site of the conspicuous refineries visible to the north of Highway 20 a few miles east of Anacortes. Turn north off Highway 20 just west of the twin Swinomish Channel bridges onto the March Point Road. After about 0.75 mile, bear right across the railroad tracks. Continue about 2.5 miles farther to the end of the point. Launch anywhere between the boat ramp and the oil tanker pier underpass. Public access to these gravel beaches is by the grace of Shell Oil Company. Many recreational vehicles park here during the warmer months.

ROUTE

The one-way distance from March Point to Saddlebag Island is 2 miles. Currents along this route are slight until the vicinity of Hat Island, where an east-flowing flood or west-flowing ebb current may be encountered. Tide rips may occur in this area. Hat Island makes a nice first landfall along the route, though you should not land on this privately owned island. Its steep rocky sides make interesting alongshore paddling. Dot Island, located just southeast of Saddlebag Island, is a wildlife refuge, so stay 200 yards offshore from it. Eagles are often seen in its trees.

Saddlebag Island, with Dot Island on the right
(Randel Washburne)

Good landings on Saddlebag Island are found at both the north and south beach at the center of the island, or at a more secluded pocket beach on the west side which requires a steep climb to the meadows above.

Campsites are scattered throughout the isthmus area. There are vault toilets, but no water. The most secluded camping is the designated Cascadia Marine Trail sites above the low bluff facing the south beach. Those near the north beach are the most accessible from the water, and are the most protected from southerlies during the off-season. As is typical with most islands in this area, the south side has rocky meadows on both its east and west hills, accessed by informal trails. The north side is more wooded.

27 CYPRESS ISLAND

The wild ruggedness of Cypress Island, the chance for a hike to catch the panoramic views from Eagle Cliff, and the three public camping areas with Cascadia Marine Trail sites almost evenly spaced around the island contribute to its popularity with kayakers. It has an added bonus unique in the San Juan Islands: Ferry trips are not required. In 1989 the Department of Natural Resources purchased the majority of the island. It now owns about four-fifths of it and manages the resource primarily for recreation.

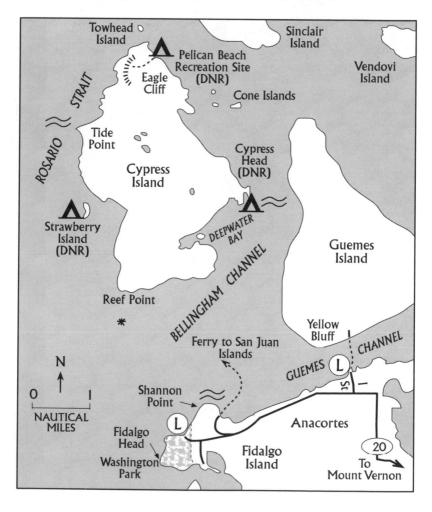

Duration: Overnight to two nights.

Rating: *Moderate +*.

Navigation Aids: NOAA charts 18423 SC or 18421 (both 1:80,000), 18430 (1:25,000); Rosario Strait current tables (with corrections for Bellingham Channel, Strawberry Island, Guemes Channel, or Shannon Point, depending on your location) or the Canadian *Current Atlas*.

Planning Considerations: This is a popular route in the San Juan Islands, and campsites may not be available on weekends at Pelican Beach—the kayaker's favorite—during the peak season. Also the trail to Eagle Cliff is normally closed from January to mid-July because of peregrine falcon breeding activities. Strong currents can create very dangerous localized conditions off Cypress Head in Bellingham Channel; avoid big tides or aim for slack current in this area. Currents strongly affect traveling speeds on all sides of the island; in general use floods for going north and ebbs for the return.

GETTING THERE AND LAUNCHING

You can choose between launch sites at the Guemes Island ferry landing on Guemes Channel just west of Anacortes or at Washington Park, a city park about 1 mile west of the San Juan Islands ferry terminal.

Pelican Beach, Cypress Island (Randel Washburne)

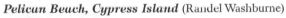

As detailed below, the currents dictate paddling schedules from both of these launch sites to and from Cypress Island.

Guemes Island Ferry Landing: To reach this ferry landing in Anacortes, drive north through town and then left as indicated for the San Juan Islands ferry. Go about 0.25 mile and then turn right on I Street. Go straight ahead and downhill to the Guemes Island ferry terminal. Park in the unpaved lot just west of the ferry lot and launch on the sand and rock beach.

Washington Park: To reach this city park in Anacortes, follow the signs through town to the San Juan Islands ferry terminal about 4 miles past Anacortes. At the top of the hill above the ferry terminal continue straight at the Y where ferry traffic bears right, and go another 0.5 mile to Washington Park.

Overnight parking is allowed in lot "B." To get closest to the beach, drive down to the day use parking lot "A" to unload, then carry your boat across the lawn to the gravel beach. Move your car to the overnight "B" lot. There is a daily parking fee.

ROUTE

A complete circumnavigation of Cypress Island is approximately 15 miles. Use the Canadian *Current Atlas* to visualize and plan your trip around the currents in Bellingham and Guemes Channels and in Rosario Strait. The stage of the tide affects which launch point is the more practical for starting out at that time.

The launch point at the Guemes Island ferry landing is probably safer and more versatile for starts at different tide stages than the Washington Park put-in near Fidalgo Head. Currents sweep strongly around this body of land, and the crossing from here to Cypress Island is more than 2 miles. As the ebb current sets southwest, reaching Cypress Island from the Fidalgo Head/Shannon Point area on even average tides can be almost impossible. There is a good possibility of being swept out into Rosario Strait in the process. This situation would be very rough with a southerly wind.

On strong ebb currents the Guemes Island ferry launch offers a safer and easier option. Cross the 0.5-mile-wide Guemes Channel, usually possible on most tide stages, and then work west along Guemes Island and up its western shore. Wait until the current slacks before crossing Bellingham Channel to Cypress Island.

On flood currents, Washington Park may be an easier launch point as the current flowing northward can be ridden into Bellingham Channel. From the Guemes Island ferry landing you will have to fight the

Northwest side of Cypress Island (Carey and Jeanne Gersten)

east-flowing flood current, though generally weaker than the ebb, in Guemes Channel until rounding the corner into Bellingham Channel.

Midway up Bellingham Channel is Cypress Head. This protuberance creates back eddies, strong eddy lines, and associated rips that can be very dangerous, particularly on large ebbs. In 1984, a double kayak capsized in this turbulence and the paddlers fortunately were rescued after a considerable time in the water. If you approach while the current is flowing, hug the shoreline. The back eddy extends 100 feet off Cypress Head and the safest route is right along the shore inside the kelp.

Cypress Head is a DNR recreation site with Cascadia Marine Trail designation. Campsites are in the woods on the head and at the neck connecting it to the main island—a great place to watch the action in a big ebb exchange. Landings are at the rock and gravel beaches on both the north and south sides of the neck. You will also find a dock and float on the north side during the warmer months. The three campsites on the west end of the neck are the most convenient from the beaches, but the more distant sites in the woods offer better weather protection. There are the usual vault toilets, but water is not available.

About 0.5 mile east of the northern end of Cypress Island is Pelican Beach, another DNR area designated with Cascadia Marine Trail status. This area was originally developed with help from the Pelican Fleet: owners of a type of beachable cruising sailboat often found hauled up on this fine pebble beach. One of the nicest features here is Eagle Cliff, a spectacular 840-foot overlook of the entire Rosario Strait area, and very popular with campers who climb up for the sunsets. The trail is a little more than 1 mile long. The climb is easy except for the last few hundred yards. The open-meadowed uplands around Eagle Cliff invite independent exploration with an alternative loop to another overlook. The trail to Eagle Cliff is closed, however, from January through mid-July because of falcon nesting there. There are other walks that are accessible from the campground such as to Duck Lake or to Eagle Harbor.

At the beach there are five to ten camping spaces. Though more can be accommodated, the narrow beach strip quickly becomes crowded, typically with kayakers. Behind is a covered picnic shelter and vault toilets. Water is not available. Camping is not allowed on the beach beyond the campsite limits, and fires must be built only in the firepits.

The currents along the Rosario Strait side of Cypress Island are strong enough to merit planning around them, though there are enough eddies in this irregular shoreline to work against them for most of the distance. Topography is at its most impressive here; Eagle Cliff and other precipices are far above.

Strawberry Island is yet another DNR recreation area with Cascadia Marine Trail status. It provides simple campsites along the southwest side of this 0.25-mile-long island. Access is via a small beach at the south end which is gravel at high tide but rocky at low water. As elsewhere

Paddling to the WWTA campsite on Strawberry Island
(Carey and Jeanne Gersten)

along Rosario Strait, be wary of huge breaking wakes from passing tankers when you beach your boat.

Camps are up to 100 yards north; those with the best weather protection are the most distant. A trail continues north up the island to an overlook. Water is not provided. There are vault toilets.

If Fidalgo Head is your destination from Reef Point at Cypress Island's southern end, formulate tactics for crossing. Keep the powerful offshore currents in mind. On a flood tide, crossing to the Washington Park area can be exhausting, even impossible. Ebbs, however, make this easy barring any strong southerly winds and with some course correction to counteract westerly drift.

If you are bound for Guemes Channel, use a slack or early flood current to cross to Yellow Bluff on Guemes Island. Then get a lift from the flood up Guemes Channel to the ferry landing. In calm weather the crossing to Guemes Channel can be made directly and quickly from Reef Point with the right timing. You use the last of the ebb to cross toward Washington Park and position yourself to catch the southerly portion of the new flood current that will sweep into Guemes Channel rather than north up Bellingham Channel.

28 LUMMI ISLAND

Though it has most of the amenities of the San Juan Islands, including a Cascadia Marine Trail campsite, Lummi Island is sufficiently off the beaten cruising path to be overlooked by many power boaters, but is now very popular with sea kayakers. The southern end has all the ruggedness that makes alongshore paddling so interesting, and a campground to match. This trip could be extended to Clark Island, covered in a separate chapter, which has an alternative route via Lummi Island.

Duration: Overnight.
Rating: *Moderate* or *Exposed*. The *Moderate* route involves currents and some open-water paddling in a channel that can become very rough with southerly winds. The *Exposed* route involves more of the same with potential commitment to miles of paddling in rough conditions.
Navigation Aids: NOAA charts 18423 SC, 18421 (both 1:80,000), or 18424 (1:40,000); Rosario Strait current tables or Canadian *Current Atlas*.

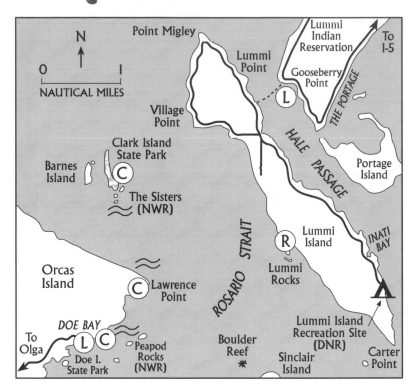

Planning Considerations: *Moderate* currents in Hale Passage affect paddling ease along these shores. Strong currents along Lummi Island's southwest shores can be hazardous against a contrary wind.

GETTING THERE AND LAUNCHING

Launch from Gooseberry Point in the Lummi Indian Reservation. From Interstate 5 take Exit 260 (Lummi Island–Slater Road) and turn west onto Slater Road. After almost 4 miles turn left onto Haxton Way. Follow Haxton Way for 6.5 miles to the Lummi Island ferry landing at Gooseberry Point.

Parking and access to the beach at Gooseberry Point have been in contest at various times, as this is within the Lummi Indian Reservation; ask in the store next to the ferry landing. Parking is probably most appropriate in the lot south of the ferry dock in an out-of-the-way spot so as not to conflict with ferry parking. Launch from the sandy beach next to the dock.

Lummi Rocks (Carey and Jeanne Gersten)

Carter Point, Lummi Island (Carey and Jeanne Gersten)

As an option you might paddle across Bellingham Bay. (See the Chuckanut Bay chapter.)

ROUTES

Hale Passage Loop: *Moderate.* The total paddling distance is about 13 miles. This pleasant overnight trip follows Lummi Island's east shore south to a campsite at one of the more interesting DNR recreation sites. Return can be by the same route or, for a little variation and weather permitting, across Hale Passage to Portage Island for the return to Gooseberry Point.

Although the crossing from Gooseberry Point to Lummi Point is only about 0.65 mile, swift currents of up to 2 knots can make paddling to the opposite shore tiring, and it can be dangerous in winds opposing the current. Hence, time this crossing for near the slack and then catch the ebb down Lummi Island's shore if possible. Though the alongshore currents are not terribly swift, they are persistent with few eddies to assist, and tiring against a contrary tide.

Northern Lummi Island is a mixture of farms and residences. There is little wild shoreline on the northeastern side. Along Hale Passage homes become sparser as you come abreast of Portage Island on the opposite shore. They gradually diminish as the shoreline steepens and disappear altogether just north of Inati Bay. Here there is also a large gravel pit. Round one more point of land and after this you will find that Lummi Island is wild to the south.

Inati Bay is a fine spot for a stretch onshore, though it is likely boats will be moored there during the cruising season. The Bellingham Yacht Club leases the head of the bay for a boaters' shore stop and has installed vault toilets and fire rings. The woods behind are well worth a walk inland, and there is an old road that eventually leads to the main road from the north.

Lummi Island DNR Recreation Site is less than 1 mile south of Inati Bay nestled among rocky shores that have gradually become steeper as you travel south. This DNR site, which also carries Cascadia Marine Trail status, is a particularly interesting one as it is fitted into the rocky benches of a steep hillside. Steps and switchbacking trails connect two tiny coves to upland campsites that make use of every level spot. The result is a charming campsite especially attractive to kayakers because it provides poor moorage for other boats with no protection against southerly blows. The campsites are more secluded than those at similar recreation areas, making this a nice resting place even if others are present. As with other DNR sites there is no water service, but garbage cans, picnic tables, and vault toilets are provided. In the summer months this site has become increasingly busy due to its easy access from the mainland.

At this point the Hale Passage loop route turns back to the north. You can opt to cross to Portage Island for the return if currents will be against you. They will probably be slower along the shallow eastern shore of Hale Passage. Portage Island, part of the Lummi Indian Reservation, is quite wild with beaches fronting on woods and meadows beyond. Landings are prohibited for nontribal members without permission. The island is connected to the mainland by a spit that dries at midtide, and cars frequently drive across it.

Lummi Island Circumnavigation: *Exposed.* The total paddling distance is approximately 19 miles. The portion from Gooseberry Point south along Hale Passage is described above. The description continues south from Lummi Island Recreation Site.

Venturing south toward Carter Point and around to the southwest side of Lummi Island takes you into a world of unforgiving rocky shorelines and steep, narrow beaches backed by talus slopes. There are few opportunities for anything but an uncomfortable emergency bivouac should the weather turn against you. After rounding the point, the shore is a continuous scree slope punctuated by cliffs that rise abruptly to the ridgeline. It gradually ascends toward 1,600-foot Lummi Peak as you move north.

There are few haulouts until opposite Lummi Rocks where the country gradually flattens. Lummi Rocks, owned by the Bureau of Land Management and leased to Western Washington University for research and education, is a nice spot for a lunch stop and a stroll over its grassy knolls. There are no facilities here and camping is not recommended.

Pastoral and residential developments appear gradually as you move north from Lummi Rocks, though most are kept at bay from the shore by bluffs until you start approaching Village Point.

Rounding Point Migley the shore is low, mostly sandy beach with residential housing. If a stiff north wind is blowing, crashing surf can easily build.

As you return to your start at Gooseberry Point, the same considerations for current hold in Hale Passage as at the trip's beginning. Try to cross at near slack and time your return with an ebb to make for easy southward paddling.

29 CLARK ISLAND

Because moorings here are somewhat exposed, Clark Island gets fewer overnight boaters than other state park islands in the northern San Juans. Going ashore, kayakers will find that this little jewel includes paths winding through madrona bordering its shores, a gravel beach on one side and sand on the other, plus extensive tide pools to explore. Its location allows radically different approach routes. The southern route from Doe Bay on Orcas Island is the shorter, though it requires a ferry ride from the mainland. The launch point at Doe Bay Resort offers opportunities to camp, rent a cabin, or just take a soak in their hot tubs on the way home. The northern route originates in the Lummi Indian Reservation between Bellingham and Ferndale. Few kayakers think to use this northeastern approach to the San Juans; it has significant advantages.

Duration: Full day to overnight.
Rating: *Exposed*. Both routes require 1.5- to 2-mile crossings through a strong current with possible shipping traffic on the northern route. Tide rips are likely along either route.
Navigation Aids: NOAA charts 18423 SC or 18421 (both 1:80,000), or 18430 (1:25,000); Rosario Strait current tables with local corrections or the Canadian *Current Atlas*.
Planning Considerations: For the southern route aim for times of least current in the area between the north shore of Orcas Island and Clark Island. Pay heed to the behavior of the eddies in this area and accompanying hazards described below. For the approach from Gooseberry Point around Lummi Island plan for times of

minimal current in Rosario Strait. Also try to avoid current flow conflicting with the likely wind direction. Currents in this area have no precise secondary reference station in the NOAA current tables. The station 1.5 miles north of Clark Island is closest. The Canadian *Current Atlas* is most useful for gauging the timing and strength of the currents on this crossing.

GETTING THERE AND LAUNCHING

Doe Bay Village Resort: From the Orcas Island ferry landing follow Orcas-Olga Road north to Eastsound and then about 16 miles to Olga. Turn left on Olga–Point Lawrence Road and go another 4 miles to the resort. Long a popular retreat for people with an inclination toward natural foods and living, Doe Bay's cabins, saunas, and hot tubs are busy year-round. An area for tent camping is nearby. There is also a café and a natural-foods general store. The management asks a nominal fee to camp and launch there. A soak in the hot tubs is an additional fee.

Gooseberry Point: See the Lummi Island chapter for directions to the Gooseberry Point launch. For Bellingham or Vancouver, B.C., residents, this northern approach is the most convenient access to the northern San Juans as well as Sucia, Maria, and Patos Islands. Seattle-area dwellers wishing to access this area will find it takes less time to drive to Gooseberry Point than to ferry to Orcas Island. Plus, it's certainly less expensive. During busy summer weekends, the time saved may amount to a half-day or more due to San Juan Islands ferry traffic backups.

ROUTES

Doe Bay to Clark Island: *Exposed.* The distance from Doe Bay to Clark Island is about 4 miles. Though the shoreline of Orcas north from Doe Bay makes pretty paddling, consider a detour 0.5 mile offshore to the Peapod Rocks when weather permits and currents are favorable. This San Juan Islands National Wildlife Refuge unit has abundant bird life, seals, and sometimes sea lions. Remember no landings are permitted, and keep a distance of 200 yards from these and other refuge rocks.

Lawrence Point is DNR land and, though open to camping, is not a particularly good place for it. There are no facilities. The grassy point does make a pleasant lunch stop or a place to watch the swirling currents to wait for favorable ones. Access is via two narrow pebble beaches on the south side of the point.

The 1.5-mile crossing to Clark Island from Lawrence Point can expose you to hazards created by strong currents. Both flood and ebb tides produce large eddies around Lawrence Point, and powerful rips may occur at the boundaries with the main current streams. The Canadian *Current Atlas* gives the best picture of the complex flows in this area. Note that strong east-flowing currents move along the shore of Orcas Island on large flood exchanges in this area, the opposite of what might be expected, and flow the same way on large ebbs too! The current can produce strong tide rips as it passes over a shoal not shown on chart 18423 SC, just east of a line between Lawrence Point and Clark Island. Hence, time your crossing to the Lawrence Point area to arrive at slack time. Also avoid this area on ebbs if southerly winds are likely. Because there are eddies near the point, a close-in route is usually safest if you must pass by while the current is running.

Gooseberry Point to Clark Island: *Exposed*. The paddling distance is approximately 7 miles each way around the north end of Lummi Island. The south end makes a much longer but interesting alternative, adding about 13 miles to the trip with a possible overnight stop at Lummi Island Recreation Site (see the Lummi Island chapter for details).

For the northern route, begin with the 1-mile crossing of Hale Passage. Realize the currents can be as strong as several knots. A flood current is advantageous for reaching the north end of the island; you can gradually work across while the moving water carries you north. The Lummi Island shore is mostly residential until you round Point Migley. From there it dwindles as bluffs prevent development along the water and conceal it from view.

The 2-mile Clark Island crossing from Village Point is exposed to the Strait of Georgia to the north and Rosario Strait to the south. Swift currents with possible tide rips and busy shipping in Rosario Strait, particularly tankers en route to Ferndale's Cherry Point terminal, make this segment of the route challenging.

Currents move very swiftly around both ends of Clark Island and nearby privately owned Barnes Island. Watch out for tide rips. The Sisters Islands to the southeast of Clark Island are units of the San Juan Islands National Wildlife Refuge. Landings are prohibited; keep 200 yards distance to avoid disturbing the residents.

Paths circle the low bluffs around the southern end of Clark Island with open madrona woods onshore and extensive tide pools and flats exposing themselves at low tide. There are no trails to the brushy north end, but rounding the cliffs and offshore rocks makes a nice paddling excursion. There is a sand beach on the island's west side and a gravel one on the east. The west beach sites are for picnicking; camping is allowed on sites most easily reached from the eastside.

Approximately six campsites are spaced out along the east beach and are low enough that a loaded kayak can be dragged over the smooth gravel right into camp. No water is available on the island, nor is there a camping charge. The beach sites are vulnerable to bad weather; two sites in the woods at the narrowest point of the island are best at those times.

30 CHUCKANUT BAY

The rocks make this Bellingham area trip a delightful exploration. Convoluted hollows and the delicate lacework of saltwater-eroded Chuckanut sandstone formations, fossilized remnants of ancient palm trunks, and even a long-gone artist's sculpture on a seaside rock award the curious paddler.

Duration: Part to full day.

Rating: *Protected* or *Moderate*. The longer *Moderate* route is exposed to southerly seas. Rocky shores could make landings difficult if the weather takes a bad turn.

Navigation Aids: NOAA charts 18424 (1:40,000) or 18423 SC; Port Townsend tide table (add about 45 minutes) for launch at Chuckanut Park.

Planning Considerations: The shorter excursion from Chuckanut Bay is feasible only at high tide.

GETTING THERE AND LAUNCHING

All four launch points are accessible from Highway 11, also called Chuckanut Drive.

Harris Street: The northernmost is the Harris Street boat ramp in Fairhaven, really part of south Bellingham. Take Harris Street west from Highway 11 0.25 mile and turn right just before Fairhaven Boatworks. Keep right, outside the chain-link fence, to the boat ramp. Kayaks are available for rental next door.

Marine Park: This tidy little park with picnic tables and rest rooms is at the end of Harris Street just past the Alaska Marine Highway ferry terminal and a boat yard. There is usually ample parking. Launch, best at mid- or low tides, on the sand and gravel beach. If you plan an overnight, pull your car back out onto the street or park in the gravel lot across from the ferry terminal.

Chuckanut Park: The park is located in a cove in the northern part of Chuckanut Bay and provides the only access for the "protected" route

San Juan Islands Area

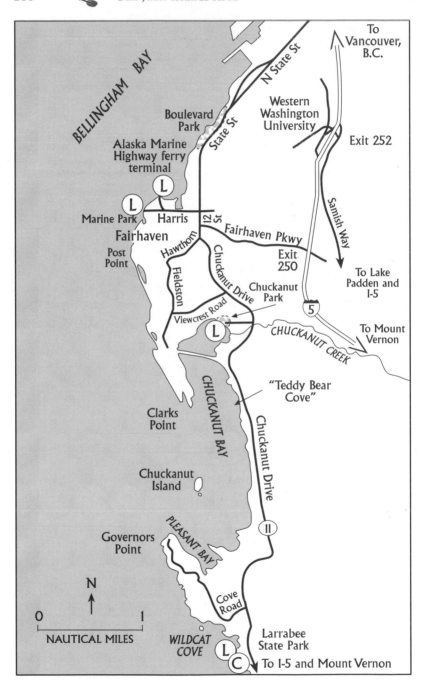

Chuckanut Island (Carey and Jeanne Gersten)

in the bay. However, this cove dries to extensive mud flats, so high-tide use is required. Follow Highway 11 1.5 mile south from Fairhaven to 21st Street. In 0.4 mile the road dead-ends at the water's edge. Parking is limited. There are no facilities at this park.

Wildcat Cove: About 1 mile south of Chuckanut Bay, Wildcat Cove is part of Larrabee State Park. Follow Highway 11 south from Fairhaven 5 miles to Cove Road. Follow it downhill, turn left after crossing the railway, and go straight into the boat launch area. Launch on the gravel beach next to the boat ramp. Camping is an option at Larabee State Park.

ROUTES

Chuckanut Bay: *Protected*. Make loops as long or as short as you like. Stay within the shallow cove at Chuckanut Park or paddle up to 4 miles around the entire bay. With the exception of the park and Chuckanut Island, all shorelines are private with some Burlington Northern right-of-way. There are fine rocks to view within the cove before paddling under the railroad bridge to the larger bay. Clarks Point has a very attractive inner bay with four fossilized palm-tree trunks in the rocks. They are easily examined from your boat. Across Chuckanut Bay east of Clarks Point is a rocky outcrop and some small beaches along the railroad. This area is known as Teddy Bear Cove; Bellingham area residents use it as a nude sunbathing and swimming area.

Chuckanut Island is owned by The Nature Conservancy, which allows stops ashore but no camping or fires. There are no facilities on the island, and they ask that you stay on the trail that rings the island. At high tide a small beach on the southwest side is the best landing with a steep scramble to the island above. On lower tides beaches on the north and southeast are uncovered. The latter landing is surrounded by interesting rocks but lacks access to the upper island.

Fairhaven to Wildcat Cove: *Moderate.* This 5-mile trip is best done with a 6-mile car shuttle between the Harris Street or Marine Park launch and Wildcat Cove. It can be shortened 1 mile with a high-tide launch at Chuckanut Park. The Fairhaven end can begin with a tour of shipyards and the southern terminus of the Alaska Marine Highway.

To the south the railroad parallels the shore with two miniature coves behind it. They can be reached under low bridges. The second provides an exciting sluice under the bridge at midtide. Beyond, watch for a rock just above high tide that a sculptor rendered many years ago. Add as much of Chuckanut Bay as you like to the route (see *Protected* route above for features). Governors Point defines the south end of Chuckanut Bay. South of here the eroded rocks take on a delicate lacy quality.

31 JAMES ISLAND

Rugged James Island State Park has plenty of trails and enough secluded coves to keep you busy for more than an overnight stay. Camping includes a Cascadia Marine Trail site along with general public camping facilities. For variety coming and going, there are two ways to get there from Lopez Island. And if you feel up to it, you can make the exposed Rosario Strait crossing from Fidalgo Head to James Island and avoid San Juan Island ferry hassles. This trip could be combined with one to Obstruction Pass (see the Obstruction Pass chapter) and Doe Bay or perhaps with a circumnavigation of Blakely Island.

Duration: Overnight.
Rating: *Moderate* or *Exposed*. The *Moderate* route involves some

currents and possible tide rips. The *Exposed* route requires a 3-mile open-water crossing with currents, tide rips, and shipping traffic.

Navigation Aids: NOAA Charts 18423 SC, 18421 (both 1:80,000), or 18430 (1:25,000); Rosario Strait current tables with corrections for Thatcher Pass.

Planning Considerations: Currents affect ease of travel and safety on both routes. See specifics about each.

GETTING THERE AND LAUNCHING

The two approaches begin from either Washington Park on Fidalgo Head in the Anacortes area or Spencer Spit State Park on Lopez Island.

Washington Park: Continue west through Anacortes approximately 4 miles following signs to the San Juan Islands ferry. At the top of the hill above the ferry terminal continue straight at the Y intersection where ferry traffic bears right and go straight another 0.5 mile to Washington Park. To get closest to the beach, drive down to the day use parking lot "A" to unload at the gravel beach, then move your car to lot "B" for extended parking. A daily fee is charged.

Lopez Island: Starting from Lopez Island requires driving a car aboard the ferry, as there is no public access to the beach at the Lopez Island ferry terminal for foot passengers with kayaks. Drive south from the ferry landing a little more than 1 mile to Port Stanley Road which is across the highway from Odlin County Park. Turn left and follow this road for approximately 3 miles as it winds past Shoal and Swifts Bays. Turn left onto Baker View Road and follow this road another mile to the state park entrance.

Within Spencer Spit State Park, use the gravel road to the right at the park office to reach the beach. This narrow road drops steeply to a small lot just south of the lagoon. There is a 50-yard carry to the beach. After unloading boats and gear, move cars back up to the main road. Go right to the parking lot and park just past the rest rooms on the left.

Spencer Spit State Park also hosts a Cascadia Marine Trail campsite. You must paddle to the site, not drive, to use it.

ROUTES

Spencer Spit to James Island: *Moderate.* One-way paddling distance via Thatcher Pass is 4 miles or 7 miles via Lopez Pass around the south end of Decatur Island.

Currents west of Blakely Island are weak and the waterway there is fairly well protected from wind-driven seas. However, Eastsound, to the north and almost bisecting Orcas Island, can develop very strong,

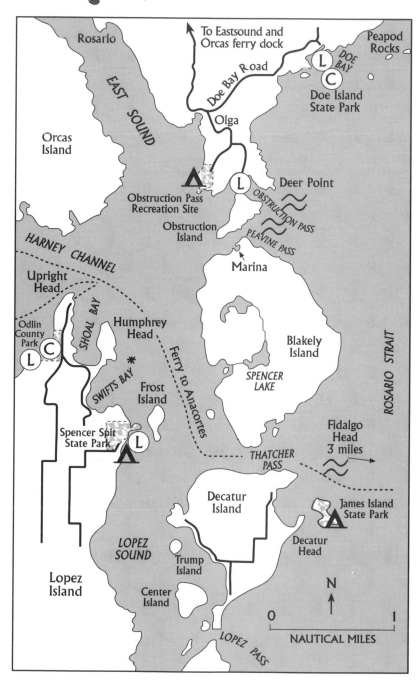

Rosario

To Eastsound and
Orcas ferry dock

Peapod
Rocks

Doe Bay Road

DOE
BAY

L

C

Doe Island
State Park

EAST SOUND

Olga

Orcas
Island

Deer Point

L

OBSTRUCTION PASS

Obstruction Pass
Recreation Site

Obstruction
Island

PEAVINE PASS

Marina

HARNEY CHANNEL

Upright
Head

Blakely
Island

ROSARIO STRAIT

Odlin
County
Park

L

C

SHOAL BAY

Humphrey
Head

SPENCER
LAKE

Ferry to Anacortes

SWIFTS BAY

Frost
Island

Spencer Spit
State Park

L

Fidalgo
Head
3 miles

THATCHER
PASS

Decatur
Island

James Island
State Park

LOPEZ
SOUND

Decatur
Head

Lopez
Island

Trump
Island

Center
Island

N

↑

0

1

LOPEZ PASS

NAUTICAL MILES

intensified northerly winds that may extend south as far as this route on warm, fair-weather afternoons. Currents in Thatcher Pass rarely exceed 1 knot and it can usually be paddled safely in any stage of the tide. However, currents are strong enough to be worth coordinating with the flow direction. The flood current flows west through Thatcher Pass.

The longer alternative route, looping south around Decatur Island, offers narrow inter-island passageways to thread through and views of this quiet and pastoral island. As with Blakely Island to the north, there is no public ferry service to Decatur. Places to go ashore here include a small, undeveloped island state park just north of the spit east of Lopez Pass and extensive publicly owned tidelands bounded above by private property. These tidelands include the shores of Center Island, which has some gravel pocket beaches. Another public tideland covers over 2 miles of sand and gravel beach, with one intermediate strip of private tideland, on the east side of Decatur between Lopez Pass and Decatur Head. The shore break here can be quite large when a southerly wind is blowing.

James Island has three camping areas with multiple sites at each, including one with Cascadia Marine Trail status. There is a network of trails over the island's steep, rocky hills and a secluded beach on the south shore. Its drawback is the rapacious raccoon population that lurks in wait for all visitors. Campsites are accessible from either the eastern or western coves. A fee is charged for those not staying at a marine trail site or lacking a water trails permit. Water is not available on the island. The central area between the coves is the most popular with boaters, and it has a small picnic shelter. However, wind can howl across this isthmus from either direction. At the east side campsites, the southern side of the cove offers more protection.

The secluded Cascadia Marine Trail site at the southern side of the west cove is the most popular with kayakers. The trees that surround the site also make it the best protected in bad weather. Beyond the outhouse, a trail leads across the island to the eastern cove.

Fidalgo Head to James Island: *Exposed.* The one-way distance is 3.5 miles, 3 miles of which are open Rosario Strait waters. Currents in this area of the strait can exceed 2.5 knots and are usually strongest on the southern flowing ebb. Hence, southerly winds can make this an extremely dangerous body of water on a falling tide, while tanker and tug-and-barge traffic add to the hazard. Crossings should be made only in auspicious conditions; otherwise use the ferry. Be especially careful in the area north of James Island where dangerous rips can form when the westward-flowing ebb from Thatcher Pass and the southward current in the strait meet an opposing wind. One kayak fatality here was apparently due to this situation. NOAA chart 18423 SC provides the following warning for Rosario Strait, presumably applying to Thatcher, Lopez, Peavine, and Obstruction Passes: "On the ebb tide, southerly winds cause dangerous tide rips off the entrance to the passes."

If conditions and your skills are appropriate for the Rosario crossing, time your start relative to the currents. Since your drift from the current will be considerable in all but very small tides, start the crossing about 30 minutes before slack so the currents will be minimal and will cancel each other out before and after the slack. They are particularly swift off Fidalgo Head.

32 OBSTRUCTION PASS

Convoluted shores and steep hillsides of madrona and rocky meadows make Obstruction Pass prime San Juan Islands paddling country. Currents in its passageways are strong enough for some exciting rides and require a measure of caution. Alternative launch points around this area make a variety of trips possible from short local paddles to one-night or longer adventures. By adding another day to the itinerary you could combine it with the Cypress Island route to the west or the James Island route to the south (see the Cypress Island and James Island chapters).

> **Duration**: Part day to overnight.
> **Rating**: *Moderate*. Area has currents with associated tide rips and eddy lines, though the areas of swiftest flow can be avoided.
> **Navigation Aids**: NOAA Charts 18423 SC, 18421 (both 1:80,000), or 18430 (1:25,000); Rosario Strait current tables with corrections for Obstruction Pass.
> **Planning Considerations**: See the Fidalgo Head to James Island route in the James Island chapter for safety considerations in the passes leading to Rosario Strait and including Obstruction Pass.

GETTING THERE AND LAUNCHING

Launch from Lopez Island at Spencer Spit (see the James Island chapter for details) or from two alternative places on Orcas Island.

Obstruction Pass: The closest launch site is the Obstruction Pass boat ramp. This site is approximately 20 miles from the Orcas Island ferry dock by road. After leaving the ferry, follow the road to Eastsound and then to Olga. Approximately 0.25 mile before Olga turn left where signs point to Obstruction Pass and Doe Bay. After another 0.25 mile there is a fork in the road; go right for Obstruction Pass. Left leads to Doe Bay. There are about twenty-five free parking spots, but this is a very busy place. Use this ramp only for day-trip paddling, as there is no overnight parking for the general public here. Nearby is a resort and marina that offers kayak and other boat rentals, and has most of the amenities you might need.

Doe Bay Village Resort: This is the other Orcas Island alternative. See the Clark Island chapter for details about launching and other services offered at Doe Bay.

ROUTES

Spencer Spit to Obstruction Pass: *Moderate.* The one-way distance is 4 miles. After crossing from Spencer Spit and Frost Island, this route follows the rocky shores of Blakely Island. The uplands of this large island are privately owned, but most of its tidelands are public. To avoid conflicts with residents, do not land in the coves along the western shore or near homes elsewhere. There are a number of fine, secluded gravel beaches along its predominantly wild shores. Stay below the high-tide line.

Blakely Island Marina at the west end of Peavine Pass has the only groceries on this route. The store operates on limited hours during the off-season. Land on the beach to the left of the fuel float.

Obstruction Pass Recreation Site, now with Cascadia Marine Trail status, provides camping and a chance for some walking on the extensive trail system. Located in a cove about 0.5 mile west of the pass, it is also accessible from the road via a 0.5-mile-long trail. Above the pebble beach are primitive campsites and vault toilets, but no water.

Unless you are confident of your boat-handling skills for fast currents, use Obstruction Pass instead of Peavine Pass for travel to and from Rosario Strait. Currents in Obstruction Pass average about 1 knot; they average over 2 knots on the ebb in Peavine Pass. Both flow east on the flood toward Rosario Strait. Interestingly, this is opposite from the flow in Thatcher Pass which is westerly on the flood.

Doe Bay to Obstruction Pass: *Moderate.* The one-way distance is 4 miles. This and the previously described route from Spencer Spit could be combined into a longer 8-mile overnight trip. However, traveling into the San Juans by ferry the day before would probably be required to leave enough time for paddling.

Doe Island is a six-acre state park located about 1 mile south of Doe Bay. It has a float during the summer season and mixed rock and gravel beaches on the northwest and southeast sides. There are two campsite areas; the best is in a hollow on the north end of the island. No water is provided.

The Orcas Island shoreline is private between Doe Bay and Deer Point. However, most of the tidelands are public with occasional gravel pocket beaches along the predominantly rock coast. You should be able to find beaches away from nearby homes.

Blakely Island Circumnavigation: *Moderate.* The distance starting from Spencer Spit is about 12 miles, 8 miles of which are from Obstruction Pass to Spencer Spit via the east side of Blakely Island. A leisurely two-night trip could be made by a second stop at James Island.

The eastern leg of the circumnavigation is significantly more exposed: fewer places to go ashore, strong currents, probable tide rips, and exposure to wind waves from either north or south. Tidelands are public along the entire east shore of Blakely Island and steep, rocky slopes above limit the residential use of this side. But they also limit the number of pocket beaches you will find. There may also be shore break on these beaches; be especially watchful for breaking tanker wakes. A powerful eddy line and associated tide rips may form during strong ebb currents in Rosario Strait at the easternmost point of Blakely Island. The current here is reported to turn to the flood an hour later than at Strawberry Island to the east. See the discussion of potentially dangerous conditions off Thatcher Pass and Peavine Pass for the Fidalgo Head route in the James Island chapter.

33 JONES ISLAND

Sandy beaches, trails that meander through madrona groves and meadows, and a resident deer herd that mingles with campers make Jones Island one of the most popular San Juan Islands destinations for kayakers. Other boaters enjoy it too, so much so that campsites are often scarce on summer weekends. For ferry foot-passengers with kayaks, this trip offers a route alternative using a launch at the public dock next to the Friday Harbor ferry terminal on San Juan Island. This area can also be combined with a circumnavigation of Shaw Island (see the Shaw Island chapter).

Duration: Overnight.
Rating: *Moderate.* The trip involves a 0.5-mile open-water crossing in currents up to 2 knots.

Navigation Aids: NOAA charts 18423 SC or 18421 (both 1:80,000), and 18434 (1:25,000); San Juan Channel current tables or the Canadian *Current Atlas* in particular are useful for route timing with favorable flows.
Planning Considerations: Arrive early to secure a campsite on summer weekends. Coordinate with currents in Wasp Passage, Pole Pass, and, if Friday Harbor is a trip terminus, San Juan Channel.

NOTE: For kayakers wheeling their watercraft aboard the ferry, convenient water access is now limited to Friday Harbor. Launching near the ferry dock at Shaw Island is no longer possible, and at Orcas Island tenuous. However, two routes are still described using these landings as starting points in the hopes that they or near alternatives will be made available through the efforts of organizations such as the Washington Water Trails Association. Including these routes also allows the kayaker the option to integrate these routes into the Shaw circumnavigation described in the next chapter or as segments into trips of their own design.

GETTING THERE AND LAUNCHING

Take the San Juan Islands ferry to either Orcas or San Juan Island, depending on the launch site to be used.

Deer Harbor on Orcas Island: This launch site provides the closest access to Jones Island. Driving to Deer Harbor to launch reduces the one-way paddling distance to Jones Island to about 2 miles. Water access is at Deer Harbor Marina and Resort. They charge a fee to launch and to park. All the basic amenities are there including rest rooms with showers, water, a small store for essential provisions, public telephone, and even a sailboat and bike rental.

Orcas Island Ferry Landing: Access at the ferry landing is not possible, although local paddlers have reported that it is possible to use the nearby private oil company dock through advance arrangement.

Friday Harbor: Launch from the public dock a few hundred yards north of the ferry landing using the floats nearest shore. There is a small launch fee. Parking in Friday Harbor is extremely scarce during the summer.

Shaw Island Ferry Landing: As stated, launching here is no longer possible. The closest access point is at Shaw Island County Park on the south side of the island. It is too far to wheel a kayak unless you are extremely determined. The distance is 2 miles. Plan on driving if you use this option as access to the waters of the San Juan Islands.

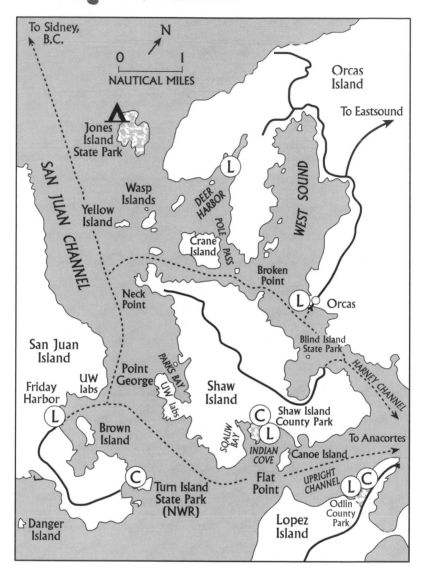

ROUTES

Deer Harbor to Jones Island: *Moderate*. The paddling distance is just shy of 2 miles. Follow the western shore of Deer Harbor toward Steep Point passing rocky shores covered with madronas, cliffs, and occasional homes. All of the shoreline along this route is private, so plan to stay in your boat until you reach Jones Island. This route would qualify for a *Protected* rating if not for the Spring Passage crossing. Here currents can reach almost 2 knots. You may need to ferry upstream at a large angle to hold your position during the crossing. Seas in the passage can get quite rough when the wind opposes the current. Tide rips are also possible. To be safest, time this crossing when currents will be flowing in the same direction as the probable wind direction.

Jones Island State Park is a very popular destination for kayakers and other boaters. Campsites are difficult to find on summer weekends, but fortunately there is a Cascadia Marine Trail group site with room for three to four tent sites on the west side of the island. A composting toilet serves this group site.

Generally, most power boaters prefer the more protected northern cove where there is a dock. There are other sites scattered around the island, connected by the 2 miles of island trails. At all the regular public campsites, only those designated with a numbered picnic table may be used for camping. Pay the camping fee at the self-registration stations at the north and south ends. Though drinking-water faucets are provided at both places, the shallow well usually runs dry in midsummer. The water is shut off between October and March when fees are not in effect.

Friday Harbor to Jones Island: *Moderate.* The paddling distance is 4.5 miles. This is a route often used by kayakers riding the ferries as foot passengers. Aside from Yellow Island (described below) there are no public shorelines along the route, but with favorable current and wind, this trip should take less than two hours. Currents in this part of San Juan Channel can attain about 1 knot. Planning to use them is worthwhile.

The shoreline of Shaw Island is probably the more interesting side to follow (see the circumnavigation route in the Shaw Island chapter for details) and, under the appropriate conditions, you can cross to the San Juan Island side at Point George. Point George and Parks Bay behind it are part of a University of Washington biological preserve. Landings are not allowed.

At Friday Harbor the public dock north of the ferry landing provides the closest place to the ferry to get ashore.

Launch sites are no longer available for the following routes:
Orcas or Shaw Ferry Landings to Jones Island via Pole Pass: *Moderate.* The paddling distance is 4 or 4.5 miles from the Orcas or Shaw ferry landings, respectively. This is a good route for learning to use currents for efficient travel. The possible exception is paddling Spring Passage when wind opposes the current. It is rarely fast enough to be hazardous, but can substantially affect paddling effort. Currents in the passages between Shaw and Orcas Islands generally flow westward

Loading up on the west beach at Jones Island
(Randel Washburne)

during the flood tide and eastward during the ebb.

Pole Pass is a little tide race that can run at more than 2 knots for a short distance. It is rarely dangerous, but boat wakes in the riffles on the downstream side can make it quite rough. It is possible to go through against the current because it is quite weak in the approaches. There are eddies to use on the Orcas Island side with a hard push required for the short distance in the narrows against the flow. Be especially wary of boat traffic in Pole Pass, as it is difficult to see what is coming the other way as you approach.

With the exception of Blind Island State Park (see the Shaw Island chapter for details) and the public tidelands at Broken Point, there is no public access ashore along this route. However, it can be covered in less than two hours with favorable currents.

Orcas or Shaw Islands to Jones Island via the Wasp Islands: *Moderate.* The paddling distance is about 5 miles. This slightly longer alternative to the Pole Pass route makes a nice return from Jones Island with a stop to see the unique flora at The Nature Conservancy's Yellow Island. The western end of this route is more exposed to southerly or northerly winds, so opt for the Pole Pass route if the weather seems chancy.

The Wasp Islands south of Jones Island, scattered with rocks and islets, make for interesting and scenic paddling. Most of the Wasp Islands are privately owned and a few smaller ones are part of the San Juan National Wildlife Refuge in which landings are prohibited.

Currents in this area are moderate. Wasp Passage runs swiftly enough to produce rips in the area of Crane Island. The major hazard here is the ferry that takes this route between Friday Harbor and Orcas Island. It can come around the corner quite suddenly from either direction. Do not dawdle in midchannel at Wasp Passage and keep your group tightly together for all channel crossings. Also watch out for ferry wakes colliding with an opposing current (when the ferry is traveling against the current), as these can become steep and nasty breakers. The wake will smooth out after entering eddies along the sides of the passage.

The Shaw Island shore of Wasp Passage is a fine place to practice using shore eddies to travel against the current, especially if you need to do so! Note that the currents in this area run counter to what might be expected; they flow west into San Juan Channel on the flood tide.

Yellow Island, owned by The Nature Conservancy, is managed to perpetuate the island's floral communities. The main attraction is the spring flowers that begin to bloom in late March and are at their best from mid-April through early summer. Resident caretakers live in the cabin on the southwest shore.

Kayakers should be aware that Yellow Island is not a public park. Visits are permitted only under stringent conditions to ensure that the primary goal of preservation is not compromised. Landings are limited to the south beach at Dodd Cabin. You are asked not to land on the spits at the ends of the island. Visits should be short and only for the purpose of viewing the island. Stay on the trail that meanders around it. Collecting plants or intertidal life, smoking, pets, camping, picnicking, and fires are prohibited. In addition, there are no public toilets. The Nature Conservancy management has been concerned about kayakers using the meadows as toilets, and the island may be closed to kayak groups if the problem continues. Groups greater than six must have prior permission to visit Yellow Island. Obtain permission by calling The Nature Conservancy in Seattle at 206-343-4345, extension 320, which is the reserve manager's voice mail box.

A caretaker's cabin on Yellow Island, near Jones Island
(Randel Washburne)

34 SHAW ISLAND: CIRCUMNAVIGATION

Located in the heart of the San Juan Islands, the waters around Shaw Island usually have the highest concentration of kayakers in the area. Mild currents and alongshore paddling with few crossings make some routes here popular for less-experienced paddlers, particularly those trying kayak camping for the first time. Route options include an easy day, a short overnight, and a longer circumnavigation of Shaw Island with stops at neighboring parks and Cascadia Marine Trail sites. The circumnavigation can easily include Jones Island (see the Jones Island chapter).

Duration: Full day to multiple nights.

Rating: *Protected* or *Moderate*. A one-day protected route can be made from Odlin County Park to Indian Cove and back. The *Moderate* circumnavigation route involves currents and some open water that may become quite rough, particularly when current and wind directions oppose each other.

Navigation Aids: NOAA charts 18423 SC or 18421 (both 1:80,000), and 18434 (1:25,000). San Juan Channel current tables or the Canadian *Current Atlas* are helpful for the circumnavigation route; Port Townsend tide tables (add about 30 minutes) are handy if Indian Cove is included as a launch point or stop.

Planning Considerations: For kayakers wheeling their watercraft aboard the ferry, convenient water access is now limited to Friday Harbor. Access at the Shaw ferry landing is no longer possible, and at Orcas not always certain. Timing with currents will greatly affect your speed and travel effort on the circumnavigation route. It is a fairly complex task in this area made easiest by the *Current Atlas*. Plan a high-tide arrival or departure at Indian Cove to avoid walking the mud flats. Campsites at Indian Cove and Jones Island are usually all spoken for on summer weekends. It is strongly suggested you arrive early.

GETTING THERE AND LAUNCHING

The route described starts from Odlin County Park on Lopez Island. Drive a little more than 1 mile south from the Lopez ferry terminal to Odlin County Park. There is easy access to the sandy beach. A campground is nearby. Cars may be parked for a daily fee paid to the caretaker at the residence near the entrance.

As an option, the circumnavigation route can also start and end at the ferry stop at Friday Harbor or from Deer Harbor. See the Jones Island chapter for a description of these launch sites.

ROUTE

The total distance of the Shaw Island circumnavigation is approximately 14 miles, beginning at Odlin County Park and proceeding counterclockwise. Add 2 miles for a side trip to Turn Island and 3 miles for Jones Island. Add 2 miles if you launch at Deer Harbor. Five places to camp are distributed around and on Shaw Island—Odlin County Park, Blind Island, Jones Island, Turn Island, and Indian Cove—allowing you to partition the trip into two or three fairly equal-length paddling days.

The distance across Upright Channel from Odlin County Park to Indian Cove is about 2.2 miles. The most interesting route follows the Lopez shore south from Odlin County Park to Flat Point, then heads across the 0.25-mile-wide narrows to Canoe Island and finally Indian Cove.

A little more than 1 mile south of Odlin County Park is the Upright Channel Recreation Site, an undeveloped DNR parcel with no facilities. This 700-foot-long public gravel beach with forested uplands is located just east of the residences near Flat Point.

Watch carefully for boat traffic before crossing from the spit at Flat Point to Canoe Island, particularly the ferries going to and from Friday Harbor. Currents in Upright Channel generally are weak, but may have some force locally here. The flood flows north. Though Canoe Island beaches are public below mean high tide, the uplands are not, and owners who operate a youth camp specializing in French language and culture strongly discourage visitors.

Shaw Island County Park, encompassing western Indian Cove and part of the peninsula that separates it from Squaw Bay, has opportunities for camping, picnicking, or more secluded stops ashore. Because the foreshore in Indian Cove dries for a considerable distance becoming a muddy tide flat, plan around low tides for arrival and departure if possible.

Campsites are located along a road that starts near a low bank to the east and climbs as the bank increases to a bluff to the west. There are steps at intervals along the beach to the campsites, but the most westerly ones are not readily accessible from the water. Camping fees are per site for as many as four people with an additional charge for more individuals. If you wish to share a site with others, a definite possibility during peak weekends, there is a shared camp area just west of campsite number nine. The fee here is a nominal charge per person.

Water, vault toilets, and a cooking shelter are provided.

To make this a one-day trip of a *Protected* rating, you can return the same way you paddled or make a loop by following the Shaw Island shore north along Upright Channel. Then, opposite Odlin County Park, make the direct 1-mile crossing back to your start.

The Shaw Island shore north of Indian Cove is rocky and for the most part wild, continuing so west into Harney Channel. Currents in Harney Channel are stronger than in Upright Channel, but still pose few problems for travel. The flood current here flows west.

Blind Island State Park with a designated Cascadia Marine Trail group site is about 0.5 mile west of the Shaw Island landing. Facilities on this three-acre island are simple—a composting toilet and picnic tables, but no water. There is no fee for the two general campsites, while the Cascadia Marine Trail group site with four tent sites requires a Water Trail Permit. Landings can be made on rocky beaches at the southwest end or at the southeast corner of the island. Trees on the island are few, but include cherry, apple, and filbert from an old homestead. The only wind protection is chest-high brush that shields some of the sites. Because it is small, Blind Island can become crowded with only a few parties camped there.

For the route west from Blind Island to Neck Point, including a possible side trip to Jones Island via Yellow and the Wasp Islands, see the Jones Island chapter above.

The small islets north and south of Neck Point are very popular with seals. It is not uncommon to see two dozen or so hauled out on the islands. Both islets are part of the San Juan Islands National Wildlife Refuge, so do not approach closer than 200 yards.

Rounding Neck Point and heading southeast along Shaw Island's west facing shore, the San Juan Channel current can be quite strong, especially at the points that protrude into the waterway. There are eddy systems along shore for much of the way with extensive eddies in the vicinity of Parks Bay. Though most of the northern portion of this shore is developed with summer residences, there are some points of interest. Beginning at Point George is a 1,000-plus-acre biological preserve, owned by the University of Washington, that extends south and west almost to Squaw Bay. Managed by the University of Washington Friday Harbor Laboratories, this preserve is off-limits to all public use in the uplands and tidelands. Nonetheless, as you paddle by you can still enjoy the forests and meadows.

Turn Island State Park, located a little over 1 mile south of Shaw Island across San Juan Channel, is a side-trip opportunity for camping or a respite along this otherwise no-access portion of the circumnavigation. It would also make a good first night destination for an afternoon start from Friday Harbor.

Be careful making the crossing of San Juan Channel to and from Turn Island. Currents are strong enough to require significant course adjustment to offset your drift, and steep seas can develop when the current opposes winds from either north or south. Watch for ferries and other heavy boat traffic associated with nearby Friday Harbor.

Turn Island is a unit of the San Juan Islands National Wildlife Refuge. A portion of the west end is leased to the Washington State Parks and Recreation Commission. Camping is allowed only in this park area with fees levied through the self-registration station. There are composting toilets, but no water is available. A rough trail circles the island. Keep in mind that public use of this refuge island is provisional on compatibility with wildlife. Avoid any nesting sites.

Rounding the southernmost point of Shaw Island you come upon Squaw Bay. The tips of both points forming the bay are private land, but two pocket beaches on the west side of the bay make more secluded landing spots. There is, however, a spur road down the rocky slopes providing land access to the beaches.

Head east to Indian Cove. From here it is usually an easy, protected paddle across Upright Channel back to your starting point at Odlin Cove.

35 SOUTH AND WEST SAN JUAN ISLAND

Kayakers come here for two distinct reasons. The first is whales: Haro Strait is the best place to see orcas during the summer months. Lime Kiln State Park was developed primarily for public observation of the whales that pass offshore regularly. The second is the barren beauty: the largely treeless southwestern coast of San Juan Island is unique for the Northwest. The exposure to southerly and westerly winds and big seas along its beaches make it all the wilder. But to the north, western San Juan Island has a gentler face with inter-island channels and the accessible historical attractions of British Camp.

Duration: Part day to multiple nights.
Rating: *Moderate* or *Exposed*. *Exposed* routes involve strong currents with probable tide rips, characteristically strong winds with fully developed seas, and resulting surf on the beaches. See the description

of wind patterns under the South Beach to Griffin Bay Route.
Navigation Aids: NOAA charts 18423 SC or 18421 (both 1:80,000), or 18433 and 18434 (both 1:25,000); San Juan Channel current tables.
Planning Considerations: Avoid mid- to late afternoon for paddling west of Cattle Point, when westerlies from the Strait of Juan de Fuca are strongest.

GETTING THERE AND LAUNCHING

There are many points of access here, but some car shuttling or walking will be needed unless you return to the launch point or commit to a 30-mile, multiday circumnavigation of San Juan Island. For the latter, kayakers who wheel their kayaks aboard the ferries as foot passengers can choose Friday Harbor. Their launch is the dinghy dock at the public wharf north of the ferry landing.

San Juan Island's Cattle Point (Randel Washburne)

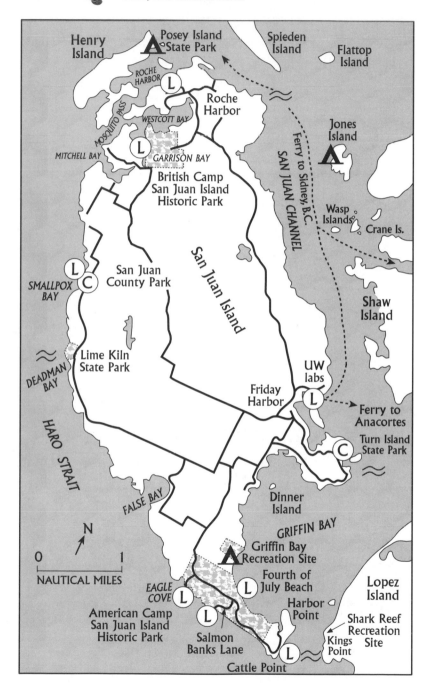

Henry Island

Posey Island State Park

Spieden Island

Flattop Island

ROCHE HARBOR

L

Roche Harbor

WESTCOTT BAY

L

MOSQUITO PASS

MITCHELL BAY

GARRISON BAY

British Camp San Juan Island Historic Park

Jones Island

Ferry to Sidney, B.C.

SAN JUAN CHANNEL

Wasp Islands

Crane Is.

San Juan Island

L C

SMALLPOX BAY

San Juan County Park

Shaw Island

Lime Kiln State Park

DEADMAN BAY

HARO STRAIT

UW labs

L

Ferry to Anacortes

Friday Harbor

Turn Island State Park

C

FALSE BAY

Dinner Island

GRIFFIN BAY

N

0   1

NAUTICAL MILES

Griffin Bay Recreation Site

Fourth of July Beach

Harbor Point

Lopez Island

EAGLE COVE

L

American Camp San Juan Island Historic Park

L

Salmon Banks Lane

L

Shark Reef Recreation Site

Kings Point

L

Cattle Point

Roche Harbor: Starting from the north, Roche Harbor is a popular launch spot for a number of routes (see the Stuart Island chapter for directions and details on launching here).

British Camp: This launch is about 9 miles from Friday Harbor. From the ferry landing follow Spring Street to Second Street on the right. Follow this street and go left where it becomes Guard Street. This eventually becomes Beaverton Valley Road and then West Valley Road. Turn off to the left for the entrance to British Camp and go down the hill to the lot. Boats will have to be carried several hundred yards along a gravel walkway and lawn, smooth enough for carts, to the sand and cobble beach. The park provides rest rooms and interpretive facilities that are open during the summer months.

San Juan County Park: Directions for the park are the same, except that you turn left onto Mitchell Bay Road about 7 miles from town. Then turn left where it becomes the West Side Road and follow it to the park at Smallpox Bay. There is a parking lot with easy access to the gravel beach. Rest rooms and water are available.

Eagle Cove: This launch point is located just north of the American Camp portion of San Juan Island National Historic Park. To reach the area from the Friday Harbor ferry landing, follow Spring Street three blocks to a Y intersection and go left on Argyle Street. This becomes Cattle Point Road and reaches the park after about 5 miles. Turn right onto Eagle Cove Road and go 0.5 mile to the parking lot. Boats must be carried 100 yards downhill on a sometimes slippery path to the gravel beach. This launch point will have more protection from surf than the beaches at Salmon Banks Lane farther south.

Fourth of July Beach: Traveling south in the park, the next launch spot is Fourth of July Beach. It provides access to the southeast shore of the island in Griffin Bay. Turn left off Cattle Point Road 1 mile south of the park entrance and drive to the picnic area lot. The beach is a short distance below.

Salmon Banks Lane: With three parking lots giving easy access to continuous gravel beaches facing southwest, this launch is reached by turning off Cattle Point Road onto Pickett's Lane a short distance south of the Fourth of July Beach intersection. Launches could be rough here in even a moderate wind.

Cattle Point Picnic Area: This launch gives access to the southern tip of the island. Continue 0.75 mile past the point where you leave the national park to the lot on the right. Boats must be carried 50 yards down rather steep rocks. Cattle Point itself offers some protection against surf at the west end of the beach.

ROUTES

South Beach (Salmon Banks Lane) to Griffin Bay via Cattle Point: *Exposed.* The paddling distance is 5 miles. Logistically this is the easiest route, as the 1.5-mile walk between the launch and take-out points can eliminate the need for a car shuttle. A lunch stop could be taken at Cattle Point Picnic Area. Plan for plenty of time in Griffin Bay to explore its three lagoons.

The *Exposed* rating is based on both currents and wind. Currents at San Juan Channel's south entrance can reach 5 knots when heavy tide rips are likely, especially around Goose Island and Deadman Island on the Lopez Island side. Staying close inshore on the San Juan Island side may prove best. The current usually flows east off Cattle Point because a large eddy forms there during the ebb cycle. This, combined with the typical daily fair-weather wind pattern, suggests paddling from west to east. A flood current is most favorable.

The Haro Strait side of southern San Juan Island is exposed to bad-weather winds from the south and is a very windy area in fair weather as well. When high pressure builds, strong offshore in-flowing winds in the Strait of Juan de Fuca often produce westerlies of up to 25 knots in the afternoon. They are strongest from about 2:00 A.M. to 6:00 P.M. A little farther north in the strait they become southwesterlies. At the north end of San Juan Island the effects of the strait are less where northwesterlies blow. Pacific swells can penetrate through the Strait of Juan de Fuca and, amplified by local wind, develop considerable surf on southwestern San Juan Island beaches, such as Salmon Banks Lane. Surf is likely to be smallest in the morning on sunny days.

If wind makes travel west around Cattle Point imprudent, consider beginning at Cattle Point Picnic Area, which cuts the paddling distance to 3 miles. There is plenty to explore in Griffin Bay. There are three high-tide lagoons and a maze of old roads meandering through the woods above and between them. If the currents are close to slack you can add 2 miles to the route by paddling across the channel narrows to Lopez Island. Here you can visit undeveloped Shark Reef Recreation Site just south of Kings Point.

Smallpox Bay (San Juan County Park) to Lime Kiln Point: *Exposed.* The round-trip paddling distance is 4 miles. This route can be paddled one-way with a 3-mile car shuttle to Deadman Bay just south of Lime Kiln State Park. Please respect private property above the beach.

This is the best coastline for whales. Facilities and interpretive displays at Lime Kiln State Park are geared toward whale watching. At least three separate extended Orca families, known as pods, pass close by daily.

Minke and pilot whales, Dall and harbor porpoise, and even occasional gray whales are sighted here. Be sure to observe "Orca etiquette" while paddling near them. Do not approach within 100 yards or try to position yourself in their path of travel. If so inclined, they will come to you. Shores along the way to Lime Kiln Point are consistently rocky with residences here and there. In a bight just north of the point are the old lime kilns which are easily identified by the white piles of material on the hillside. To go ashore at the park, continue around the point and land on the north end of the beach at Deadman Bay.

Roche Harbor to English Camp via Mosquito Pass: *Moderate.* The round-trip paddling distance is 5 miles or half that for one-way paddling with a 4-mile car shuttle. This entire route is very well protected from winds and an excellent route for most weather conditions. However, currents in Mosquito Pass can be strong and erratic. There are no predictions for them in the current guides. Paddlers not experienced with currents should stay close to the eastern side of the channel near Mosquito Pass. This is probably the easiest route for going through against the current. South of the pass, turn left to enter even more protected waters in Garrison Bay. Land on the beach next to the blockhouse. There is a visitor center in the white barracks building just inshore from the blockhouse. Rest rooms are nearby.

Great San Juan Island Tour: *Exposed.* The circumnavigation distance is about 30 miles. Shorter partial circuits include Cattle Point to Roche Harbor (17 miles) and Smallpox Bay to Friday Harbor (20 miles). Campsites around San Juan Island are sparse and irregularly spaced with a 14-mile gap at the southwest portion. Choices include: Turn Island State Park just south of Friday Harbor (see the Shaw Island chapter for details), Griffin Bay Recreation Site, San Juan County Park at Smallpox Bay, or Posey Island north of Roche Harbor (see the Stuart Island chapter for details).

The Griffin Bay campsite, a Cascadia Marine Trail site, is located just south of Low Point in a meadow area directly inshore from Halftide Rock. Water, vault toilets, picnic tables, and the single campsite are 400 yards inland at the trees. The grassy path is smooth enough for boat carts if you feel the need to keep your boat nearby. There is no formal access to this recreation site from the road, and private property borders it.

San Juan County Park in Smallpox Bay is a very popular campground often full during the summer months. Fortunately, they have a reservation system. Information can be obtained by calling 360-468-4413 or writing to the park at 380 Westside Road North, Friday Harbor, Washington 98250.

36 POINT DOUGHTY ON ORCAS ISLAND

Accessible only from the water, this little DNR Recreation Site at Orcas's northwest tip has attractive madrona and fir woods, tide pools, and spectacular cliffs complete with a small sea cave or two on the north side. A Cascadia Marine Trail campsite rounds out the scene.

> **Duration**: Full day to overnight.
> **Rating**: *Moderate.* A north wind can create rough conditions and surf along the Orcas north shore. Current and tide rips are likely off the point.
> **Navigation Aids**: NOAA charts 18423 SC or 18421 (both 1:80,000), 18431 (1:25,000); Canadian *Current Atlas.*
> **Planning Considerations**: Aim for times of least current to avoid tide rips while rounding Point Doughty.

GETTING THERE AND LAUNCHING

There are two launch opportunities. From the Orcas Island ferry dock, drive north to Eastsound. At Eastsound, drive north on North Beach Road.

North Beach Road End: Launch from the gravel beach at the end of North Beach Road. Parking is free and allowed along the road, but is restricted to maybe five cars. Do not expect to find space as it is an extremely popular launch.

Bartwood Lodge: Turn right off North Beach Road onto Anderson Road. Go 0.75 mile, taking a left at the Bartwood Lodge sign. Parking and boat launching are permitted, each for a separate daily fee. They have water and a phone, but rest rooms are not available for general public use.

ROUTE

The round-trip distance from North Beach to Point Doughty is about 6 miles. Follow the beach west past occasional homes and small resorts. A mile short of the point the shore begins to rise, and interesting cliffs line the remaining distance. Rocks and shoals are extensive off the point, and together with swift currents produce significant tide rips. A close inshore route around the point may avoid them if the seas are smooth enough to allow it.

An unprotected moorage and largely rock beach limit visits by other

Looking east from Point Doughty at Orcas Island's northern shore
(Randel Washburne)

boaters, though the point is popular with scuba divers. Access is via a small beach on the south side of the point. At midtide or above, landings are on pebbles and gravel; low tide approaches are rocky and may be hard on the boat if there is a southerly sea running.

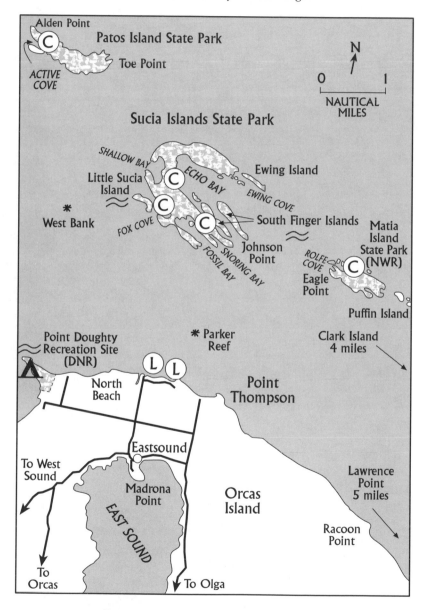

There are two campsites both with Cascadia Marine Trail designation, but open to the public-at-large on a first-come-use basis. Included are vault toilets, picnic tables, and garbage cans, but water is not available. One campsite has good views to the south and west, but poor weather protection. The other is tucked into the trees and is a good all-weather camp, but without views. Trails lead east from the campsites along the south bluffs and eventually to the YMCA's Camp Orkila, 1 mile to the east, though there is no public access by land.

37 PATOS, SUCIA, AND MATIA ISLANDS

This chain of state park and wildlife refuge islands is famed for its intricate geology as well as its potentially treacherous waters. Separated by miles of sea from other islands in the San Juan group to the south, and open to the expanse of the Strait of Georgia, they are relatively isolated and very beautiful.

Duration: Overnight to multiple nights.

Rating: *Exposed*. Though this area is sometimes millpond smooth, it is also well known for producing strong but erratic currents and big seas that develop from northerly winds on fair afternoons. This is no place for inexperienced paddlers!

Navigation Aids: NOAA charts 18423 SC or 18421 (both 1:80,000), or 18431 (1:25,000); Rosario Strait current tables or the Canadian *Current Atlas*.

Planning Considerations: All routes to these islands put paddlers at the mercy of the weather and strong currents during long crossings. Definitely consult forecasts and be prepared to lay over in the islands during bad weather. Currents are strong throughout the area but not reliably predictable (see the discussion in the North Beach to Sucia Island route).

GETTING THERE AND LAUNCHING
See the Point Doughty chapter for directions to launch sites.

ROUTES
A weekend trip from North Beach to Sucia Island (about 0.5 mile round-trip), with an optional excursion to Matia (add another 2 miles) is one of the most popular kayak outings in the San Juan Islands. Including

Patos Island in the agenda adds another 5 miles or more to the total distance and usually merits another overnight on that island.

North Beach to Sucia Island: *Exposed.* The round-trip distance is about 5 miles, depending on your destination on Sucia Island. The crossing from North Beach to the nearest point on Sucia Island is 2 miles. The greatest hazard en route is Parker Reef. It consists of two separate shoals located less than halfway across. The area around the reefs can develop dangerous rips in strong currents, sometimes exceeding 2 knots, which are made worse by contrary winds. As a warning, a kayaking fatality has occurred here.

Generally, the west-flowing ebb current is considered the most dangerous. The Canadian *Current Atlas* shows the flood currents coming around the east and west sides of Orcas Island, meeting and weakening in this area. Timing of these currents is somewhat unreliable. There have been reports of slacks varying greatly from their predicted times and current even flowing reverse of what was predicted.

Nonetheless, this route attracts large numbers of paddlers during the summer months, including novices. As the record shows, more than a few first-time kayakers have had bad experiences between Sucia and Orcas, with some lucky to escape with their lives. To that point this route deserves an *Exposed* rating; the potential for risk remains very high and must be considered into the planning of this trip.

Sucia Island is the hub of cruising in the northern San Juan Islands for yachts and kayaks alike. You are least likely to find solitude in the summer on Sucia Island, but other attractions make up for it. This island complex, in actuality at least six separate islands, can absorb a day's exploring by kayak and another day by foot along the extensive trail system. Be sure to avoid Little Sucia Island, which is managed as an eagle preserve. The bizarre formations of water-dissolved rock are unsurpassed; seals abound on and around them.

The majority of visitors to Sucia Island are found in Fossil and Echo Bays where there are extensive campsites with drinking water and solar composting toilets. The low banks and mixed shell and gravel beaches make attractive camping for kayakers in Fossil Bay or in adjoining Fox Cove. Echo Bay and Shallow Bay just across the island to the west have similar camps with drinking water nearby at the picnic shelters in northern Shallow Bay.

Fossil Bay and Echo Bay complexes are the best campsites for the off-season, more so since driftwood for fires piles up in Echo Bay during the winter. Kayakers visiting Sucia Island during the summer generally prefer Ewing Cove or Snoring Bay for the relative isolation from other boaters and campers that these areas afford. Camp only at sites designated with a

Ewing Cove, Sucia Island (Randel Washburne)

fire ring and/or a picnic table. Camping elsewhere is prohibited.

Campsites are often full to capacity at Sucia on busy summer weekends. As a Washington state park, a reservation service is provided through Reservations Northwest. There is a fee for making a reservation, and it is best done well in advance by calling 800-452-5687.

North Beach or Sucia Island to Matia Island: *Exposed.* The crossing from Orcas to Matia Island is slightly longer, about 2.5 miles, and may involve strong currents, though the problems of the shallows at Parker Reef are easier to avoid.

Located a little more than 1 mile from Sucia Island, Matia Island is hard-pressed to maintain its wild quality in the face of nearby boating activity. Management of the island is something of a conundrum. Matia Island is owned entirely by the federal government as a national wildlife refuge for bald eagles and pelagic cormorants. Yet five acres at Rolfe Cove are formally leased to the Washington State Parks and Recreation Commission, which also manages the rest of the island for the U.S. Fish and Wildlife Service.

Camping is confined to Rolfe Cove. It affords well-protected sites above the gravel beach and low bluffs. A solar composting toilet is nearby, but no water is provided on the island. Fees are collected through a self-registration station. Nearby Eagle Cove is outside the state park lease area and closed to camping. Exploring ashore should be confined to a trail loop that runs down the center of the island and returns on the south side.

Around Matia Island are numerous coves best visited by boat to comply with refuge objectives of least on-shore disturbance. On the south side is the "hermit's cove" where remnants of a solitary island dweller's structures dating to the 1920s can still be seen. At the southeast corner are coves with pebble beaches. Refuge managers ask that you avoid the cove at the east end of the island facing Puffin Island because of the eagles that nest there. Keep at least 100 yards distance from Puffin Island to avoid disturbing that refuge as well.

North Beach or Sucia Island to Patos Island: *Exposed.* Patos Island can be reached from North Beach by following the Orcas shore west to Point Doughty, then crossing slightly over 4 miles of open water. Strong currents and tide rips are possible along this route. The safer but longer alternative is to head for Sucia Island first, then cut across to Patos Island at the time of slack water. Both routes are safer and far easier on the flood current. Watch for rips in the area of West Bank marked by an extensive kelp bed.

Patos Island is one of the wildest islands in the northern chain. The island is owned and managed by the Washington State Parks and Recreation Commission. Four acres at Alden Point are dedicated to a Coast Guard light station and are off-limits to the public.

All recreational use is confined to the west end of the island; the remainder is managed to enhance bald eagle nesting habitat. The eastern end has also been designated a Heritage Area by the DNR for the preservation of plant communities. Campsites are located at Active Cove with vault toilets, but no water or garbage service. The state does not charge for their use.

Patos Island does merit a circumnavigation, taking care to avoid disturbing the eagles along the way. On the south shore are bluffs and low cliffs with the weirdly eroded conglomerate rocks that characterize this island chain. The east end has two coves with pebble beaches and long rock reefs. They are revealed at low tide a long distance from shore, giving Toe Point its name. These beaches characterize the majority of the northern shoreline.

Great Rectangle Route: *Exposed.* The paddling distance is about 25 miles. This string of Patos, Sucia, and Matia Islands can be integrated into a large box route including Clark Island (see the Clark Island

chapter) with the fourth side formed by the entire north shore of Orcas Island. Camping is at the three islands described above, Clark Island, and Point Doughty on northwestern Orcas Island (see the Point Doughty chapter). Plan on two or, better yet, at least three nights for this trip. Getting from Matia Island to Clark Island involves a 4-mile crossing with active currents between Clark and Orcas Islands, making both crossings precarious in unfavorable conditions. (The Clark Island chapter includes a description of currents between Clark and Orcas Islands.) In unsettled weather it's safer to cut this area out of the rectangle.

The north shore of Orcas Island forms the return leg of the rectangle route. Though this 6-mile-long linear shoreline between Lawrence Point and North Beach appears unexciting on the chart, it is gratifying to follow. However, there are few spots for an emergency camp, so do your best to plan for fair weather during this leg of the journey. Most of the shore is very steep with either wooded scree slopes or cliffs rising right from sea level. There are occasional narrow gravel beaches at the base, but rarely anywhere to go above.

The coast is wild—look for otter and hauled-out seals—and has a few surprise bits of history. At one point there is an old limestone kiln fitted into the steep slope so unobtrusively that most other boaters probably miss it. Farther on is an extensive, overgrown quarry long since covered by a vigorous young fir forest. Near the tiny extension of Moran State Park that reaches the sea is a rarity for the San Juan Islands—a waterfall spilling into the sea at high tide. Houses finally appear during the final third of the way to North Beach.

38 STUART ISLAND

Paddling to Stuart Island is among the "wildest" of the San Juan Island trips for two reasons: this destination is in a rarely experienced natural state, and the tidal forces are some of the strongest. This is no place for novices. You are likely to generate some excitement just paddling to and from Stuart Island, but its shorelines, two park areas, and Cascadia Marine Trail tent sites are sure to make the visit a pleasure.

Duration: Overnight or longer; two nights recommended.
Rating: *Exposed*. Strong currents and tide rips are likely throughout this area.
Navigation Aids: NOAA charts 18423 SC, 18421 (both 1:80,000),

or 18432 (1:25,000); San Juan Channel current tables with corrections for Limestone Point, Admiralty Inlet current tables with corrections for Turn Point, or the Canadian *Current Atlas*.

Planning Considerations: Currents in this area are very strong, and powerful tide rips form in all weather conditions. Coordinating travel with currents is essential for both efficiency and safety, particularly when there are larger-than-average tides.

GETTING THERE AND LAUNCHING

Launch from San Juan Island at either Roche Harbor or Friday Harbor.

Roche Harbor: Drive from the Friday Harbor ferry landing two blocks through town to Second Street South and turn right. After three blocks bear left on Guard Street. Turn right onto Tucker Avenue. At the fork bear left onto Roche Harbor Road. The total distance is about 10 miles.

Launching at Roche Harbor is allowed by the Hotel de Haro resort at the ramp or the adjoining grassy area about 100 yards south of the hotel. There is a "stiff" charge to launch here. Parking is in a pay lot across the street. Rest rooms, a shower, water, and a grocery are available. Kayaks are also rented at the resort.

Friday Harbor: Use the public dock east of the ferry landing. There is a nominal fee. Overnight parking is very limited and almost unobtainable in Friday Harbor during the summer. Check in the port office at the public dock for possibilities.

An alternative launch point is Orcas Island (see the Jones Island chapter).

ROUTES

Roche Harbor to Stuart Island: *Exposed*. The round-trip paddling distance is 10 miles. This is the shortest, least hazardous, and most popular approach to Stuart Island. Add 10 miles to the round-trip distance if launching from Friday Harbor.

Paddling between San Juan Island and Stuart Island probably requires more careful timing with the currents than anywhere else in the San Juan Islands. Though the crossings are generally 1 mile or less, the strong currents that run through these channels and the associated tide rips earn this trip its *Exposed* rating. However, since tidal cycles are predictable, careful planning and timing can make this a safer trip than those trips with the same rating due to longer crossings and associated bad-weather exposure.

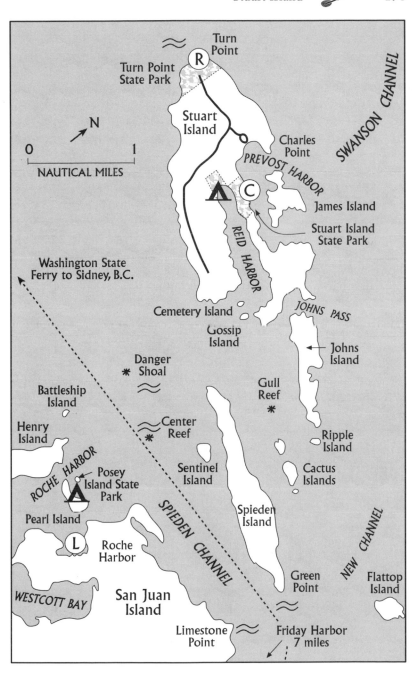

Turn Point

R

Turn Point
State Park

Stuart
Island

Charles
Point

PREVOST HARBOR

SWANSON CHANNEL

N

0   1

NAUTICAL MILES

C

James Island

Stuart Island
State Park

REID HARBOR

Washington State
Ferry to Sidney, B.C.

Cemetery Island

Gossip
Island

JOHNS PASS

Johns
Island

Danger
Shoal

Gull
Reef

Battleship
Island

Henry
Island

Center
Reef

ROCHE HARBOR

Posey
Island State
Park

Sentinel
Island

Ripple
Island

Cactus
Islands

NEW CHANNEL

Pearl Island

L

Roche
Harbor

SPIEDEN CHANNEL

Spieden
Island

Green
Point

Flattop
Island

WESTCOTT BAY

San Juan
Island

Limestone
Point

Friday Harbor
7 miles

The primary hazards occur in Spieden Channel. At the eastern end between Green Point on Spieden Island and Limestone Point on San Juan Island is some of the fastest water in the San Juan Islands; it runs over 5 knots on the year's biggest tides. Most significant are two powerful and extensive tide rips that form off both points on both the flood and ebb sets of the tide. The rip off Limestone Point forms 100 yards or more offshore, but the Green Point rip extends in quite close to Spieden Island's shoreline. There are less severe rips at the western end of the channel in the vicinity of Danger Shoal, Center Reef, and Sentinel Island.

The channels north of Spieden Island on either side of the Cactus Islands also run very swiftly, though you will find no local reference stations for them in the current tables. Currents here and in the northern San Juan Channel are somewhat fickle, particularly after the tide changes when patterns of flow around each side of San Juan Island are not yet established. One kayaker bound for Jones Island from Flattop Island reported being carried to Spieden Island on the flood current when it should have been flowing in the opposite direction.

Since the total distance from San Juan Island to Stuart Island is too far to paddle in a single slack current period, give most low current priority to Spieden Channel. Then you may round Spieden Island in whichever direction is the most convenient, keeping in mind the possible rips close to Green Point. Currents in Spieden Channel are slower between Davison Head and Sentinel Island than farther to the east. At the tail end of a flood tide is a good place to start, next riding the ebb current west along Spieden Island, and finally taking advantage of that same ebb current to reach Reid Harbor by compensating to the northeast against its flow.

Most of the small islands and rocks north of Spieden Island are within the San Juan Islands National Wildlife Refuge; do not approach them. If you make a late start from Roche Harbor or run late on the return, the Cascadia Marine Trail group site on tiny Posey Island State Park outside the harbor's two approaches makes a suitable overnight spot. A composting toilet and a couple of picnic tables are provided; water is not available. The tent sites are located on the south, east, and west sides, with wind protection from the trees and brush at the center depending on wind direction. The maximum number of campers allowed at one time is sixteen, and it is strictly enforced on this fragile island. Since Posey Island is close to Roche Harbor's many summer homes, you can expect company in the summer months from young party-makers bringing their music with them.

For camping at Stuart Island, both Reid and Prevost Harbors are suitable for kayakers. Both locations are within Stuart Island State Park, one of the few marine parks in the San Juan Islands where you can count on finding fresh water; the well rarely runs dry. The fee for camping is levied through a self-registration station or by holding a Cascadia Marine Trail permit.

The Cascadia Marine Trail tent sites at Reid Harbor are on either side of the marsh at the head of the bay. The beach here dries for a fair distance—great for clam diggers, but not so good for gear-laden kayakers on minus tides. The three or four campsites on either end of the beach have water. Be advised that the walk to the self-registration station is long and arduous, about 0.5 mile up and over the steep hill to the north, whereas it is only a 150-yard paddle to the dock just below it, so take care of this detail before stashing your boat.

There are sites above the dock at Reid Harbor, but the only access to the top of this steep shoreline is via the twisting dock ramp—not an easy carry for a kayaker. Nonetheless, this access is easier for getting your craft across to Prevost Harbor or the campsites there than the 4.5-mile paddle via Johns Pass.

As in Reid Harbor, there are campsites above Prevost Harbor's dock and float. However, the bank is lower and an easy path leads up from the beach next to the dock. The four sites about 100 yards to the west are especially appealing, as they have their own beach access. This area also has sanitary facilities and a water faucet.

Allowing a day layover at Stuart Island for some exploration by foot or boat is strongly recommended. Hiking the island's ample trails and little-used, unpaved country roads is a pleasure. There are also fine opportunities for day-long paddling loops, each skirting the island from one harbor to the other via Johns Pass to the east or Turn Point to the west.

If you circumnavigate Stuart Island, note that the currents flow around both ends of the island on their way to or from the Strait of Georgia. With the right timing both trips can be made with favorable currents for almost the entire distance. Consult the Canadian *Current Atlas* for specifics.

Reid Harbor to Prevost Harbor via Johns Pass One-day Loop: *Protected.* The total paddling distance is 4.5 miles. The Johns Pass loop is easier and shorter than the Turn Point loop (below). Most of this shoreline is residential. Except for Johns Pass, currents along the shore are usually benign, hence the *Protected* rating. Tiny state-owned Gossip Island and Cemetery Island at Reid Harbor's entrance are the only opportunities for shore exploration along this route.

Reid Harbor to Prevost Harbor via Turn Point Loop: *Exposed.* The paddling distance is 7 miles. The western circuit around Turn Point is exceptionally appealing. The wild, rugged shores and boisterous Haro Strait waters provide a setting unmatched in our inland waters. But remember, the steep shores with few safe landings, the strong currents that race around the point, and the open north and south fetches with potential for rough seas require kayakers with good skills and experience.

From Prevost Harbor the pastoral civility of Stuart Island is left behind at Charles Point. From there to Turn Point is a progression of rocky kelp beds, sea crags, and overhanging vegetation. Extensive eddies occupy most of these beds all the way to the point, and progress is fairly easy even against the current. These waters are prime fishing grounds for both bottom fish and salmon.

Turn Point is a 10-acre Coast Guard light station reservation surrounded by a 53-acre state park. The light facility is now automated and diverse tenants such as Stuart Island teachers and whale researchers occasionally occupy the former residences. The parkland is undeveloped with no recreational facilities. Camping is not allowed. However, it does provide excellent day hiking and is a popular 5-mile round-trip hike from the Reid and Prevost Harbors via an unpaved road.

Turn Point provides few easy landing sites for visiting the light station. Though the rocks have eroded into fairly flat shelves, you will have to be adept at landing on rocks in the waves that are usually present. Also beware of the powerful wakes of ships that pass quite close offshore.

A much more practical landing with a rough trail access to the point is found at a small gravel beach about 0.25 mile to the south, just beyond some spectacular sea cliffs and still within Turn Point State Park. Secure your boat well above the drift logs and passing freighters' wakes. Plan to be gone for at least one hour if you intend to visit the point.

The rough, little-used trail switchbacks steeply up from the beach. Follow the gully above the beach uphill for about 100 yards to a well-defined trail that climbs across the hillside to the left through open fir and madrona woods. It then trends upward for another 300 yards, passing open, grassy meadows above and below, a perfect spot for secluded sunbathing. Finally it reaches a high, bald hilltop with sweeping views over Haro Strait, Boundary Pass, and the Canadian Gulf Islands beyond. Walking down to the cliff edge you can see Turn Point light station below. A few yards behind this bald hilltop is the old road linking the light station to Reid and Prevost Harbors. Follow it to the left and downhill to the point.

GULF ISLANDS (BRITISH COLUMBIA)

39 PORTLAND ISLAND: PRINCESS MARGARET MARINE PARK

Convoluted shores, lots of nearby islets, seemingly endless meadows lined with red-barked arbutus—known as "madrona" in the United States—and remnants of old orchards make this one of the jewels of the Gulf Islands. If you come here to camp, allow lots of time to explore the extensive trail system around and across the island. This excursion is easily integrated into the D'Arcy Island loop (see the D'Arcy Island Loop chapter) to the south for a multiple-night trip.

Duration: Full day to overnight.
Rating: *Moderate.* Currents can be strong enough to produce tide rips and rough seas when opposing wind. Boat and ferry traffic is heavy.
Navigation Aids: Canadian Hydrographic Service chart 3310 (small craft strip charts in folio) or 3441 (both 1:40,000); Canadian Hydrographic Service current tables (volume 5) for Race Passage with corrections for Swanson Channel, or Canadian *Current Atlas.*
Planning Considerations: This island receives heavy camping use. Arrive early to secure your site on summer weekends. Travel with current flow; the flood moves north.

GETTING THERE AND LAUNCHING
Launch sites at either Sidney or Swartz Bay are respectively adjacent to the Washington State (to/from Anacortes) or B.C. ferry terminals. Follow signs to the appropriate one.

Sidney: Use the beach next to the launching ramp in Tulista Park located just south of the Washington State Ferries terminal. If driving off that ferry, turn left after reaching the highway and then left again into the park in about 0.2 mile. Park in the area for vehicles launching boats. If

Boat Passage on Saturna Island (Randel Washburne)

walking off the ferry with your boat, follow the vehicle route around the terminal, except follow the paved path across the lawn immediately after passing the terminal, about a 0.25-mile carrying distance. There is also a rough path to a narrow gravel beach in front of the terminal; turn toward the water just after exiting the terminal. This is a much shorter carrying distance, but space on the beach is limited at high tide and the shore break here may be much larger than behind the breakwater at the park.

    Swartz Bay: Use the beach below the public dock just east of the terminal. If exiting the ferry by car, make a left turn where allowed soon after the terminal and follow the road back past the parking area. Turn left about 100 yards past the terminal onto a short street that dead-ends at the dock. Park along the street or, if it's full, at the terminal. Foot passengers can take a shorter route (requiring a 0.25-mile carry) with their boats after leaving the ferry by cutting across the vehicle lanes to a gate at the main terminal building below the "control tower," and going east through the parking area.

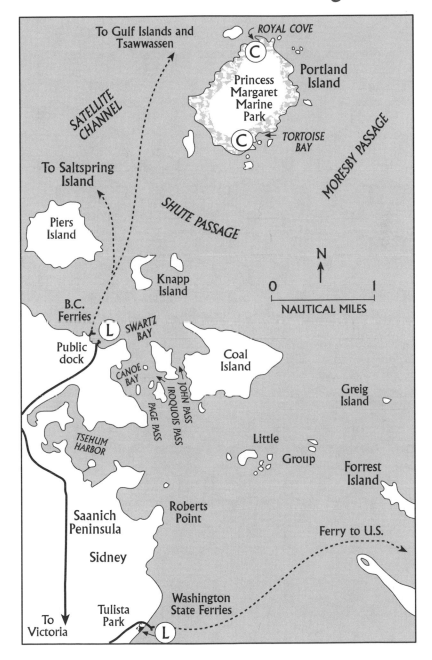

ROUTE

One way distance from Swartz Bay to Portland Island is 2 miles; it's 4 miles from Tulista Park in Sidney. Those originating from Sidney can sightsee through John, Iroquois, or Page Passes where sumptuous homes and moored yachts line the shores. Paddlers starting from either place should go east of Knapp Island to avoid the busy ferry lanes on the west. Currents in Shute Passage flood northwest at up to 1.5 knots, and in the opposite direction at the same speed on the ebb, requiring a substantial ferry-angle course adjustment to control the amount that you are set by it. The Canadian *Current Atlas* is very helpful for timing with this current.

Portland Island has picnicking and camping facilities, including tables and pit toilets, at several points along its shore, and an extensive trail system. Water is available from a hand-operated pump in the center of the island. For orientation and access to the water, stop at Tortoise Bay, called Princess Bay on some charts. There is a map here and at Royal Cove at the north end of the island. Boats moor at both of these locations and traffic ashore is heaviest there. Camping is best on the south and east-to-northeast sides of the island, accessible from beaches or eroded sandstone shores, although the latter may be difficult in rough southerly conditions. If a fire ban is not in effect, campfires can be built in designated rings, but it's best to rely on your cook stove on this wildfire-prone island.

40 PENDER, SATURNA, AND MAYNE ISLANDS

This part of the southern Gulf Islands offers the most opportunities for small-channel paddling, but with swift currents in some passages that are inappropriate for the inexperienced. There are many route variations, especially for those who carry kayaks aboard the B.C. ferry, and can use different island stops to begin and end their paddling trip.

Duration: Part day to overnight.
Rating: *Moderate* or *Moderate +*. Currents in parts of this area are strong, with at least two local tide races. The most challenging one is avoidable.
Navigation Aids: Canadian Hydrographic Service chart 3310 (1:40,000 small craft strip charts in folio), or 3442 (1:40,000) and 3477 (1:15,000); Canadian Hydrographic Service current tables

(volume 5) for Active Pass with corrections for Georgeson and Boat Passages, current tables for Race Passage with corrections for Swanson Channel, or the Canadian *Current Atlas*.

Planning Considerations: Travel with current flows as much as possible. The flood goes northward in Pender Canal and northwest in Plumper Sound. These have no current predictions but can be estimated from those in Swanson Channel.

GETTING THERE AND LAUNCHING

Unless you integrate this trip with the Portland Island route to the west (see the Portland Island chapter), you will have to use the B.C. ferries to either Pender, Mayne, or Saturna Islands. If coming from the mainland at Tsawwassen you will have to transfer ferries at Mayne Island to reach Saturna Island, or at Swartz Bay if the schedule works out to be better.

Pender Island: Those who drive aboard can access the center of this paddling area via Pender Island, allowing a shorter and more sheltered route between the two Pender Islands or across to Saturna. Launch at Browning Harbour public dock. To get there from the ferry landing, take Otter Bay Road east to Bedwell Harbour Road, turn right, and follow it to the intersection of Razor Point Road. Turn left and follow that about 1 mile to the public dock. Limited parking is available along the road.

Mayne Island: Foot passengers can wheel their boats on and off at Mayne Island at Village Bay or Saturna Island. At Village Bay, turn left immediately after leaving the ferry through a gate leading to a path to the beach.

Saturna Island: Turn left to the public dock next to the ferry landing. A store is located just above the ferry dock at Saturna.

ROUTES

There are three options. You may paddle locally in Port Browning and Bedwell Harbour, make a full day of exploring between Saturna and Mayne Islands, or take an extended overnight route that includes both of the above. If you choose the last option you should camp at Beaumont Marine Park by beginning at Village Bay, and either return there or re-board the ferry at Saturna Island for the return.

Port Browning and Bedwell Harbour: *Moderate +.* The round-trip distance is 4 to 6 miles. This could be a day trip or an overnight, with camping at Beaumont Marine Park, the only camping facility in this area.

This trip would fall within the *Protected* rating were it not for the current in Pender Canal which can run at up to 4 knots for a short

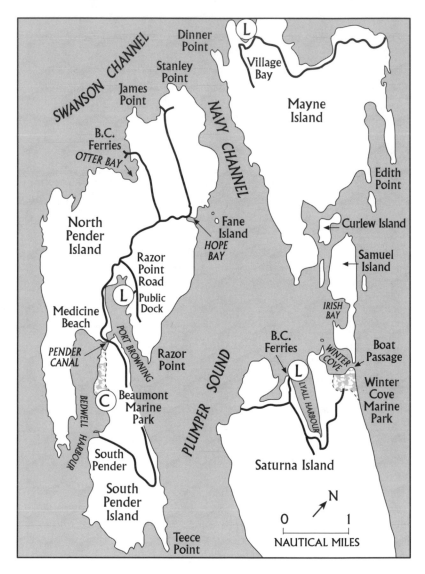

distance under the bridge. There are no predictions about the current's schedule other than it flows north on the flood. This passage requires some care, but should be no problem for paddlers with average boat-handling skills. Whether going through with or against the current, look carefully for powerboats going through the cut, as they must maintain speed to have maneuverability in the current and have limited deep water in which to avoid you. Bigger boats going through against the current make large breaking wakes on the beaches. If you are going through against the flow, you may need to walk your boat under the bridge in the shallows or carry it along the beach. You should be able to find eddies in both the north and south approaches to the canal.

The canal area, which was a portage until being dredged at the turn of the century, was a long-used Salish townsite. An archaeological team dug here for a number of years. However, little remains to be seen.

Beaumont Marine Park begins on the northern shore of Bedwell Harbour at Ainslie Point. There are several nice beaches for a break ashore with trails that connect with the developed part of the park farther south. The shell beaches there and shells in the soil above attest to the history of Indian use in the camping and picnic areas. Pit toilets, tables, and a water pump are the extent of the facilities.

About 1 mile farther south on the shore of Bedwell Harbour is South Pender. It has a full service marina/resort complex and acts as a Canada Customs office during the busy summer months.

Between Mayne and Saturna: *Moderate.* The distance from Saturna ferry landing can be as little as 3 miles round trip to Winter Cove or lengthened to about a 7-mile circumnavigation of Samuel Island. A trip to Winter Cove avoids significant currents, but allows a close-up look at fast water in little Boat Passage, sometimes reaching up to 8 knots. The east side of Winter Cove is a marine park that is restricted to day use. A gravel beach just east of Boat Passage gives access to trails for a view of the passage and the Strait of Georgia beyond.

Circumnavigating Samuel Island should be attempted only if you are comfortable with strong currents and sharp eddy lines, or if you plan to traverse its tide races at slack, especially Boat Passage. If your skills are up to it, Boat Passage can be run in midstream with few problems. Going through against the flow is difficult without portaging, as there are no eddies. Currents at the western end of Samuel Island are slower, but still provide challenging eddies and possible tide rips between Samuel and Curlew Islands.

Village Bay, Winter Cove, and Bedwell Harbour Triangle Loop: *Moderate.* This loop trip involves about 20 miles of paddling. Travel in the Pender Islands and between Mayne and Saturna is as described above. Use Swanson Channel predictions for Plumper Sound and Navy Channel, but note Navy Channel floods east at a maximum of 3 knots from Swanson Channel, meeting the west-flowing flood current from Plumper Sound off Hope Bay. Current speeds in Plumper Sound between Saturna and South Pender Island can reach 3 knots.

41 D'ARCY ISLAND LOOP

This loop avoids the more crowded cruising grounds of the Gulf Islands. With the exception of popular Sidney Spit, you are more likely to find solitude in the D'Arcy Island or Isle-de-Lis Marine Parks than elsewhere on a summer weekend. Sparser use has more to do with the lack of facilities than with their lack of appeal. Including Portland Island (see the Portland Island chapter) in the route extends the loop 4 miles to the north.

> **Duration**: Overnight to multiple nights.
> **Rating**: *Moderate*. Currents here can be strong enough to produce tide rips and rough seas when opposing wind from either the north or south.
> **Navigation Aids**: Canadian Hydrographic Service chart 3310 (small craft strip charts in folio) or 3441 (both 1:40,000); Canadian Hydrographic Service current tables (volume 5) for Race Passage with corrections for Sidney Channel, or Canadian *Current Atlas*.
> **Planning Considerations**: Travel with current flows as much as possible; the flood goes north. Exploring the lagoon at Sidney Island requires high tide (use Canadian tide table for Fulford Harbour).

GETTING THERE AND LAUNCHING

Use Tulista Park in Sidney, which is accessible for foot passengers with boats coming from the United States on the Washington State ferry (see the Portland Island chapter for details).

ROUTE

Total loop distance is about 18 miles, and can be shortened to 15 miles by eliminating Mandarte Island and Isle-de-Lis Marine Park. An early start and coordination with currents makes this loop feasible as an overnight. A more relaxed itinerary would allow an additional stop at either Sidney Spit or Isle-de-Lis (also called Rum Island) Marine Parks. Water may be available at Sidney Spit, but since the well does run dry in summer, bring enough to last the entire trip.

Sidney Spit makes an interesting, if populated, stop for lunch or a somewhat inconvenient campsite. The campground is located some 0.2-mile distance from the water and up the hill south from the dock and picnic area. The path is smooth enough for boat carts above and below the stairs leading to the sites. The spit makes interesting exploration on foot at low tide or by paddle. The large lagoon to the south makes great

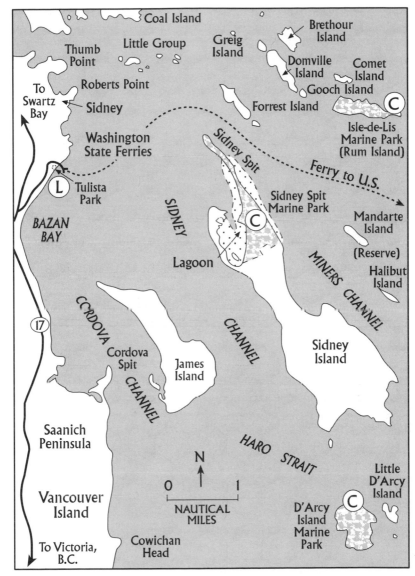

high-tide paddling with small channels to explore along the south side. Please avoid the private dock on the north shore and several buildings at the base of the surrounding spit. If you are en route to D'Arcy Island from Sidney Spit, consider paddling down the lagoon if the tide is right, and then portaging across the spit at the southwest end. It's about 75 yards across and too rough for boat carts because of old logs.

Isle-de-Lis Marine Park, Rum Island (Randel Washburne)

The remainder of Sidney Island is largely undeveloped, though privately owned. Only an occasional home is visible along its attractive shorelines or on the bluffs above.

D'Arcy Island Marine Park has no facilities and is much more lightly visited than either Sidney Spit or Princess Margaret (Portland Island) parks to the north. Its south and east sides are the most appealing with a number of gravel beaches fronting woods and meadows. There are a half-dozen or so areas that are suitable for camping. Remains of buildings are found on the brushier west side; a leper colony operated here until the mid-1920s. Due to the chronic fire hazard on this dry island, rely on camp stoves.

A return route via the north side of Sidney Island takes you toward an island that is conspicuously different from all the other islands around it. Mottled chalky sides and a few snags along its crest give slender Mandarte Island the appearance of a derelict dreadnought. In fact, this steep and rocky island is home to countless nesting birds, including gulls, pigeon guillemots, and rhinoceros auklets. Their droppings give the island its whitewashed appearance and stunt the tree growth. Landings are not allowed on this reserve. Ornithology researchers use the small buildings on the north side and blinds along the crest.

About 2 miles farther north from Mandarte Island is Isle-de-Lis Marine Park. It is located on Rum Island, joined to Gooch Island by a short gravel spit. This steep, rocky island has no facilities, but does have suitable tent sites along the south side. There are marginally useful landing sites along that steep and rocky shore, but these will be made precarious by southerly winds, especially at higher tides. You might do better to land on the leeward side of the spit and follow the up-and-down trails over the island.

OLYMPIC PENINSULA

42 INDIAN ISLAND

Bands of seals, Navy ships, weird nodules in sandstone formations, a fast sluice through a 4-foot-high culvert: all this and more are found along Indian Island's shores. This naval base won a conservation award for management of its wildlands, but look, don't touch: landings are not allowed. No matter—there are a lot of fine opportunities to land and camp elsewhere along this route with several conveniently located Cascadia Marine Trail sites.

> **Duration**: Part to full day.
>
> **Rating**: *Protected* or *Moderate*. *Moderate* route involves some fast-water paddling and possible tide rips for a short distance.
>
> **Navigation Aids**: NOAA charts 18423 SC (1:80,000), 18471 (1:40,000), or 18464 (1:20,000); Port Townsend tide table and Deception Pass current table with corrections for Port Townsend Canal.
>
> **Planning Considerations**: Coordinating your launch time with high tide will dramatically reduce the carrying distance at the Marrowstone Island–Indian Island causeway and will aid in catching favorable currents. At low tide the portage is at least 300 yards of tide flats; high tide reduces it to as little as 50 feet.

GETTING THERE AND LAUNCHING

Drive to Chimacum, turn east, and drive to Hadlock. Turn right at the stop sign in Hadlock, and then bear left after 0.8 mile to Indian Island.

Indian Island County Park: Drive approximately 0.75 mile beyond the Indian Island bridge. Ample parking is available with launching on sand or gravel beaches, which are dry for a considerable distance at low tide. This also happens to be a popular clamming spot if you are so inclined.

Marrowstone Island–Indian Island Causeway: Use the county park waysides nearby, probably the most suitable start for the Indian Island circumnavigation if the launch is at high tide (see Planning Considerations above). There are a series of wayside turnoffs and paths to the beach on Oak Bay to the south between Indian Island County Park and the causeway. The one about 0.2 mile before the causeway has off-highway parking and a short path, giving access to the Kilisut Harbor tide flats. This is the best site for a high-tide launch starting to the north or for access to the beach on Oak Bay.

Nordland on Marrowstone Island: Use the Mystery Bay Recreation Area. This state park area has ample parking and easy access to a sand and gravel beach.

Fort Flagler State Park: Located at the north end of Marrowstone Island, use the park's boat launch area on Kilisut Harbor. There is parking and easy access to the ramp, as well as the sand and gravel beaches. A fee is required to park overnight if you are not camping.

ROUTES

Indian Island Circumnavigation: *Moderate*. The total paddling distance is 11 miles. Time your trip for high tide at the causeway whether you start there or not.

An effective plan for this trip is to launch at the wayside west of the causeway just after high tide and then head north into Kilisut Harbor.

Indian Island's sandstone nodules (Randel Washburne)

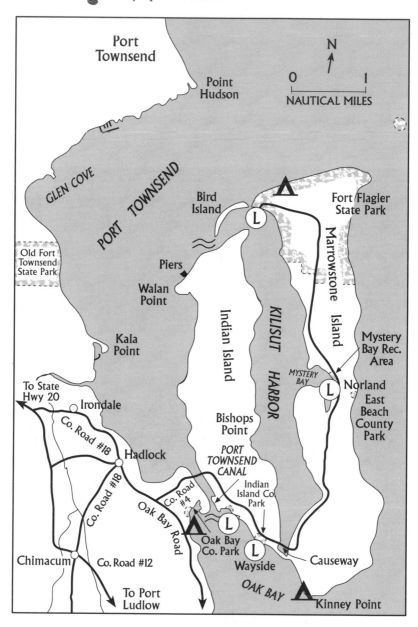

Starting off to the north gets you across the extensive tide flats of the harbor at high water. Also, the Oak Bay beach is not nearly such a long carry at lower water when you return. Time your progress paddling north so as to catch the ebb current out of Kilisut Harbor at Fort Flagler State Park. Aim for either the slack or the beginning of the south-flowing flood current in the Port Townsend Canal.

If you catch the tide level at the causeway just right, you can ride the current through one of the two four-foot-wide culverts under the highway. Be careful! The current through here is fast. Be sure that you will have enough headroom and enough water to avoid hanging up on the rocks at either end. But if you opt for discretion instead of this little thrill, the carry over the highway is easy.

Indian Island is an interesting blend of attractive "forbidden fruit," a restricted government property, surrounded by accessible public lands. Most of the island is occupied by the Naval Undersea Warfare Engineering Station, which stores ships' ammunition, reportedly nonnuclear. There are piers and buildings along the northwestern shore, but the remainder of the shoreline is remarkably pristine. The Navy employs a wildlife biologist to manage the island's habitat, and the station won national honors in a Department of Defense conservation award for its management.

However, *landings within the station boundaries are strictly prohibited*. Nonetheless, cruising along the station's shorelines is a pleasant interlude with a largely undisturbed environment. Plus, there are plenty of places on non-Navy property to stretch your legs. Look for river otter along the rocky shores.

The southern end of Indian Island, on both sides, has interesting sandstone formations with embedded nodules of harder rock that have eroded into studded surfaces, some forming tiny bridges like handles. Look for these south of Bishops Point on the Kilisut Harbor side and just north of the Port Townsend Canal on the west side.

Mystery Bay Recreation Area on Marrowstone Island is the first chance for a shore stop, about 2 miles north of the causeway. There are toilets, picnic facilities, and a store nearby at Nordland. If you use this as a launch point, there is a ramp fee.

Following the west shore of Indian Island south out of Kilisut Harbor involves an hour or so of paddling along shores with no opportunities to get out. A good plan is to take a stretch break at Fort Flagler beforehand. It has a wonderful beach over a mile in length. Besides a Cascadia Marine Trail site, Fort Flagler has picnic facilities, bathrooms with running water, and a concession stand that sells snacks during the summer months. The six Cascadia Marine Trail tent sites are secluded in the woods just east of the main campground.

The western edge of the harbor is a low sand spit covered with grass and connected to the park at low tide. Called Bird Island locally, its southern end is a popular place for large groups of seals to haul out. Paddling out through the channel you may find yourself surrounded by 50 or more of them.

Be sure to honor the Navy's requirement that you stay 600 feet from their docks at Walan Point. The next complex of docks, at Crane Point about 1 mile south, has no such distance restriction, but do not land. Just beyond is an inviting park facility, but it's for naval personnel only.

You could make a 1.5-mile detour west to Hadlock before entering Port Townsend Canal. There is a private marina, a very popular shoreside café and the town's center a few blocks up from the water.

The Navy's property line on Indian Island turns inland at the mid-point of a shell beach just north of the narrows of Port Townsend Canal. Immediately south are excellent stops ashore in the beginning of the county's parklands. Also south of the beach is the old Indian-Marrowstone ferry landing.

Port Townsend Canal has currents of up to 3 knots. Shore eddies form, except between the jetties at the southern end, where you have no choice but to fight the current if it is against you. Otherwise, if the water level is high enough, you can opt to paddle behind the jetty on the Indian Island side. Fairly large rips can form in the channel at the downstream end of the narrows, which may be dangerous for paddlers inexperienced with rough water.

Adjoining the southern end of the canal are Oak Bay County Park on the west side and Indian Island County Park on the east side. The sand and gravel tide flats are productive clamming areas.

Both parks have outhouses, picnic tables, and fresh water. Oak Bay County Park is also the location of a Cascadia Marine Trail group area with two tent sites. Beware, during higher tides the sites may flood. A camping fee must be paid at the pay station as the state's Water Trail Permit does not apply at county parks.

From the south entrance of Port Townsend Canal, it is but a brief paddle back to your start at the Marrowstone Island–Indian Island causeway.

A Cascadia Marine Trail campsite is planned for Kinney Point, at the south end of Marrowstone Island, beginning in the 1999 season. Please check with WWTA or DNR before planning on camping.

Fort Flagler State Park Local Paddling: *Protected.* Choose your own paddling distance. This area is popular for short trips in the warmer protected waters. It is also a good place for new paddlers to work on their skills. Be careful of the entrance channel to Kilisut Harbor, which can run at more than 1 knot.

Near Hadlock on Port Townsend Harbor (Carey and Jeanne Gersten)

43 MATS MATS BAY

This quiet little bay north of Port Ludlow is just right for paddling practice or touring anchored yachts. The mood is pastoral with residences
generally low-key and set back from the shore. A narrow, tree-lined entrance leads out to interesting offshore rocks less than 0.5 mile away.
They are popular with divers. You can extend this trip by paddling to or
from Port Ludlow about 3 miles away.

> **Duration**: Part day.
> **Rating**: *Protected*.
> **Navigation Aids**: NOAA chart 18445 SC (1:80,000, see 1:40,000
> inset).
> **Planning Considerations**: Go anytime.

GETTING THERE AND LAUNCHING

From Highway 104, turn north on Paradise Bay Road just west of the
Hood Canal Bridge. Follow this 6 miles, passing Port Ludlow, to the intersection with Oak Bay Road. Turn right and go another 2 miles and turn
right on Verner Road. Go 0.5 mile to the launching ramp in Mats Mats Bay.

Boat launch at Mats Mats Bay (Randel Washburne)

ROUTE

Suit your fancy here. The bay and entrance, plenty to see on their own, make a 2-mile loop if you follow the shore. Optionally, paddle out to Klas and Colvos Rocks if the weather isn't too windy, as these are

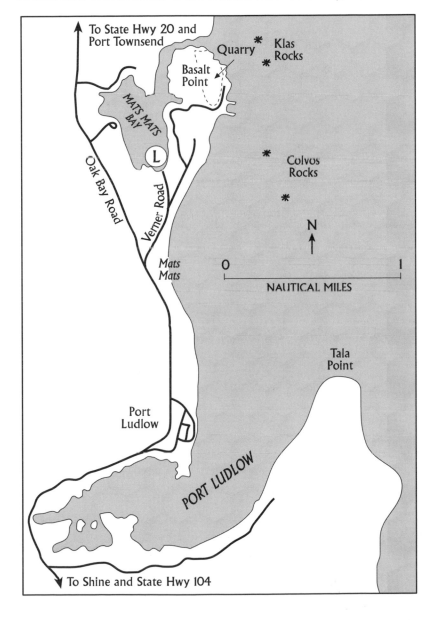

nicest to explore on calm days. You might also paddle south toward Port Ludlow. Colvos Rock, the largest of the offshore rocks in the area, is a poor place to get out of your boat—it's about 50 feet across, barren, and too steep for easy landings. The round trip to Colvos Rock from the Mats Mats Bay boat launch is 3 miles.

The entrance to the bay narrows to less than 100 yards with range markers to guide larger craft through. There are a few homes on the northern shore, while the naturalness of the south side is marred by the scars of a quarry seen through the trees.

The quarry and gravel operation occupies the real estate for almost a mile south of the bay entrance. Though there are a few beaches unaffected by the work behind, do not go ashore.

44 PORT GAMBLE

Established in 1853, Port Gamble at the mouth of Hood Canal had the oldest operating sawmill in North America until it finally ceased operation in 1996. At the turn of the century this bay was busy with lumber schooners, like Seattle's *Wawona*, being loaded for destinations up and down the Pacific Coast. Paddling by this once-bustling mill, you can still see the historic Victorian buildings in the background. Future plans call

Sawmill at Port Gamble (Randel Washburne)

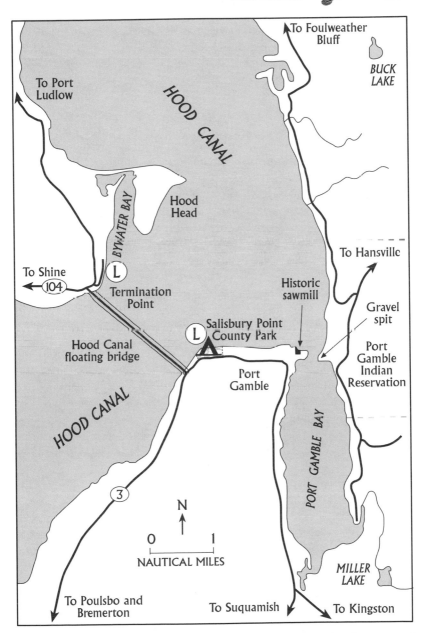

To Foulweather Bluff

BUCK LAKE

To Port Ludlow

HOOD CANAL

BYWATER BAY

Hood Head

To Shine

104

Termination Point

L

Historic sawmill

To Hansville

Gravel spit

Hood Canal floating bridge

HOOD CANAL

L

Salisbury Point County Park

Port Gamble

Port Gamble Indian Reservation

PORT GAMBLE BAY

3

N

0   1

NAUTICAL MILES

MILLER LAKE

To Poulsbo and Bremerton

To Suquamish

To Kingston

for the continued preservation of the mill town and the development of marina facilities. This route could be combined with Hood Head (see the Hood Head chapter) using launch sites on either side of Hood Canal

(the crossing would rate a *Moderate*). At Salisbury Point County Park, just west of Port Gamble on the Hood Canal side, a Cascadia Marine Trail site has been established.

Duration: Part day.
Rating: *Protected*.
Navigation Aids: NOAA charts 18445 SC, 18441 (both 1:80,000), or 18477 (1:25,000); Seattle tide table (subtract five minutes).
Planning Considerations: Go anytime.

GETTING THERE AND LAUNCHING

Use Salisbury Point County Park, located 0.5 mile north of the Hood Canal bridge. Launch either at the ramp, the more difficult choice if there is a shore break, or the sand beach in the south end of the park, which requires a 100-yard carry across the lawn.

ROUTE

The one-way distance to the entrance to Port Gamble Bay is about 1.5 miles. Paddle as far as desired into the bay. Note that there are no public tidelands or shores on this route once you leave the county park. The entrance to the bay narrows to a little more than 100 yards, with the silent mill's docks on the west and a gravel spit to the east. The spit and lands north and south of the bay's entrance on the east side are part of the Port Gamble Indian Reservation—only open to access with permission. The north end of Port Gamble Bay is mostly residential and farmland. The south end is largely undeveloped and wooded with occasional barge hulks and beaches. Just south of the sawmill's log storage area is a section of the Hood Canal floating bridge. Others were kept here while the bridge was undergoing rebuilding following its destruction in the winter of 1979–1980.

The Cascadia Marine Trail site at the county park has room for four to five tents. Fresh water, rest rooms, showers, picnic tables, and fireplaces with grills make this a pleasant stopover.

45 HOOD HEAD

An interesting lagoon and a gravel spit, both preserved in an undeveloped state park, plus easy access make this a nice afternoon's destination for western Puget Sound residents. Ducks, herons, and other waterfowl are plentiful in the lagoon during the winter months. The alongshore paddling and largely protected waters constitute a suitable trip for new kayakers. It could be combined with others in the area, such as the Salisbury Point–Port Gamble or Port Ludlow–Mats Mats Bay trips (see the Port Gamble and Mats Mats Bay chapters).

Duration: Part day.
Rating: *Protected.*
Navigation Aids: NOAA chart 18477 (1:25,000) or 18445 SC (1:80,000); Port Townsend tide table.
Planning Considerations: Midtide or higher required to explore the lagoon.

GETTING THERE AND LAUNCHING

Access is simple: just turn down Termination Point Road immediately north of the west end of the Hood Canal bridge. Follow it north past a Puget Power substation to Shine Public Tidelands. Managed by the Washington State Parks and Recreation Commission, this area has parking, vault toilets, and twenty RV-style campsites along the shore. Launch on the gravel beach.

ROUTES

Lagoon Round Trip: *Protected.* The paddling distance is 4 miles. Follow the beach north to the entrance just short of the spit connecting Hood Head to the mainland. You may encounter some current at the entrance to the lagoon, but probably not enough to cause any problems. At higher tides you can paddle southwest to grassy flats bordering alder forest that make a good spot for a picnic stop, some bird-watching, and exploration ashore in this undeveloped state park. An abandoned house is concealed in the brush on the west side of the lagoon.

Hood Head Circumnavigation: *Protected.* Add 2 miles to the lagoon round trip. Rounding Hood Head, perhaps on your way back to the launch point, will give you some different perspectives on Hood Canal— a fine view north toward Marrowstone Island and south along the canal past Bangor. You might also get as close as you ever will to a passing Trident submarine, certain to be an awesome and intimidating sight from your little craft. You will be able to paddle across the spit only on the highest tides; otherwise a short carry is needed above midtide. The mud flats are extensive south of the spit on the lowest tides. Some of the tidelands south of Point Hannon are privately owned and are marked accordingly.

46 CENTRAL HOOD CANAL: QUILCENE AND DABOB BAYS, DOSEWALLIPS, PLEASANT HARBOR, AND SCENIC BEACH

With the Olympic Range towering overhead, this part of Hood Canal is the epitome of the meeting place of land and sea. When you can take your eyes off this gorgeous backdrop, there is plenty to look at up close: rich estuaries, lagoons, and a tideland that is renowned for its oysters. Be careful where you collect them; most tidelands in Hood Canal are private. Oysters are usually open to harvesting from mid-September to mid-July. Remember the general rule is to shuck and leave the shells where taken. Check current Department of Fisheries regulations for the current season and local exceptions in this area.

> DURATION: Part to full day.
> RATING: *Protected* or *Moderate*. *Moderate* route involves crossing 1.5 to 3 miles of open water.
> NAVIGATION AIDS: NOAA charts 18476 (1:40,000) or 18445 SC (1:80,000); Seattle tide table (add 5 to 15 minutes).
> PLANNING CONSIDERATIONS: Best at high tide.

GETTING THERE AND LAUNCHING

Launch from either the east or west shore of Hood Canal, depending on which is most convenient. On the west side, at least five alternatives are off Highway 101 between Quilcene and Pleasant Harbor.

Quilcene Boat Haven Ramp: This is the best launch for exploring upper Quilcene Bay. From Rogers Road take a left on Linger Longer Road. Follow it 1.5 miles to this small boat harbor.

Point Whitney: Start here for access to Dabob Bay or for paddling south toward Dosewallips and Pleasant Harbor. From Quilcene follow Highway 101 south 8 miles to Bee Mill Road, which is marked for Point Whitney. Turn left and go 2.5 miles to the Washington Department of Fisheries Shellfish Lab at Point Whitney. The gravel beach next to the boat ramp is fine for launching in all but strong northerly winds when shore break may be quite large. Public rest rooms are nearby.

Though roads lead directly to the shores of upper Dabob Bay, launching there to paddle this interesting area is not advised since both the tidelands and shores are private. Local owners are concerned about trespassing on the rich oyster beds.

Dosewallips State Park: Launch in the high-tide channels adjacent to the day use area.

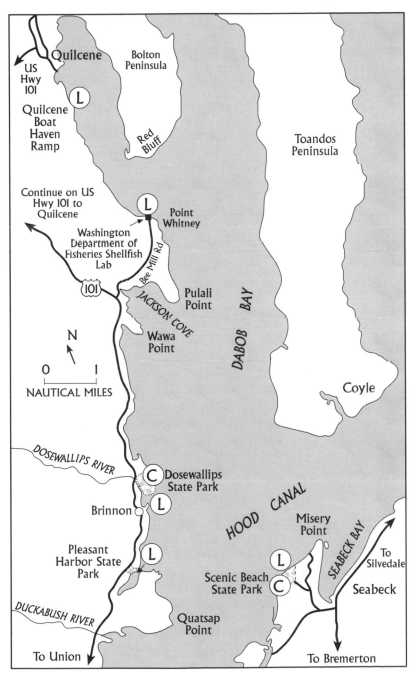

Quilcene

US
Hwy
101

Bolton
Peninsula

Quilcene
Boat
Haven
Ramp

Red
Bluff

Toandos
Peninsula

Continue on US
Hwy 101 to
Quilcene

Point
Whitney

Washington
Department of
Fisheries Shellfish
Lab

101

Bee Mill Rd

JACKSON COVE

Pulali
Point

Wawa
Point

DABOB BAY

N

0   1

NAUTICAL MILES

Coyle

DOSEWALLIPS RIVER

Dosewallips
State Park

HOOD CANAL

Misery
Point

Brinnon

Pleasant
Harbor State
Park

Scenic Beach
State Park

SEABECK BAY

To
Silvedale

Seabeck

DUCKABUSH RIVER

Quatsap
Point

To Union

To Bremerton

Pleasant Harbor: Use the dock at Pleasant Harbor State Park. This otherwise undeveloped park is not well marked from Highway 101. About 2 miles south of Dosewallips State Park turn left off Highway 101 onto a narrow lane next to a deserted building about 0.25 mile north of Pleasant Harbor Marina. Descend carefully to the small, unpaved parking lot.

Scenic Beach State Park: On the east shore use Scenic Beach State Park near Seabeck. It is open from April 1 to October 1. From the small center of Seabeck, the closest store to the launch point, go south 0.5 mile and turn right on Scenic Beach Road. Follow the park signs, driving another 1.5 miles to the park. Continue straight past the park entrance to the last lot. Carry boats through the picnic area about 150 yards to steps leading to a small gravel beach. Water and rest rooms are provided.

ROUTES

Scenic Beach–Dosewallips–Pleasant Harbor Triangle: *Moderate.* The distance is 8 miles. Start at any of the three points of this triangle. Both Scenic Beach and Pleasant Harbor are fine at any stage of the tide, but access to the water at Dosewallips is feasible only at high tide. Stops there are much more pleasant when the extensive tidal flats of this estuary are covered. All three make pleasant lunch stops. Scenic Beach State Park has the most extensive and convenient facilities.

Amenities at Dosewallips are a short walk from the water if you are able to paddle up the river of the same name about 0.25 mile or up one of the dead-end side channels to the south of the river at high tide. The river channel enters Hood Canal in the southern portion of the estuary. The park's day use facilities are located on the south side of the river. The portion of the estuary north of the river channel is primarily private land.

Tiny Pleasant Harbor is worth a little time to explore its back reaches and to look over the variety of yachts and working boats that use this all-weather shelter. The park is just inside and west of the narrow entrance. It consists primarily of the dock, a dusty parking lot above it, and an outhouse.

Quilcene to Dosewallips: *Protected.* The distance is 5 miles. Start from Point Whitney with a possible short side trip into the narrow lagoon entered from the end of the beach just west of the laboratory buildings. The rocky and largely undeveloped shores south of the lab to Pulali Point are some of the more interesting ones in the area. Make a wide swing around the flats of the Dosewallips estuary to the south side before going ashore to avoid private land.

Quilcene to Dabob Bay: *Protected.* The round-trip distance is from 3 to 10 miles depending on how deep you care to explore into northern Dabob Bay. The only place you can go ashore is the public tidelands at the southeast end of the Bolton Peninsula, east of Red Bluff. This 0.5-mile state tideland is best identified by the lack of private tidelands signs that define its limits. The shores above are private. All other tidelands in Dabob Bay are private as well, so remember that you will be trespassing anywhere that you touch bottom.

47 SOUTHERN HOOD CANAL: ANNAS BAY

Annas Bay, the elbow of the Great Bend of Hood Canal, has the largest river estuary, the Skokomish River, in the area. Set against the spectacular backdrop of the immediately adjacent Olympics, this maze of winding

Annas Bay (Randel Washburne)

channels and grassy banks abounds in bird life and seals. At high tide a meandering route can be followed all the way across the estuary through these watery convolutions and miniature islets. Especially stunning are the fall colors of the wetland deciduous trees and shrubs in brilliant contrast against the mountains' greens.

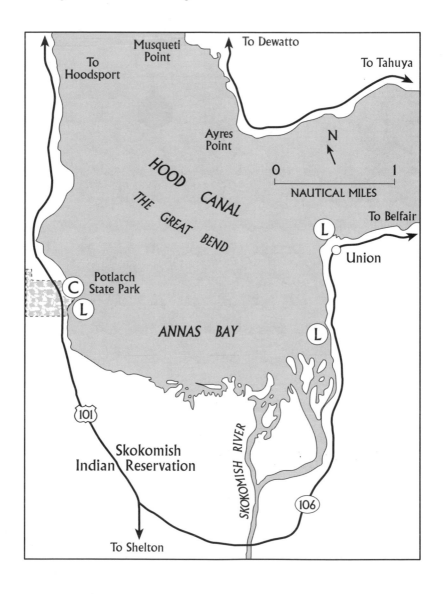

Duration: Part day.
Rating: *Protected*.
Navigation Aids: NOAA charts 18476 (1:40,000) or 18445 SC (1:80,000); Seattle tide table (add 10 minutes).
Planning Considerations: Best at high tide.

GETTING THERE AND LAUNCHING

Launch from sites in or near the town of Union along Highway 106 or at Potlatch State Park on Highway 101. The car-shuttle distance between these areas is about 5 miles.

Union: Use the public boat ramp and lot. An informal roadside pullout along Highway 106 about 1 mile south of Union gives the closest access to the eastern end of the estuary.

Potlatch State Park: Use the beach in the day use area.

ROUTE

The one-way paddling distance across the estuary is about 2.5 miles. Add another mile if you start from Union. The tidelands in the estuary are the property of the Skokomish Indian Reservation. There may be many gill nets set across the river channels during the fall salmon runs.

Depending on the tide height, pick your route along the fringe of channels and islands defining the northern edge of the estuary. If the water level is fairly high you should be able to make it all the way across, except at the estuary's center where a causeway requires you to skirt to the outside open water.

48 SEQUIM BAY

This quiet bay has the backdrop of the Olympics to the south and Protection Island and distant Dungeness Spit to the north. A huge lagoon almost landlocked by two sand spits at its entrance, Sequim Bay provides unlimited opportunities for exploring its wooded and residential shorelines or the sand spits. These and an associated tidal lagoon allow plenty of shallow-water paddling and stops ashore at two public beaches. Using a shuttle (road distance is 5 miles), a 3-mile paddle along bluffs to the bay's entrance can be made, beginning at Marlyn Nelson Park north of Sequim Bay and ending at John Wayne Marina inside of it. This could be extended another 2 miles by ending at Sequim Bay State Park deeper inside the bay.

Duration: Part day.

Rating: *Protected*. Confined waters and alongshore routes make this a good place for new kayakers. The paddling is easy and scenic with few likely challenges.

Navigation Aids: NOAA chart 18465 (1:80,000) or 18471 (1:40,000); Port Townsend tide table (subtract 30 minutes).

Planning Considerations: A rising tide is best for exploring the lagoon behind Gibson Spit. Launch from John Wayne Marina and stay within the bay and lagoon if seas to the north of Travis Spit are rough.

GETTING THERE AND LAUNCHING

John Wayne Marina, Sequim Bay State Park, and Marlyn Nelson Park are launch alternatives for this route.

John Wayne Marina: On land donated to the county by the actor, the launch is off Highway 101 about 2 miles east of Sequim. The turn

Travis Spit, looking west toward Gibson Spit (Randel Washburne)

from the highway is well marked; just follow signs about 1 mile to the marina. Use the ramp for launching.

Sequim Bay State Park: The park lies on both sides of Highway 101 about 4.75 miles east of Sequim. Turn east off the highway, toward the water, and follow the road downhill through the campground to the boat launch. An alternative is to turn right to the picnic area and launch on the beach.

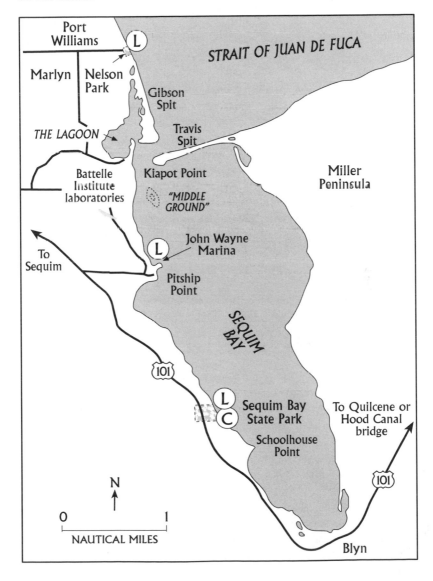

Marlyn Nelson County Park: The park is reached by turning north from Highway 101 onto Brown Road about 0.5 mile east of Sequim. Follow it 1 mile to Port Williams Road, turn right and go about 2.5 miles to the park. Launch from the gravel beach.

ROUTE

Beginning at either Sequim Bay State Park or John Wayne Marina, paddle north along the beach. Shores between these points and the bay's entrance are wooded with occasional homes above the gravel beaches. About 1 mile north of the marina are Battelle Institute's laboratories. They are located just inside the dredged entrance that skirts Kiapot Point at the end of Travis Spit. The spit is a long sand and gravel obstruction that extends from the east shore nearly to the bay's western side. Just north is a smaller one, Gibson Spit, running perpendicular to Travis Spit from the north. It further constricts the entrance. At the laboratories, you can either cut across to explore the north side of the spit or continue along the shore to the lagoon and Gibson Spit. This is a narrow dredged channel, so stay close to shore to assure that larger boats will have the room they need.

The two spits have public tidelands: on the north side of Travis Spit and the east side of Gibson Spit. The areas above the mean high-tide line on both spits are the property of Battelle Institute. Their scientists do research there from time to time and they ask that you not trespass.

The lagoon is a fine place to ride in on a rising tide starting about midtide. The bird viewing is good with a pastoral backdrop of farmlands. At high tide you should be able to follow the tidal channels for a mile or so. The tidelands in the lagoon west of Gibson Spit are also research areas, as is the drying shoal called Middle Ground south of Travis Spit. Stay in your boat except on the public tidelands. Though shellfish are plentiful in Sequim Bay, they cannot be harvested because of contamination.

The route from Gibson Spit to Marlyn Nelson Park follows the gravel beach north. Bluffs begin at the foot of the spit less than 1 mile south of the park. The park's present site was once Port Williams where steamers called with freight and passenger service for the community of Sequim.

There are alternative routes in Sequim Bay. For instance, you could make an upper bay loop from either the marina or Sequim Bay Park by paddling the 1.5 miles of open water across the bay to the largely residential east shore. Then you could follow the shore around the south end, cutting back across at your discretion.

49 DUNGENESS SPIT

This 5-mile-long spit is a national wildlife refuge set aside for waterfowl and shorebirds. As many as 10,000 birds winter in the refuge, particularly the black brant. Sandpipers and other shorebirds scour its beaches for food. Shallow Dungeness Bay, south of the spit, harbors clams and oysters, as well as the crab that takes its name. Paddling the full length of the spit makes a fine day trip with a stop for lunch at the New Dungeness Lighthouse National Historic Site near the end.

> **Duration**: Part to full day. No landing or camping is allowed along these shorelines.
>
> **Rating**: *Protected* or *Moderate*, depending on route. *Moderate* route may involve exposure to rough seas, beach surf, and tide rips.
>
> **Navigation Aids**: NOAA chart 18471 (1:40,000); Port Townsend tide tables (subtract about 45 minutes).
>
> **Planning Considerations**: Best on higher tides. Tideflats south of the spit and in the lagoon are extensive at low tide. *Landing is by required reservation and only allowed at the boat landing zone south of the lighthouse.*

On the beach at the end of Dungeness Spit (Randel Washburne)

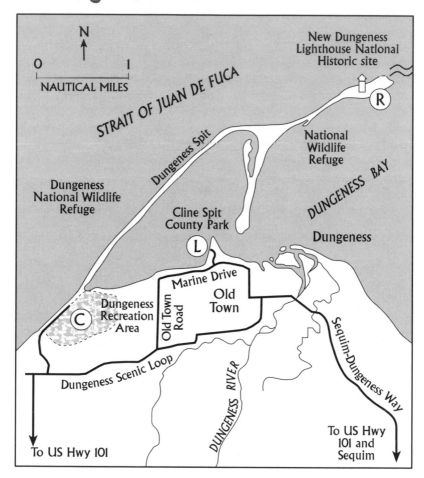

GETTING THERE AND LAUNCHING

From Highway 101 in Sequim, turn north on Sequim Avenue and go 6 miles. This becomes Sequim-Dungeness Way and later Marine Drive. After 6 miles the spit comes into view on the right. Turn down a side road that drops sharply over the bluff to Cline Spit County Park and launch from the gravel beach north of the parking area.

If you plan to go ashore, you must make advanced reservations by calling 360-457-8451. The only point of access allowed is the boat landing zone on the beach south of New Dungeness Lighthouse.

No camping is allowed in the refuge. The closest is Dungeness Recreation Area, a Clallam County park. To get there, continue driving on Marine Drive beyond the turn-off to Cline Spit County Park, which then

The New Dungeness Lighthouse National Historic Site
(Conrad Fiederer)

turns left becoming Old Town Road. Turn right on the Dungeness Scenic
Loop and follow it to the park entrance. Camping is too far from shore
for paddle-in use.

ROUTE

In windy weather you may prefer to stick to the lagoon north and
east of Cline Spit, which affords sheltered paddling yet easy viewing of
the shoreline south of the spit. The south side of the spit usually is calm
except in southerly winds. The waters on either side of Graveyard Spit are
closed from October 1 to May 14; call ahead to confirm these dates.

The manned lighthouse at the end of the spit is open to the public
for daily tours. The climb up the tower's spiral staircase is worthwhile in
its own right; the view along the spit is even better.

In calm weather, consider paddling around the end of the spit into
the Strait of Juan de Fuca proper. The feasibility of this depends on the
sea conditions. If too big, retreat to the south side of the spit. Currents

passing over the bar at the end of the spit and interacting with the eddies behind it can produce bad tide rips on both the flood and ebb. You may be able to avoid them by cutting across close to shore unless seas are rough.

Paddling the northern side of Dungeness Spit allows a close-up look at this wild, driftwood-strewn beach, staying as close in as the surf or, where enforced, a 100-yard buffer allows. Keep an eye offshore for wakes from the constant stream of ships passing in and out of the Strait of Juan de Fuca, as these will break farther out. With an eye to seaward you can play "chicken" with the surf, gauging your distance from the beach to position yourself just beyond where the waves break. The rapid rise and fall of a steepening wave is exhilarating, and the feel of the wave as it breaks beneath your shoreward paddle blade is a little thrill. Be ready to cut to seaward for bigger waves, or else you will be washed onto the beach and probably drenched.

50 CRESCENT BAY TO FRESHWATER BAY: STRIPED PEAK AREA

Here is a taste of Washington's outer coast just a few miles west of Port Angeles. Swells penetrating the Strait of Juan de Fuca are still large enough to make challenging surf on the area's beaches and pack enough power to bore a double sea arch along this route. Depending on the swell size, landings are possible on many tiny gravel beaches along the way that are inaccessible from the cliffs above. Preservation of the uplands as the Department of Natural Resources' Striped Peak Recreation Area makes this one of the wildest stretches along the Strait of Juan de Fuca coast.

> **Duration**: Part day (add time for car shuttle or double the route distance for a paddled return).
> **Rating**: *Exposed*. Surf and strong currents are likely. Surf may prevent landings along the route and commit you to paddling in the current while possibly exposed to the effects of wind and opposing current for the full distance between Crescent and Freshwater Bays.
> **Navigation Aids**: NOAA chart 18465 (1:80,000); Race Rocks current table (adjusted for Angeles Point) or the Canadian *Current Atlas*.
> **Planning Considerations**: Travel with the current direction or at times of little current as forecasted in the current tables or the *Current Atlas*. Alongshore currents can exceed 2 knots. Breaking swells may prevent using inshore eddies to work upstream. A large swell

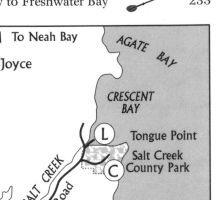

may produce big and unavoidable surf at Crescent Bay, and may also prevent landings along the way. Avoid weather conditions when strong east or west winds are forecast for the Strait of Juan de Fuca.

GETTING THERE AND LAUNCHING

This route can be accessed from either Freshwater Bay to the east or Crescent Bay to the west. Neither launch point allows overnight parking. However, camping is provided at Salt Creek County Park at Crescent Bay. An easy 9-mile vehicle shuttle can be made between them.

Freshwater Bay: Drive Highway 112 west from its junction with Highway 101 just a few miles west of Port Angeles. After 5 miles turn right on Freshwater Bay Road and follow it 3 miles to Freshwater Bay

Crescent Bay from Tongue Point (Randel Washburne)

County Park. Launching is on a gravel beach next to the launching ramp.

Crescent Bay: Continue another 3 miles beyond the turn-off to Freshwater Bay on Highway 112 to Camp Hayden Road. Turn right and go 3 miles to Salt Creek County Park. Continue straight for the park or turn left for the launching point.

The park provides a large number of campsites, many of which are sited spectacularly at the edge of sea cliffs with panoramic views of the strait, and offers access to extensive tide pools at Tongue Point. This area has unique coast defense artillery installations that are well worth a visit. These were built during World War II rather than prior to the First World War, as in the case of others farther inland.

The best launch point in Crescent Bay is from a small parking lot next to Salt Creek. At low tide it is necessary to follow the creek, often too low to float a kayak, for about 300 yards down the beach to the water. Surf can be significant depending on swell size and weather, though refraction behind the rocks near Tongue Point may give some protection at midtide.

If conditions appear too daunting at Crescent Bay, a shorter trip out of Freshwater Bay is probably wiser and certainly less effort. Protected from the west, Freshwater Bay usually offers calm launching and a chance to visit as much of the wild coast to the west as is comfortable. Generally, swells and shore break increase to the west toward Crescent Bay.

ROUTE

The *Exposed* rating is merited by the swells and current. They can make landings along this 4-mile route difficult and can commit you to reaching one end or the other if the weather takes a turn for the worse.

Planning with the current is more important here than along other routes where it is possible to use eddies to travel against contrary flows. Extensive kelp beds border this entire coastline. Unless the swells are very small, surge and shore break prevent using the eddies inside the kelp. This can commit you to traveling along the outside of the beds where the current is strong.

Cliffs with tiny gravel pocket beaches here and there are continuous between Observatory Point at Freshwater Bay and Tongue Point at Crescent Bay. You will also find a couple of small sea caves just wide enough to paddle into if the tide and sea conditions are right. The most interesting landing spots are at the midpoint of the route near a double arch best reached from a beach just to the east.

Be especially watchful for intermittent breakers on offshore rocks while rounding Tongue Point. Since swells vary in size, these rocks may allow smaller ones to pass without breaking, making them unnoticeable until a big one arrives. Note their position on the chart and try to spot them when they do break, giving them a wide berth.

A WWTA/DNR campsite on Lummi Island
(Carey and Jeanne Gersten)

APPENDIX I: Useful Publications

A number of excellent how-to books, manuals, guidebooks, and references are available to the sea kayaker. I have listed a few that are favorites—essential, extremely helpful, or otherwise just enjoyable to read—for the practical information and knowledge they impart.

Broze, Matt, and Gronseth, George. *Sea Kayaker's Deep Trouble: True Stories and Their Lessons from Sea Kayaker Magazine.* New York: McGraw-Hill, 1997. Not only do the authors give a very readable and exciting account of the incidents, they also clearly dissect the underlying factors contributing to the incidents and how they could have been prevented, in a compassionate voice.

Burch, David. *Fundamentals of Kayak Navigation.* Seattle: Pacific Search Press, 1993. The acknowledged choice for learning not only the fundamentals of navigation, but also the practical tricks.

Canadian Hydrographic Service. *Current Atlas: Juan de Fuca Strait to Strait of Georgia.* Ottawa: Canadian Hydrographic Service Department of Fisheries and Oceans, 1983. This atlas provides the most accurate and detailed information on tidal currents in this complex region. For a given hour and tidal range, the user is directed to a chart showing currents at that time. Calculations required to arrive at the correct chart make this resource a bit difficult to use. (See *Washburne's Tables* for a simplified method of finding the proper current chart.)

Chettleburgh, Peter. *An Explorer's Guide: Marine Parks of British Columbia.* Vancouver, B.C.: Maclean Hunter, 1985 (out of print). Some of the best detail available on the history and attractions of these parks, especially those not covered in other resources listed here.

Cummings, Al, and Bailey-Cummings, Jo. *Gunkholing in the Gulf Islands.* Edmonds, Washington: Nor'westing, 1989 (out of print). This boater's guide includes a lot of local lore not found elsewhere. It is written in a friendly and entertaining style.

————. *Gunkholing in the San Juans.* Edmonds, Washington: Nor'westing (out of print). Done with the same wit and eclectic detail as their Gulf Islands book.

Department of Natural Resources, State of Washington. Public tideland
booklets: *North Puget Sound*, 1978; *San Juan Island Region*, 1985;
South Puget Sound, 1978; *Strait of Juan de Fuca*, 1984 (all booklets out of print). These booklets are handy for identifying public
tidelands and DNR upland picnic or camping facilities, if you can
track down copies of them. The tidelands are primarily of interest
for shellfish gathering or just a place to stretch your legs at low
tide. They are of little use to you when the tide is high because the
uplands are usually private.

Dowd, John. *Sea Kayaking: A Manual for Long Distance Touring.*
Seattle: University of Washington Press, 1997 (revised). Another
classic manual from a man who, enviously, has been sea kayaking
longer than most of us probably ever will.

Dutky, Paul. *The Bombproof Roll and Beyond!* Birmingham, Alabama:
Menasha Ridge Press, 1997. A difficult skill is dissected and explained
well. It's the next best thing to a personal coach on the subject.

Harrison, David. *Kayak Camping.* Toronto: Hearst Marine Books,
1995. This is a straightforward and clear presentation of the
specific camping skills a sea kayaker should have before setting out
on an overnight adventure.

Hutchinson, Derek C. *The Complete Book of Sea Kayaking.* Connecticut: Globe Pequot Press, 1995 (revised). A great presentation of
the subject with a British perspective. It also includes interesting
history about the origins of sea kayaking and its development into
a modern pursuit.

Ince, John, and Kottner, Hedi. *Sea Kayaking Canada's West Coast.*
Vancouver, B.C.: Raxas Books, 1992 (revised). The original sea
kayaker's classic guidebook for the coast, with trips liberally
scattered up and down the British Columbia coast, including the
Gulf Islands.

Island Canoe Company. *Current and Tide Tables for Puget Sound,
Deception Pass, the San Juans, Gulf Islands, and Seymour Narrows.*
Bainbridge Island, Washington: Island Canoe Company, published
annually. This collection of local tide and current information is
otherwise available only in large NOAA volumes.

————. *San Juan Current Guide Including the Gulf Islands and Strait of Juan de Fuca*. Bainbridge Island, Washington: Island Canoe Company, 1987. The charts in this publication show currents with correction factors for local slack times and speeds.

————. *Puget Sound Current Guide*. Bainbridge Island, Washington: Island Canoe Company, 1996. This publication includes the same information for Puget Sound as found in the above publication.

Lilly, Kenneth E., Jr. *Marine Weather of Western Washington*. Seattle: Starpath School of Navigation, 1983. Lilly's book provides some of the most helpful information ever for understanding the patterns and idiosyncrasies of western Washington's weather and learning about how weather features happen. It is essential if you want to go beyond just listening to forecasts for weather prediction, and it also includes useful information on waves. The publication is only available from:
Starpath School of Navigation
311 Fulton Street
Seattle, WA 98109
206-284-8328

McGee, Peter, editor. *Kayak Routes of the Pacific Northwest Coast*. Seattle: The Mountaineers, 1998. A beautiful compendium of sea kayaking trips spanning the coast from Washington state to the upper reaches of the British Columbia coast, including the Queen Charlotte Islands.

The following five companion volumes provide comprehensive coverage of each area; almost any place worth mentioning is included. They also include good information about facilities and services on shore.

Mueller, Marge and Ted. *Middle Puget Sound Afoot and Afloat*. Seattle: The Mountaineers, 1997.

————. *North Puget Sound Afoot and Afloat*. Seattle: The Mountaineers, 1995.

————. *The San Juan Islands Afoot and Afloat*. Seattle: The Mountaineers, 1995.

———. *Seattle's Lakes, Bays & Waterways: Including the Eastside.* Seattle: The Mountaineers, 1998.

———. *South Puget Sound Afoot and Afloat.* Seattle: The Mountaineers, 1996.

Nyberg, Carl, and Bailey, Jo. *Gunkholing in South Puget Sound: A Comprehensive Cruising Guide from Kingston/Edmonds South to Olympia.* Seattle: San Juan Enterprises, Inc., 1997. As with previous books in the Gunkholing series, this guide cannot be beat for the extensive useful information provided alongside more obscure history and legends of the region.

Obee, Bruce. *The Gulf Islands Explorer.* North Vancouver, B.C.: Whitecap Books, 1997 (revised). A good how-and-where reference for the major islands, with information and ideas for kayaks and canoes.

Renner, Jeff. *Northwest Marine Weather: From the Columbia River to Cape Scott.* Seattle: The Mountaineers, 1994. Not only a popular Seattle TV weatherman, Renner is also an outdoor enthusiast who hikes, skis, and sea kayaks, as well as pilots an airplane. He knows the importance of paying attention to what the skies are doing and going to do. His book lucidly teaches boaters weather awareness, mechanics, and the general principles of forecasting.

Snowden, Mary A. *Island Paddling.* 2d ed. Victoria, B.C.: Orca Book Publications, 1997. This guidebook provides not only extensive and necessary information about logistics, but also a wealth of interesting lore and history to make the paddler's journey come alive.

Tidelog: Puget Sound Edition. Tiburon, California: Pacific Publishers, published annually. This is a useful combination of tide and current information for the year. It provides daily tidal curves that show slacks and associated current strengths and lunar and solar phases as they affect tides. It also includes current charts for Puget Sound and current schedules for Deception Pass and The Narrows at Tacoma.

U.S. Department of Commerce, National Oceanic and Atmospheric Administration. *Tidal Current Tables: Pacific Coast of North America and Asia.* Washington, D.C.: Government Printing Office, published annually. This volume includes current information for local points throughout the Northwest, as well as the rest of the Pacific Coast. See Island Canoe Company publications if you are interested in Washington's inland waters only.

Washburne, Randel. *The Coastal Kayaker's Manual: A Complete Guide to Skills, Gear, and Sea Sense.* 3rd ed. Old Saybrook, Connecticut: Globe Pequot Press, 1998. A classic manual that covers the spectrum of topics in the sport of sea kayaking, and then some.

Washburne's Tables. Bellevue, Washington: Weatherly Press, published annually. Use these tables in conjunction with the helpful Canadian Hydrographic Service's *Current Atlas: Juan de Fuca Strait to Strait of Georgia.* These tables provide direct access to the proper current chart at any hour of any day without need for calculations or adjustment for daylight saving time.

APPENDIX II: Quick Trip Reference

Trip	Rating	Duration	Launching	Camping
South Puget Sound				
1. Hammersley Inlet	*Moderate* or *Moderate* +	Full Day to Overnight	Boat Ramp along Pine Street in Shelton Jacoby Shorecrest County Park Walker County Park Arcadia Boat Ramp	Hope Island State Park (CMT)
2. Hope Island (south)	*Moderate* or *Moderate* +	Part Day to Overnight	Latimer's Landing Arcadia Boat Ramp Boston Harbor	Hope Island (CMT) Joemma Beach State Park (CMT) Jarrell Cove State Park (CMT)
3. Eld Inlet	*Protected* or *Moderate*	Part to Full Day	Boat Ramp on Gravelly Beach Loop Road Northwest Frye Cove County Park	
4. McMicken Island	*Moderate*	Full Day	Joemma Beach State Park (CMT)	Joemma Beach State Park (CMT)
5. Carr Inlet	*Protected*	Part Day	Kopachuck State Park (CMT) Rosedale Street Northwest in Rosedale	Kopachuck State Park (CMT)
6. Henderson Inlet	*Protected* or *Moderate* +	Part to Full Day	Woodward Bay Natural Resources Conservation Area Zittel's Marina on Johnson Point	
7. Nisqually Delta	*Protected*	Part Day	DF&W Boat Ramp at Luhr Beach	
8. Commencement Bay	*Protected* or *Moderate*	Part to Full Day	Thea Foss Waterway Thea's Park Tacoma to Point Defiance Shoreline Point Defiance Park	

Trip	Rating	Duration	Launching	Camping
8. Commencement Bay (Continued)			North Shore of Commencement Bay, Brown's Point	
9. Maury Island	Protected, Moderate, or Exposed	Part to Full Day	Dockton County Park Beach at Portage Burton Acres County Park Saltwater State Park	Saltwater State Park
10. Blake Island	Protected, Moderate, or Exposed	Full Day to Overnight	Alki Beach, Seattle Alki Point Light Station, Seattle Lincoln Park, Seattle Ramp next to Vashon Island's North Ferry Terminal Beach next to Southworth Ferry Terminal	Blake Island State Park (CMT)
11. Eagle Harbor to Bremerton	Moderate	Full Day	Eagle Harbor Beach Access next to Winslow Ferry Terminal First Street Public Dock in Bremerton	Fort Ward State Park (CMT) Manchester State Park (CMT) Blake Island State Park (CMT)
12. Eagle Harbor	Protected	Part Day	Winslow Waterfront Park Eagle Harbor Beach Access next to Winslow Ferry Terminal	
13. West Point, Shilshole Bay, and Golden Gardens	Protected or Moderate	Part to Full Day	Golden Gardens City Park	
14. Port Madison and Agate Passage	Moderate or Moderate +	Part Day	Fay Bainbridge State Park Suquamish Museum and Tribal Center Old Man House State Park Suquamish Center Boat Ramp	Fay Bainbridge State Park (CMT)

Trip	Rating	Duration	Launching	Camping
15. Lake Union	*Protected*	Part Day	Gasworks Park Sunnyside Avenue Ramp Stairs at Northwest Outdoor Center South Passage Point Park East Lynn Street Minipark Lake Union Steam Plant Chandler's Cove Development Portage Bay	
16. Duwamish Waterway	*Protected*	Part Day	End of Diagonal Street East Waterway Junction Jack Perry Memorial Viewpoint Terminal 105 Viewpoint Terminal 115 Viewpoint First Avenue Bridge Boat Launch	
17. Elliott Bay	*Moderate*	Part Day	32nd Avenue West Boat Ramp in Magnolia Washington Street Public Dock Jack Perry Memorial Viewpoint Pocket Beach #1 Bell Harbor Marina (Pier 66)	
North Puget Sound				
18. Everett Harbor	*Protected*	Part Day	Marine Park along Marine View Drive	
19. Port Susan	*Protected or Moderate*	Part Day	DF&W Boat Ramp on Hat Slough Kayak Point County Park (CMT)	Kayak Point County Park (CMT)
20. Whidbey Island	*Protected or Moderate*	Part to Full Day	Oak Harbor City Park (CMT) Captain Thomas Coupeville Park	Oak Harbor City Park (CMT)

Trip	Rating	Duration	Launching	Camping
21. Skagit River Delta	*Protected*	Part to Full Day	Blake's Skagit River Resort and Marina DNR Boat Ramp along Moore Road La Conner Boat Ramp	
22. Hope and Skagit Islands	*Moderate +*	Part Day to Overnight	Cornet Bay, Deception Pass State Park Hoypus Point Snee-oosh Beach	Ala Spit (CMT)
23. Deception Pass	*Protected, Moderate +, or Exposed*	Part Day	Deception Pass State Park: —Bowman Bay (CMT) —West Beach —North Beach —Cornet Bay	Bowman Bay (CMT), Deception Pass State Park
San Juan Islands Area				
24. Burrows Island	*Moderate*	Part Day	Skyline Marina, Anacortes Washington Park, Anacortes	Burrows Island (CMT) (to open 1999 season)
25. Padilla Bay	*Protected*	Part Day	Bayview State Park Indian Slough Swinomish Channel Boat Ramp March Point	Saddlebag Island (CMT)
26. Saddlebag Island	*Moderate*	Part Day to Overnight	March Point	Saddlebag Island (CMT)
27. Cypress Island	*Moderate +*	Overnight to Two Nights	Guemes Island Ferry Terminal Washington Park, Anacortes	Cypress Head DNR Recreation Site (CMT) Pelican Beach DNR Recreation Site (CMT) Strawberry Island DNR Recreation Site (CMT)

Trip	Rating	Duration	Launching	Camping
28. Lummi Island	*Moderate* or *Exposed*	Overnight	Gooseberry Point, Lummi Indian Reservation	Lummi Island DNR Recreation Site (CMT)
29. Clark Island	*Exposed*	Full Day to Overnight	Doe Bay Village Resort Gooseberry Point, Lummi Indian Reservation	Clark Island State Park Lawrence Point DNR Recreation Site Doe Bay Village Resort
30. Chuckanut Bay	*Protected* or *Moderate*	Part Day to Full Day	Boat Ramp at Harris Street, Fairhaven Marine Park, Fairhaven Chuckanut Park Wildcat Cove on Chuckanut Bay	Larrabee State Park
31. James Island	*Moderate* or *Exposed*	Overnight	Washington Park, Anacortes Spencer Spit State Park, Lopez Island (CMT)	Spencer Spit State Park, Lopez Island (CMT) James Island (CMT)
32. Obstruction Pass	*Moderate*	Part Day to Overnight	Spencer Spit State Park, Lopez Island (CMT) Obstruction Pass Boat Ramp Doe Bay Village Resort	Obstruction Pass Recreation Site (CMT) Doe Bay Village Resort
33. Jones Island	*Moderate*	Overnight	Deer Harbor on Orcas Island Friday Harbor Public Dock, San Juan Island	Jones Island State Park (CMT)
34. Shaw Island	*Protected* or *Moderate*	Full Day to Multiple Nights	Odlin Park, Lopez Island Friday Harbor Public Dock, San Juan Island	Odlin County Park, Lopez Island Shaw Island County Park Blind Island State Park (CMT) Turn Island State Park

Trip	Rating	Duration	Launching	Camping
35. South and West San Juan Island	*Moderate or Exposed*	Part Day to Multiple Nights	San Juan Island: —Friday Harbor Public Dock —Roche Harbor —British Camp —San Juan County Park —Eagle Cove —Fourth of July Beach —Salmon Banks Lane —Castle Point Picnic Area	San Juan County Park Griffin Bay Recreation Site (CMT) Turn Island State Park Posey Island (CMT) Jones Island State Park (CMT)
36. Point Doughty	*Moderate*	Full Day to Overnight	North Beach Road End, Orcas Island Bartwood Lodge, Orcas Island	Point Doughty DNR Recreation Site (CMT)
37. Patos, Sucia, and Matia Islands	*Exposed*	Overnight to Multiple Nights	North Beach Road End, Orcas Island Bartwood Lodge, Orcas Island	Sucia Island: Fossil Bay, Echo Bay, Snoring Bay, Fox Cove, Ewing Cove Rolfe Cove, Matia Island Active Cove, Patos Island Clark Island Point Doughty DNR Recreation Site (CMT)
38. Stuart Island	*Exposed*	Overnight to Multiple Nights	Roche Harbor, San Juan Island Friday Harbor Public Dock, San Juan Island	Stuart Island (CMT) Posey Island (CMT)
Gulf Islands (British Columbia)				
39. Portland Island	*Moderate*	Full Day to Overnight	Tulista Park, Sidney Beach at Public Dock at Swartz Bay Ferry Terminal	Portland Island: —Royal Cove —Tortoise Bay

Trip	Rating	Duration	Launching	Camping
40. Pender, Saturna, and Mayne Islands	*Moderate*	Part Day to Overnight	Browning Harbour Public Dock, Pender Island Beach near Ferry Terminal at Village Bay, Mayne Island Public Dock near Ferry Terminal on Saturna Island	Beaumont Marine Park, Pender Island
41. D'Arcy Island Loop	*Moderate*	Overnight to Multiple Nights	Tulista Park, Sidney	D'Arcy Island Marine Park Sidney Spit Marine Park Isle-de-Lis (Rum Island) Marine Park
Olympic Peninsula				
42. Indian Island	*Protected or Moderate*	Part to Full Day	Indian Island County Park Marrowstone Island–Indian Island Causeway Mystery Bay Recreation Area Fort Flagler State Park (CMT)	Fort Flagler State Park (CMT) Oak Bay County Park (CMT, Kinney Point (CMT) (to open 1999 season)
43. Mats Mats Bay	*Protected*	Part Day	Mats Mats Bay Boat Ramp	
44. Port Gamble	*Protected*	Part Day	Salisbury Point County Park (CMT)	Salisbury Point County Park (CMT)
45. Hood Head	*Protected*	Part Day	Shine Public Tidelands	Salisbury Point County Park (CMT)
46. Central Hood Canal	*Protected or Moderate*	Part to Full Day	Quilcene Boat Haven Ramp Beach at Point Whitney Boat Ramp Dosewallips State Park Pleasant Harbor Scenic Beach State Park	Dosewallips State Park Scenic Beach State Park

Trip	Rating	Duration	Launching	Camping
47. Southern Hood Canal	*Protected*	Part Day	Union Public Dock Public access along Route 106 Potlatch State Park	Potlatch State Park
48. Sequim Bay	*Protected*	Part Day	John Wayne Marina Sequim Bay State Park Marlyn Nelson County Park	Sequim Bay State Park
49. Dungeness Spit	*Protected* or *Moderate*	Part to Full Day	Cline Spit County Park Boat Ramp	Dungeness Recreation Area (no water access)
50. Crescent Bay to Freshwater Bay	*Exposed*	Part Day	Freshwater Bay County Park Boat Ramp Salt Creek at Salt Creek County Park	Salt Creek County Park

INDEX

Agate Passage 100–103
Alki Point 86–87
Allan Island 141
American Camp 181
Annas Bay 223–225
Arcadia 54
Bayview State Park 142, 143
Beaumont Marine Park 203
Bellingham 159
Bellingham Channel 148, 149
Blake Island 86–89
Blakely Island 168
Blind Island State Park 177
Boat Passage 203
Boston Harbor 59, 61
Bowman Bay 134, 136, 137
Bremerton 90–93
British Camp 181
British Columbia Marine Provincial
    Parks 32
Browns Point 79
Burrows Island 139–141
Camping 36–40
Cape Horn 54, 57
Cascadia Marine Trail (CMT) system
    13, 30, 33–36, 45
Cattle Point 181, 182
Chapman Bay 69, 72
Charts, nautical 44
Chuckanut Bay 159–162
Chuckanut Island 162
Clark Island 156–159
Commencement Bay 77–80
Commodore Park 99
Cornet Bay 131, 132, 133, 136, 137
Craft Island 128–129

Crescent Bay 232–235
Current cycles 22–23
Current hazards 25–28
Current prediction 24–25
Cypress Head 147
Cypress Island 146–151
D'Arcy Island 204–207
Dabob Bay 220, 223
Dana Passage 61
Decatur Island 163, 164, 165
Deception Island 137
Deception Pass 133–138
Deer Harbor 171–172
Distance planning 44
Doe Bay 156, 157, 167, 168
Doe Island State Park 167
Dosewallips State Park 220, 221, 222
Dot Island 144
Dungeness Spit 229–232
Duwamish Waterway 100, 111
Eagle Harbor 90–96
Eddy-hopping 29
Eld Inlet 61, 62–65
Elliott Bay 112–114
Emergencies 51–53
Fay Bainbridge State Park 100, 101, 103
Ferries 47–48
Fidalgo Head 151, 165–166
Fort Flagler State Park 209
Fort Ward State Park 92
Freshwater Bay 232, 233, 235
Friday Harbor 168, 171, 172, 192
Goat Island 129–130
Golden Gardens 98–100
Gooseberry Point 152, 154, 155, 156
Great Bend of Hood Canal 223
Griffin Bay Recreation Site 183
Hale Passage 154–155

Kayaks at Eagle Harbor, Bainbridge Island
(Carey and Jeanne Gersten)

Hammersley Inlet 54–58, 59
Harbor Island 114
Haro Strait 182
Hartstene Island 59
Henderson Inlet 69–74
Hood Head 218–219
Hope Island (north) 130–133
Hope Island (south) 54, 58
Hypothermia 18–19
Indian Island 208–213
Isle-de-Lis Marine Park 204, 207
James Island 162–166
Jetty Island 115–118
John Wayne Marina 226–227, 228
Johns Pass 195
Jones Island State Park 168–174
Kayak Point 119–122
Kellogg Island 111
Kopachuck State Park 68–69
La Conner 126, 127, 129
Lake Union 104–107
Larrabee State Park 161
Lime Kiln State Park 182–183
Lincoln Park 86, 87–88
Lopez Island 162, 163, 175
Lopez Pass 163, 165, 166
Lummi Island 151–156
Lummi Island Recreation Site 155
Lummi Rocks 155, 156
Manchester State Park 92
Mandarte Island 204, 207
March Point 143, 144
Marine traffic hazards 19–22
Marlyn Nelson Park 225, 226, 228,
Marrowstone Island 208–209, 211, 212
Matia Island 187, 189–190, 191
Mats Mats Bay 214–216
Maury Island 81–85
Mayne Island 200, 201, 202
McMicken Island 65–67

Minimum impact 36–40
Mosquito Pass 183
Mud Bay 64
Mystery Bay Recreation Area 209, 211
National parks 31
National wildlife refuges 31
Navy Channel 203
Nisqually River Delta 75–77
North Beach, Orcas Island 184, 187–191
Oak Bay County Park 212
Oak Harbor 122–125
Oakland Bay 55, 56
Obstruction Pass 166–168
Obstruction Pass Recreation Site 167
Odlin County Park 163, 175, 176, 177
Off-season paddling 48–51
Old Man House State Park 101–102, 103
Orcas Island 166, 167, 168, 171,
    172, 173
Padilla Bay 141–143
Patos Island 190
Peale Passage 58, 61, 62
Pelican Beach 149
Pender Canal 201
Pender Island 201, 203
Penn Cove 122–125
Pickering Passage 58, 59–61
Pleasant Harbor 220, 222
Plumper Sound 203
Point Defiance 77, 79, 80
Point Doughty 184–187
Point Madison 100–103
Point Robinson 85
Point Whitney 220, 222
Pole Pass 172–173
Port Gamble 216–218
Port Susan 119–122
Port Townsend Canal 211, 212
Portland Island 197– 200
Posey Island State Park 194

Potlatch State Park 225
Prevost Harbor 195, 196
Princess Margaret Marine Park 197–200
Quartermaster Harbor 82
Quilcene Bay 220, 222, 223
Raft Island 68
Reid Harbor 195, 196
Rich Passage 90, 92, 93
Roche Harbor 181, 183, 192
Rosario Strait 156, 158, 162, 165, 166
Rum Island 204, 207
Saddlebag Island 144–145
Safety 13–14
Salsbury County Park 218
Salt Creek County Park 233, 234
Saltwater State Park 82, 85
Samuel Island 203
San Juan Channel 175, 177, 178
San Juan County Park 181, 183
San Juan Island 178–183
San Juan Islands National Wildlife
    Refuge 157, 158, 173, 177, 178, 194
Saturna Island 201, 203
Scenic Beach State Park 222
Sequim Bay 225–228
Sequim Bay State Park 225, 226,
    227, 228
Shaw Island 175–178
Shaw Island County Park (Indian
    Cove) 176
Shelton 55
Shilshole Bay 96–100
Shute Passage 200
Sidney 197–198
Sidney Spit Marine Park 204, 205, 207
Skagit Island 130–133
Skagit River 126–130
Skokomish River 223
Skyline Marina 139–140, 141
Snohomish River 115, 117

Southworth 88
Spencer Spit State Park 163–165, 167
Spieden Channel 194
Squaxin Island 54, 58, 61
Stillaguamish River 119–122
Strait of Juan de Fuca 182, 231,
    232, 233
Strawberry Island 150
Striped Peak Recreation Area 232
Stuart Island 191–196
Sucia Island 187, 188, 189, 190
Suquamish Museum and Tribal
    Center 103
Swartz Bay 198, 200
Swinomish Channel 130, 142, 143
Tacoma 77, 78, 79
Tide rips 27–29
Tillicum Village 86, 89
Tongue Point 234, 235
Towing kayaks 11–12
Trip ratings 41–43
Turn Island State Park 176, 177, 178
Turn Point State Park 196
Upright Channel 176, 177, 178
Vashon Island 81, 88
Washington Department of Natural
    Resources (DNR) areas 32–33
Washington Park 139, 140, 141,
    148, 163
Washington State Parks 31–32
Washington Water Trails Association
    (WWTA) 33
Wasp Islands 173–174
Weather forecasts 15–18
Weather patterns 15–18
West Point 96–100
Whidbey Island 122–125, 130
Winslow 93, 94, 95, 96
Woodward Bay 69–74
Yellow Island 173, 174

ABOUT THE AUTHORS

Randy Washburne is a veteran sea kayaker and the author of two other books, *The Coastal Kayaker's Manual* and *The Coastal Kayaker*, as well as *Washburne's Tables*, popular regional current guides, and numerous magazine articles on kayaking. He teaches sea kayaking and navigation and manufactures canoe and kayak accessories in Seattle, Washington.

R. Carey Gersten, who updated this book for the second edition, is an active volunteer and past president of the Washington Water Trails Association. He is also the general manager of Puget Sound Kayak Company with three waterside locations, as well as a certified Coastal Kayak Instructor with the American Canoe Association, the leading organization promoting national standards for paddled watercraft instruction and safety.

THE MOUNTAINEERS, founded in 1906, is a nonprofit outdoor activity and conservation club, whose mission is "to explore, study, preserve, and enjoy the natural beauty of the outdoors. . . ." Based in Seattle, Washington, the club is now the third-largest such organization in the United States, with 15,000 members and five branches throughout Washington State.

The Mountaineers sponsors both classes and year-round outdoor activities in the Pacific Northwest, which include hiking, mountain climbing, ski-touring, snowshoeing, bicycling, camping, kayaking and canoeing, nature study, sailing, and adventure travel. The club's conservation division supports environmental causes through educational activities, sponsoring legislation, and presenting informational programs. All club activities are led by skilled, experienced volunteers, who are dedicated to promoting safe and responsible enjoyment and preservation of the outdoors.

If you would like to participate in these organized outdoor activities or the club's programs, consider a membership in The Mountaineers. For information and an application, write or call The Mountaineers, Club Headquarters, 300 Third Avenue West, Seattle, Washington 98119; (206) 284-6310.

The Mountaineers Books, an active, nonprofit publishing program of the club, produces guidebooks, instructional texts, historical works, natural history guides, and works on environmental conservation. All books produced by The Mountaineers are aimed at fulfilling the club's mission.

Send or call for our catalog of more than 300 outdoor titles:

The Mountaineers Books
1001 SW Klickitat Way, Suite 201
Seattle, WA 98134
1-800-553-4453

e-mail: mbooks@mountaineers.org
website: www.mountaineersbooks.org

Other titles you may enjoy from The Mountaineers:

CONDITIONING FOR OUTDOOR FITNESS: A Comprehensive Training Guide, *David Musnick, M.D. & Sandy Elliot, P.T. with Mark Pierce, A.T.C.*
The most comprehensive guide to conditioning, fitness, and training for all outdoor activities, featuring a "whole body" approach by experts in the field. Includes training programs for hiking, biking, skiing, climbing, paddling, and more.

KAYAK ROUTES OF THE PACIFIC NORTHWEST COAST, *Peter McGee*
A comprehensive guide to kayaking routes and camping sites from Puget Sound to the Queen Charlotte Islands.

PADDLE ROUTES OF THE INLAND NORTHWEST: 50 Flatwater and Whitewater Trips for Canoe & Kayak, *Rich Landers & Dan Hansen*
Detailed guidebook for casual adventuring in Washington, Idaho, Montana, Oregon, and British Columbia. Perfect for families, weekenders, and novice paddlers.

AFOOT AND AFLOAT™ Series, *Marge & Ted Mueller*
The best-selling series of recreation guides for hikers, boaters, bicyclists, and car tourists, covering the entire Puget Sound and the San Juan Islands.

PADDLE ROUTES OF WESTERN WASHINGTON: 50 Flatwater Trips for Canoe and Kayak, *Verne Huser*
A flatwater paddling guide including information on location, distance, duration, shuttle details, best season to go, and more.

BOATER'S SAFETY HANDBOOK, American Outdoor Safety League
Quick help for boaters and boat emergencies.

SEA KAYAKING CANADA'S WEST COAST, *John Ince & Hedi Köttner*
A fully detailed guide to paddling the western coast of B.C., plus Vancouver Island and the southern Queen Charlottes.

CANOE AND KAYAK ROUTES OF NORTHWEST OREGON, Second Edition, *Philip N. Jones*
The definitive flatwater paddling guide to northwest Oregon, including seventy outings for canoe and sea kayak enthusiasts.

Outdoor Books by the Experts

Whatever the season, whatever your sport, The Mountaineers Books has the resources for you. Our FREE CATALOG includes over 350 titles on climbing, hiking, mountain biking, paddling, backcountry skiing, snowshoeing, adventure travel, natural history, mountaineering history, and conservation, plus dozens of how-to books to sharpen your outdoor skills.

All of our titles can be found at or ordered through your local bookstore or outdoor store. Just mail in this card or call us at 1·800·553·4453 for your free catalog.

Name _____
Address _____
City _____ State _____ Zip+4 _____-____
E-mail _____

Please send another catalog to my friend at:
Name _____
Address _____
City _____ State _____ Zip+4 _____-____
E-mail _____

607-3

Attention Western Washington residents:

Wanna go outside and play?

Join The Mountaineers today!

You may think we're just a climbing club but The Mountaineers offer a lot more. We sponsor regular outings and classes on hiking, backcountry skiing, backpacking, alpine scrambling, bicycling, first aid, photography, sailing, sea kayaking, trail maintenance, and conservation. There are activities for families, singles, and active people of all ages. Other benefits of joining The Mountaineers include the use of four terrific mountain lodges and the opportunity to join our exotic foreign excursions. And, of course, we offer hundreds of climbs each year for all levels of experience.

If you live in Western Washington, there's a Mountaineers Club near you. To receive membership information, just mail in this card today!

300 Third Avenue West
Seattle, WA 98119
206·284·6310
www.mountaineers.org

Name _____
Address _____
City _____ State _____ Zip+4 _____-____
E-mail _____

607-3

BUSINESS REPLY MAIL
FIRST-CLASS MAIL   PERMIT NO. 85063   SEATTLE, WA

POSTAGE WILL BE PAID BY ADDRESSEE

THE MOUNTAINEERS BOOKS
1001 SW KLICKITAT WAY STE 201
SEATTLE WA 98134-9937

BUSINESS REPLY MAIL
FIRST-CLASS MAIL   PERMIT NO. 75491   SEATTLE, WA

POSTAGE WILL BE PAID BY ADDRESSEE

THE MOUNTAINEERS
300 3rd AVE W
SEATTLE WA 98119-9914